ABUSED

BY

THERAPY

How searching for childhood trauma

can damage adult lives

KATHARINE MAIR

Matador
9 Priory Business Park
Kibworth Beauchamp
Leicestershire LE8 0RX, UK
Tel: (+44) 116 279 2299
Fax: (+44) 116 279 2277
Email: books@troubador.co.uk
Web: www.troubador.co.uk/matador

ISBN 978 1783060 665

British Library Cataloguing in Publication Data.
A catalogue record for this book is available from the British Library.

Typeset in Aldine401 BT Roman by Troubador Publishing Ltd
Printed and bound in the UK by TJ International, Padstow, Cornwall

Matador is an imprint of Troubador Publishing Ltd

MIX
Paper from
responsible sources
FSC
www.fsc.org   FSC® C013056

CONTENTS

Acknowledgements iv

Foreword by Professor Christopher C. French, Anomalistic Psychology Research Unit, Goldsmith's College, University of London v

Introduction: Two fathers tell their stories xi

1. The difficulty of knowing about the past 1

2. The consequences of child sexual abuse 24

3. The strange history of the dissociative disorders 46

4. Diagnosing dissociative disorders 68

5. Therapy 94

6. The consequences of therapy 112

7. Belief meets the backlash 137

8. Alternative approaches to dissociation 165

9. The campaign 189

10. The damage 211

Appendix: Dissociative Experiences Scale-II 219

Index 227

ACKNOWLEDGEMENTS

Throughout the years spent researching and writing this book I have been sustained and encouraged by my husband, John Rawles. It was he who first insisted that I should come out of retirement and make public my longstanding concerns about false memories. Since then it has been due to his continuing support, wise advice and practical assistance, not to mention his IT expertise, that I have been able to complete this undertaking. I have also been helped in a variety of ways by some generous friends. From among them I would like to give special thanks to Madeline Greenhalg, James Ost, Kevan Rudling and Julie Wyness.

In addition I am grateful to the many people who have been prepared to talk to me about their varying experiences and opinions concerning recovered memory therapy and dissociative disorders. I am sorry if some of them are distressed by the contents of this book. I am aware that my conviction that certain theories are both unfounded and damaging has caused me to contradict many dedicated and well-meaning people.

FOREWORD

This is an important book that deserves to be widely read, not just by those with a professional interest in matters of psychological health but also by members of the general public. Within this volume, Katharine Mair reveals the truth about the damage that misguided therapy can often inflict, both directly upon clients but also more widely. For it is not just the clients of such therapists that can find their lives shattered, as they come to believe that they were victims of horrendous childhood abuse. Inevitably, the lives of the alleged perpetrators are also damaged, often irreparably – and the real tragedy is, of course, that the apparent memories of abuse that have been 'recovered' during such therapy are in all probability false memories, produced by the therapeutic techniques themselves, rather than being a record of events which ever actually took place.

Fortunately, there are many forms of therapy available that do not result in the tragic outcomes detailed in this book. Many of them, such as cognitive behavioural therapy, have been shown to be effective in treating a range of psychological problems, from phobias to depression. The type of psychotherapy that potentially causes more harm than good is of a specific type. It is based, first and foremost, upon the Freudian notion of 'repression'. Freud believed, in his early work at least, that if a person experienced events of a severely traumatic nature, an automatic psychological defence mechanism kicked in that pushed the memory of those events deep into the unconscious mind. Repression was believed to be completely beyond conscious control. While the memory was repressed in this way, it could not be retrieved into consciousness by any effort of will. However, Freud claimed that it could be retrieved by the skilful application of psychoanalysis. This is the belief that underlies the 'memory recovery' work that is still used by some psychotherapists to this day.

These psychotherapists believe that memories of childhood

sexual abuse are particularly likely to be repressed. Even though they are repressed, it is claimed that such memories can still exert a toxic effect upon the victim's psychological health in later years, causing a wide range of psychological problems. It is further believed that the only way to resolve these psychological problems is by recovering the horrific memories that lie deep within the unconscious mind, bringing them into the full glare of conscious attention and then 'working through' them. As one might imagine, this is a stressful process for all concerned, but those suffering from psychological problems will often accept the counsel of their therapists and put themselves through this severe emotional (and often financial) hardship in the hope of getting better. As Katharine Mair makes clear in these pages, the assumptions which underlie this approach are not supported by any solid empirical evidence. Furthermore, there is little evidence that the clients themselves benefit psychologically from putting themselves through this gruelling process.

The notion of repression is widely accepted not only within the psychotherapeutic community but also by the public at large, despite the fact that many leading experts in memory research are dubious regarding the validity of the concept. There is no doubt that Freudian ideas have had a huge influence upon intellectual life beyond the narrow confines of the therapeutic context, including art, literature, drama, and various social sciences. Ironically, Freudian theories actually receive very little coverage within modern academic psychology courses – and when such theories are considered at all, it is often from a very critical perspective, pointing out the pseudoscientific nature of the theories. But the fact remains that in the minds of many members of the general public, Freud is considered to be a pioneer and a genius whose insights must have some validity.

It is now generally accepted that childhood sexual abuse is unfortunately much more common than was once appreciated and that it is often associated, albeit not inevitably, with adult psychological problems in its victims. The acknowledgment of this regrettable truth is to be welcomed as it makes it more likely that those at risk of such abuse can be properly protected. However, this heightened awareness of the prevalence of abuse combined with unwarranted belief in the Freudian notion of repression combine to provide the perfect context for the ready acceptance of the use of a range of 'memory recovery' techniques, such as hypnosis and guided imagery, that are accepted by many as providing valuable tools to allow the recovery of hidden traumatic memories.

While it is easy to see why an explanation of adult psychological problems in terms of repressed memories of sexual abuse would appear plausible to many people, it is worth bearing in mind that these same 'memory recovery' techniques are used in various other, more esoteric, contexts. Katharine Mair's book opens with two accounts of fathers who were accused by their adult daughters of childhood sexual abuse. The first of these accounts mentions that the troubled daughter had, during the course of her therapy, also recovered apparent memories of a past-life as an assistant in a holocaust death camp during World War II. Most people would find it much harder to accept recovered memories of a past-life as being veridical compared to recovered memories of childhood sexual abuse – but the technique used to recover both types of memory is identical. Furthermore, the same technique is also used to recover apparent memories of being abducted by extraterrestrials. Logically, if one is prepared to accept apparent memories of childhood sexual abuse in the absence of any independent supporting evidence, one should also accept the more bizarre memories of past lives and alien abduction. I suspect that most readers would not be prepared to believe the latter.

Memories of bizarre and extreme satanic abuse, believed by some therapists to be the primary cause of dissociative identity disorder (DID; formerly multiple personality disorder), are also typically 'recovered' using hypnotic regression and related techniques. This has led some professionals to promote the idea that such abuse is prevalent throughout society – even though such claims are not supported by a scrap of forensic evidence. Furthermore, the validity of the DID diagnosis itself has been called into question with many commentators arguing that it is a product of the therapy rather than a pre-existing psychiatric condition. Overall, there is scant evidence to support the use of the therapies critically examined in this book.

They say that the road to hell is paved with good intentions. That is certainly the case when it comes to the damage that can be caused by misguided forms of therapy. Everyone involved has the best of intentions. The therapy that causes the damage is often paid for by parents who want nothing more than to ease the psychological pain of their adult children. The children themselves simply want to find a way to feel happy again. The therapists firmly believe that the only way to attain that goal is to embark upon a long and difficult journey but that ultimately their clients will benefit from the experience. Unfortunately, the evidence shows that it is all too often the case that families are plunged into their own personal hell from which they may never emerge. My fervent hope is that Katharine Mair's meticulous analysis of this phenomenon will help at least some families to avoid this tragedy.

Christopher C. French
17 June 2013

INTRODUCTION

Two fathers tell their stories

These men told me their stories during October 2012. All the names have been changed, but the information remains unaltered.

Peter

Peter has been married for nearly 50 years but now lives alone. His wife, Mary, moved out more than two years ago and is now in the process of divorcing him. He has two married daughters, Janet and Emma, and they now refuse to see him. He can now see no way out of a family situation which is painful for all concerned. He believes it all came about because his older daughter, Janet, needed to find some explanation for her continuing ill health.

> "Janet contracted a serious viral infection 23 years ago and went back to work too soon afterwards, pushing herself to keep going. She started to get tired and, as the weeks went on, this got worse and worse. Her GP couldn't find anything wrong with her, so he didn't do anything about it… She was later referred to various other doctors who diagnosed Chronic Fatigue Syndrome, but were unable to help her in any way. They recommended a European specialist, but Janet had to pay for this herself. That involved lots of tests and experimental medicines and went on for a long time but with no success, and eventually she was no longer able to go to work."

18 years had now passed since Janet had contracted the viral infection that was thought to have started her decline. During this time she had been married and divorced, and had moved to another part of the country. She later married again, and continued searching

desperately for some explanation and cure for her persistent ill health. Both parents remained in close contact, and Peter grew increasingly sceptical about some of the therapies that she tried.

"We're getting into the realms of what you might call pseudo-religion. She'd gone to the Isle of Mull, where there was a religious group that was supposed to get to the inner person, the inner soul. She came back with all these fancy charts, they didn't make any sense to me, but Janet seemed to think there was something in it. She was clutching at straws basically. She'd gone to various places like this, they were not doing her any good at all. I think she was spending many hours on the computer, on the internet, searching and searching for answers. And it's there she picked up this book which is called *The Courage to Heal*. I'm not sure if she got the idea of hypnotherapy from there. We were not aware she was going to do that...

"She got in touch with this man and started with hypnotherapy and the next thing we knew was when she came to see us and told us quite categorically that she knew what she'd been in a past life. She told us that she'd been an assistant in one of the death camps during the holocaust in the last war. I sort of took this in a light-hearted way, and I think Janet could see that I didn't believe it . She reacted very aggressively, which was unusual for her, because we'd always got on fine together. I realised then that she absolutely believed it. She was deadly serious that she had been this in a past life and that was one of the reasons she was feeling the way she was feeling now."

At this point Peter's wife, Mary, showed that she was reluctant to challenge her daughter's beliefs. From now on her reactions to all of Janet's revelations would be very different from Peter's.

"Mary seemed neither to believe or disbelieve. She just took it as what Janet said. Unfortunately this is the situation with

Mary and Janet. Janet has been so successful both in her education and at work, and she was such an outgoing, positive person. Anyone would believe what she was saying, she has that sort of aura around her. Mary always looked up to her, so whatever Janet says, it must be true. Mary has always lacked the ability to question Janet.

"After this initial hypnosis, it progressed to a point where she was told or she realised that she'd actually been abused as a child. The first we knew of it was when Janet and Paul [her second husband] came to see us one weekend. Janet said, 'I've got something to tell you' and she just came out with this story that she'd been sexually abused as a child by her grandparents, Mary's parents, my in-laws. I was just staggered! Didn't know what to say, didn't know what to think. Mary just went and put her arms round Janet, which gave me the indication that she believed her. Why didn't Mary stand back and say 'Whoa! Hang on a bit. What's happening, where's this coming from?'

"Janet had been such a happy child. When she was going to see her grandparents she was always excited. She never showed any resistance to wanting to see her grandparents, never! I find it difficult to understand when all this abuse could have taken place, we didn't see them that often. Occasionally Janet stayed overnight, often with her sister, so what was she doing while Janet was being abused? Apparently both grandma and grandpa were acting together.

"They went away and left us to consider. What on earth do we do now? Mary was convinced that this had happened. I didn't know what to believe. I didn't really think it had happened, but looking back now I think how foolish I was. Why wasn't I more adamant at the time, saying this is nonsense, it *definitely* didn't happen? I regret not doing that. It's easy to say that now, it wasn't at the time. I wanted to keep the peace and I knew that if I was to go against Janet it would cause a great rift in the family. So I unwisely went along with it, trying to understand Janet, hoping all the time that she would come to her senses and realise that she had got this wrong. She had either had a dream to start this off, or the hypnotherapist had got it wrong. Then I was told that this hypnotherapist is very qualified, he knew what he was doing. All the evidence seemed to be stacked up against me not believing him.

"Then, within two weeks of this announcement I was put under pressure to get in touch with Mary's parents. [They were abroad] I wanted to wait until they got home, but the family [including the two sons-in-law] thought I should do it now, straightaway. So I did, I phoned them and told my mother-in-law, 'Janet has announced that when she was a child both you and grandpa sexually abused her'. It wasn't an easy thing to say. Mother-in-law was just totally and utterly… she couldn't believe it was me. She kept saying, 'Are you really saying that? [her husband was in the same room, she told him, then came back] 'I can't believe what you're saying to us' and she hung up. They tried to get an early ticket to come home, and when they got back Mary wanted to go and see them with Janet and all the family and confront them. I was against that, and within a month grandfather had died of a heart attack brought on by stress. Within that month he'd lost a lot of weight, he couldn't sleep well, and despite the fact that he was a strong healthy man he kept breaking down and just bursting into tears, saying, 'Why are they doing this to us, what have we done to deserve it?'And he kept on and on repeating that and eventually he collapsed and died. He went downhill from that day. When he died, Janet gave the impression of being relieved, which I found strange, she would never have behaved like that before. Mary refused to go to the funeral.

"It was after that that we started getting the details of this abuse. We now got emails from Janet, saying the most amazing things. What we learnt from one of them was that Janet was taken by her grandparents to this church, where there were other men and women, and other children of a similar age, boys and girls, and that Janet was laid on this slab, a tombstone or something, and the men and women got a pretend knife and they cut her open and used some skinned rabbits to show her that these were babies that were being taken away. There was also a lot about these people using controlling techniques that they had learnt from a manual."

After about a year and a half, the hypnotherapist referred her on to another therapist, who lived much nearer to Janet. The new therapist was a clinical psychologist who had previously worked in the NHS, where she had established a reputation as an expert on treating the survivors of child sexual abuse. She now only saw private clients. With this new therapist there were more revelations. Janet sent her parents emails detailing many new memories of abuse, and these usually coincided with her therapy sessions. She also talked to her mother about what these had entailed. Meanwhile the accused, and now widowed, grandmother had been repeatedly writing to Janet, asking her why she was making these allegations. Janet's husband had been instructed to intercept these letters and destroy them, but one of them got through and was read by Janet, who was upset. Peter thinks that he was expected to intervene at this stage, to make some protest to the grandmother. He was reluctant to do this, and now thinks that this was his big mistake.

"I said that Janet should just forget about it. I did the wrong thing. I didn't realise at the time. Janet said to Mary, 'I don't think Dad believes me', and shortly after that was when I was accused.

"I'd gone away for a few days and on my return Mary wasn't in the house, which was unusual. She left a note to say she was staying with Jenny, a close friend, and she'd be back tomorrow. The following day I got a phone call to say she wasn't coming back that day, it would be another day or so. I thought that was strange, not like Mary to behave like that... The next day she arrived, with Jenny, and they both stood there looking stone-faced and gave me a letter from Janet. Janet was accusing me of abusing her when she was a young child. No specific allegations, just general allegations of sexual abuse. My initial reaction to that was, of course, shock. But also within a few seconds I was thinking, well perhaps this is not such a bad thing after all. So my first words were 'Perhaps we can now move forward. We can do something for Janet'. And I was looking at Mary and Jenny and they were staring at me, and I said, 'Mary, you don't believe this do you?' And she said, 'I don't know what to believe'. And Jenny said 'Well I believe it.' I said, 'This is utter nonsense, you can't possibly believe this. We had a superb family life, we never had a problem like this.' And at this point they left and Mary has never been back since.

"This was the start of a very black time. I'd lost the support of all my family. My youngest daughter was being coerced by Mary and Janet, so she kept away, which meant I couldn't see my granddaughter. I haven't seen her for two years now. My own health started to decay. I didn't feel like cooking, I felt sick all the time and I didn't feel I could keep going like this. I didn't see a way forward, so I decided to end it all... I planned out exactly how I would do it: shot through the head – done, finished! But I eventually remembered that when my father-in-law died, my son-in-law said, 'He killed himself because he couldn't face the facts.' I knew that wasn't true and that gave me the courage to tell myself, if you go through with this they will say the same thing about you. And that stopped me. It didn't make it any easier, but it stopped me from doing that."

During this time Mary had been able to buy a flat of her own, using money that she could take from Peter's business account, since she kept his books. Peter says this was not the first time that they had considered divorce. They had started drifting apart at the time that their daughters left home, when they discovered how few interests they now had in common. He feels that Mary was now exploiting their unhappy situation.

"I do honestly believe that Mary was using this allegation as a lever, so she could demand whatever she wanted, knowing that I couldn't object to it because she would then publicly announce that I had been accused of abusing my daughter. That backfired because I decided that I wasn't going to hide anything. I've nothing to hide. I decided right from the beginning of all this that whatever I said would be the truth. If you start covering up and tell lies you just get yourself in such a mess, you can't remember what you said. If you tell the truth it's easy, you just carry on with the truth. All my friends and many people in the village know the situation, I've not hid it from them. It's backfired on Mary, she's not been able to use this as a lever. She could try to bring in the police, but I don't think they'd believe her anyway.

"All the time I've been supported by my friends. I can't thank them enough. I must be a pain in the neck to them, but they've been wonderful. Some of them were Mary's closest friends, and they've tried to talk to her, but she just won't listen."

It is now more than two years since Peter has been on his own. In an effort to persuade his younger daughter, Emma, of his innocence he recently took a lie detector test. This was conducted in a professional manner and the result was unequivocal: he was not lying when he answered a string of sensitive questions. The report declared him totally innocent of the charges against him. Emma now has a copy of this report and Peter knows she will have shown it to other family members, but he has heard nothing from any of them. As far as he knows, Janet is still in contact with the same psychotherapist, despite the fact that, after moving house more than three years ago, they now live hundreds of miles apart from each other. From that time they have continued their therapy sessions online with Skype.

Janet is now in her late forties, apparently still suffering, to some extent, from the chronic fatigue syndrome that she developed more than 20 years ago. Peter has little knowledge of her present activities but he has heard that she recently attended a course for abuse survivors, aimed at helping them forgive their abusers and move on. He suspects that this may be a prelude to a training course that will enable her to become a psychotherapist herself.

Peter is bleak about future prospects for himself and for his family. His friends have told him that he has to move on and find a new life for himself, but he finds it impossible to sever the emotional ties that continue to torment him.

"I can't move on. What really does concern me is that I can't see a way forward. If Janet was to recover her memory, which in a way I wish she could, then being the person that she is, a very caring, loving person, I don't know how she'd cope. If she found out that she was directly responsible for her grandpa's death and the travesty to the family that's happened since, how could she cope with that? I don't know if it's better for her to go on believing that she's been abused, or that the truth should come out… I know that if I could see Janet right now I'd just put my arms around her and tell her, 'It's alright'. Because I know that what's happened is not Janet, it's not how Janet is, it's not how Janet's been, it's not how we were. I can't blame her for it at all. But I don't know how she would cope if she learnt the truth. This is a situation where I don't think anybody's going to win."

David's story

David and his wife, Wendy, have a daughter, Jane, now in her mid-twenties, and two sons who are considerably younger. They became concerned about Jane about four years ago. She had been very upset after breaking up with her boyfriend and the dementia and death of her grandfather. She had since then shown some rather alarming mood swings. She was attending college, training to be a teacher. David persuaded her to see a counsellor at her college. He made the appointments for her and made sure that she kept them. However, after three months of counselling Jane's behaviour seemed to be getting worse rather than better, and both parents were becoming increasingly concerned. Then came the bombshell.

"One day we got a call from Wendy's brother James saying, 'I need to talk to you.' When we got there we were handed a hand-written sheet, a story by Jane saying her father had raped her when she was between the ages of 10 and 12. I was puzzled. I asked, 'Was that me?' I was told it was. I was just completely lost for words. Only a few hours before we had had a friendly text from Jane, telling us about a holiday she was planning. It just didn't make sense.

"I just went completely numb. I couldn't really process anything. I realised afterwards that James was just the messenger, and that he didn't believe this, but at the time I didn't know anything. I just couldn't compute. I offered to leave home, so that Jane could come home again. But Wendy was supportive, right from the start and didn't want that.

"I felt crushed and devastated, and for two or three weeks I was quite suicidal. I was in tears, I had to give up work and withdraw from my church activities. I couldn't sleep, neither could Wendy. I kept asking myself, had I really done these things and not known that I'd done them? What have we done to deserve this? Why would she say these things? At first I felt that I was the victim, but about two weeks later, after I had spoken to a few people I got the sense that they didn't believe Jane's story. So I said to myself, 'I've got a clear conscience'. That's when I was able to start sleeping again. But we didn't tell most people, mainly to protect Jane. We still don't talk about it, and there must be some people who have only heard Jane's side of the story who still believe it. I just don't know."

Wendy has supported Mark throughout this ordeal, and now takes up the story.

> "I never really believed it, but I did have to think, 'could this have happened?' But the stories didn't fit. She said she had been abused in the shower, but the house we were living in at that time didn't have a shower. None of it rang true. We thought she had been stolen from us. We felt she was the victim, not just David.
>
> "I did manage to speak to Jane's counsellor. She was a Christian Counsellor, affiliated to the Christian Counsellor's Association. I thought she was very sheepish. She hid behind the veil of confidentiality, but said, 'They don't make things like this up.'"

Jane had now been having counselling two or three times a week for almost three years. She broke off all contact with her family, and reluctantly followed her counsellor's advice that she should inform the police, so that she would be believed. By this time her story had grown. The abuse had gone on much longer and many new details had been added. The police arrested David and carried out an investigation lasting two months, during which they questioned Jane's younger brother. They then dropped all charges. Meanwhile Wendy was determined to try to regain contact with her daughter. She started by texting her. Three months later they had their first meeting.

> "I just couldn't recognise her. She had lost a lot of weight and looked absolutely dreadful. She was so upset, she said how much she'd missed us, kept hugging me and crying. She wasn't ready to see her dad. She had been told that once she came out with these allegations she'd get better, she'd be able to get on with her life, but she had just got worse from then on. The counselling was stopped, because she had left the college, but she was left without any support. She had been living with a couple but then she moved away to live

on her own, and she actually had a breakdown and had to give up her job. She then moved in with friends who knew that this hadn't happened. She had moved away from the people who had believed her."

After three more months Jane agreed to see her father. They were both now having help from a social worker, and they had one joint session together. By now Jane had got married and, after a few more months, she and her husband moved in with her parents for a while, while waiting for their future home to be ready. David knows that, despite this positive move, her problems are still far from over.

"She hasn't actually withdrawn her allegations, but we've got our daughter back, and that's all we ever wanted. She said, 'I'm sorry about what I've put you through.' She's sorry for the pain. It's the pain of coming to realise that what you've done is actually worse than what you thought happened in the first place. She now thinks very negatively about the people she used to live with, but I wouldn't say she's trying to blame them, she's just saying they weren't good for her... It takes time to believe these things, it doesn't just happen overnight. And now it's a process of coming out of it. She wants to block it all out and not talk about it. Her social worker thinks she should address these things in time. She does now say, 'I never want to be separated from my family ever again'. One day it will all come out. That will be part of the healing process. But we do have to go at her own pace."

1. THE DIFFICULTY OF KNOWING ABOUT THE PAST

The difference between asking and searching

Psychotherapy has been described as 'the talking cure' and, less kindly, as 'messing with people's minds'. This is therapy in which two people talk together in the hope that one of them will help the other to sort out some psychological problems. It used to be practised mainly by psychiatrists and clinical psychologists but many other professions are now joining in so that we find social workers, counsellors, psychiatric nurses and a growing band of 'alternative' therapists are also doing it. Some of them may call it counselling, or even healing, but what they are doing often involves very similar processes.

Anyone who is in the business of trying to help troubled adults may want to ask them whether they ever suffered any trauma or abuse during childhood. This is part of the routine of taking a history, since childhood suffering can sometimes throw light on current difficulties. However, one particular type of trauma, child sexual abuse, recently seems to have become a major preoccupation with some psychotherapists. They can justify this by pointing out that child sexual abuse is a regrettably frequent occurrence which was often overlooked in the past. Estimates of its prevalence vary widely, partly due to different ways of defining abuse, and different methods of enquiry. It was recently reported that child sexual abuse involving contact has been experienced by 20% of women and by 5-10% of men worldwide.[1]

The words 'child sexual abuse' cover a range of experiences which may have very different consequences for the victim:

A single glimpse of a stranger flashing his penis.
Intimate fondling by a favourite uncle.
Violent rape by a gang of men.
Enjoyable sex with an older partner during adolescence.
Repeated forced sex and other perversions with family members.

1

It is therefore not possible to generalise about the damaging effect that child sexual abuse can have on the later lives of its victims. Common sense tells us that for some victims there is probably no lasting harm, but for others the consequences may be devastating. Accordingly, it makes sense for a psychotherapist to ask clients whether they ever suffered childhood sexual abuse, especially as they may be unwilling to mention this spontaneously. In some cases this will lead to a better understanding of their current problems. In the next chapter I will be describing how research studies have shown us that there can be a link between child sexual abuse and later difficulties and disorders. However, this link is often tenuous, and we can seldom be certain that it was the abuse which caused the later problem. Similarly we can never assume that, because someone has a particular diagnosis or set of symptoms, they must have been abused as children. This book is about what can happen when therapists make this crucial mistake: when they see certain diagnoses or symptoms as signs of childhood trauma. They are then making unwarranted assumptions about the past lives of their clients. At this point therapists may stop listening to what they are being told, and start searching for the hidden trauma, driven by an unsubstantiated theory that can have very dangerous implications for their clients.

We have abundant evidence that therapists who carry out such searches will often find exactly what they are looking for. They then claim that their hunches are justified, and that they are helping their client by uncovering the previously unsuspected trauma that accounts for their present difficulties. This may sometimes be the case, but the two stories which introduce this book suggest that a search may have a less happy outcome: the 'discovery' of hidden trauma may be a complete delusion. Time and again clients have appeared to 'remember' events that can later be shown not to have occurred, or to have been physically impossible. These memories feel real, they may be vivid and painful, but they are still imaginings rather than true memories, and they lead both therapist and client hopelessly astray. Both become trapped in a web of fantasy as they try to deal with images of abuse which are often nauseating and horrific, but which never really happened. In later chapters I will be describing some of the grave, life-changing consequences for the clients, and also for their families. But first, we must consider how it is possible for false memories to emerge during therapy.

Freud's search for abuse.

Sigmund Freud was one of the first therapists to evoke demonstrably false memories of childhood abuse in his clients. He has left us a rich legacy, part of which is an understanding of the power of our unconscious fears and desires. It can be argued that he also left us some very damaging myths. He saw his practice of psychoanalysis as a means of enabling people to gain access to their unconscious minds. To do this he initially used hypnosis, but then switched to the technique of free association, in which patients were encouraged to let their minds drift, to say whatever they thought of, and to respond to any interpretation that their analyst might make of this. He believed that this was a way of overcoming the barriers of repression that prevented people being aware of the unconscious conflicts dating from childhood that had caused their current problems. He was a theoriser and was looking for some unifying explanation for a wide range of disorders, suspecting that this might be sexual trauma of some kind. Like many of today's therapists, he was driven by a theory to search for hidden trauma, and like them he usually found what he was looking for.

In 1896 he proudly proclaimed his 'seduction theory', which stated that a wide range of unexplained disorders in women, from panic attacks to epilepsy and some skin disorders, were probably the result of sexual abuse in childhood, usually by the child's father. It was not until two years later that he became embarrassed by the fact that his theory had led him to the belief that many of his respectable friends, some of whom were paying for their daughters' treatment, had committed these despicable crimes. He then claimed that what his patients had revealed to him in treatment were not memories of actual abuse but childhood fantasies of having sex with their fathers. This fitted in with his fanciful belief that boys and girls between the ages of about two and five years were sexually attracted to the parent of the opposite sex.

Freud has been credited with being among the first to acknowledge the problem of child sexual abuse. Many people believe that he started off by listening sympathetically to the women who complained of it. They castigate him for later betraying these women as fantasists when he abandoned his seduction theory.[2,3] This volte-face was indeed a betrayal, and his notion that women reporting abuse could be relaying childhood fantasies has subsequently had an extremely damaging effect. For many years psychiatrists, who were then mainly men, were encouraged by Freud's teachings to be sceptical whenever women reported sexual abuse. Until the last two decades of the twentieth century the problem of incest certainly seemed to be underestimated and many victims of child abuse failed to get the sympathetic hearing that they deserved. In 1934 John Henry Wigmore, an influential US lawyer, warned that women and girls might be 'predisposed to accuse men of good character of sexual offences' and therefore all complainants should be examined by a psychiatrist to determine their credibility, especially if they made complaints about their fathers.[4]

It becomes clear, however, when we read Freud's own words, that he did not betray women only when he abandoned his seduction theory. He betrayed them from the start. The idea that he initially believed what his clients were telling him turns out to be a complete myth. These clients never did come to him with complaints of abuse. He would not have been interested if they had, because it was only unknown abuse or trauma that concerned him. His clients came to him for help with a variety of known difficulties, but he was driven by his theory to search for problems of which they were quite unaware. He was ruthless in his quest for what he believed to be the truth. This is his account of the way his clients responded to his discoveries about their past experiences:

> Before they come for analysis the patients know nothing about these scenes. They are indignant as a rule if we warn them that such scenes are going to emerge. Only the strongest

compulsion of the treatment can induce them to embark on a reproduction of them. While they are recording these infantile experiences to consciousness, they suffer under the most violent sensations, of which they are ashamed and which they try to conceal: and even after they have gone through them once more in such a convincing manner, they still attempt to withhold belief from them, by emphasising the fact that, unlike what happens in the case of other forgotten material, they have no feeling of remembering the scenes.[5]

Freud seems to have been able to convince his patients that, despite 'having no feeling of remembering the scenes', they really had been sexually assaulted by their fathers. He was satisfied that he had proved his theory. However, he had perhaps been too successful in finding what he was looking for. Two years later he was forced to revert to common sense, and accept that it really was highly unlikely that, in a series of 18 consecutive women patients every single one of them had suffered this same fate at the hands of her father. In abandoning his seduction theory Freud never accepted that he had been wrong to believe that unconscious sexual images could be the cause of adult problems. He still thought that the answers lay in the unconscious, but in fantasies rather than memories, thus shifting the blame for what he found there from the fathers to the daughters. What he never accepted was that fantasies about child sexual abuse came only from himself, and were then imposed on his unwilling patients.

The problem of false memories

Freud used powerful techniques which evoked false memories in his clients. However, false memories are not confined to the consulting room. We all have some false memories. Strictly speaking, if an experience never happened, it is a fantasy rather than a memory; but it does feel just like a memory. That is the problem: we cannot tell true memories from these pseudo-memories, they feel the same. False memories can carry a strong emotional charge. Most of us have had the experience of waking from a disturbing dream with feelings of dread or of guilt about what we believe has just occurred. In the case of the dream we can then reflect 'Thank heavens, it was only a dream!' In our waking lives such a revelation is rarely possible, we are more likely to cling on to our beliefs until someone tells us 'That's not true, that never happened' or 'That's not how I remember it'. This is often what happens when family members get together and mull over long distant events. This tells us that remembering is an active process in which we reconstruct the past. When we think about past experiences we tell ourselves about them again, unconsciously filling in some gaps or switching some details, so that the story imperceptibly changes.

Some memories are held with more confidence than others. Memories that accompany shocking events are usually held with great confidence and seem to remain unchanged over long periods of time. These have been called 'flashbulb' memories. We all remember where we were and what we were doing when we heard the dreadful news of 9/11. Or do we? In 1986 Ulrick Neisser and Nicole Harsch started an experiment that has become famous because of its surprising results. That year, in the US, the *Challenger* space rocket exploded, killing the seven astronauts on board. The day after this shocking event, Neisser and Harsch asked 106 US college students questions about the circumstances in which they heard the news: where they were at the time, what they had been doing and who told them. Two and a half years later, almost half of these students were contacted again and asked the same questions. On comparing the students' two versions of events, it was found that only three of them were completely consistent. If we assume that their first version was accurate, this means that 93% of these students later got at least one detail wrong and 25% of them were wrong about every key detail. What was especially striking was their confidence in their altered memories. They refused to change their most recent accounts when challenged, and some even said that they must have been wrong the first time![6]

It has been argued that these memories are very different from more highly charged memories recalled in therapy. To answer these objections researchers have devised many experiments in which they attempt to implant false memories of more personally significant events, though there are obvious ethical objections to implanting memories that are anything like the distressing memories that are recalled in therapy. In one of these studies, information was obtained from the parents of 77 student subjects about upsetting events that had occurred during these students' childhood. Upsetting events were then invented, such as getting lost, being hurt in an accident or attacked and wounded by an animal. The students were subsequently interviewed three times. They were asked each time what they could remember about both the real and the invented incidents. Eventually 26% of the students said they had a complete memory of an invented incident, and a further 30% said that they had a partial memory for this distressing event that they had never experienced.[7]

A further study investigated the effect that photographs might have in prompting the experience of false memories. Once again students were used as subjects. Their parents were asked to provide verbatim accounts of two school related events that had occurred at different times during early school years. A pseudo-event was then invented, said to have occurred when the children were aged six or seven, before the true events. This involved playing a prank on their teacher, and was something that all parents thought their children had not experienced. The experimenters read this account to the students, together with the parents' accounts of the true events, giving the impression that all accounts had been provided by the parents. The students were then asked to rate their memories of all three events. As expected, the most recent event was remembered best, but a minority of the students said they did also have clear memories of the most distant pseudo-event. They were then told to try to remember as much as they could about this pseudo-event over the next week. When seen again, more of the students now said that they did have some memory of this event. These results were very much in line with what had been reported in other studies that had implanted false memories. What distinguished this study was the effect of a photograph in prompting false memories. Half the students were given a photo of their class, taken at the time of the pseudo-event. They were asked to use this to help them remember. When they were first questioned, more of the students who were given the photo said they had clear memories of experiencing the pseudo-event. When seen a week later the difference between the two groups of students was especially marked. At this time 65% of those with the photo said they had clear memories of experiencing the event and a further 13% said they had images of it, but not memories. Those who had clear false memories reported that these were just as compelling as their memories of the true events. When debriefed, and told that the pseudo-event had been invented by the experimenters, they were amazed ('I can't believe that... No way! I remember it! That's so weird!... If you didn't tell me... I would have left here thinking I did this'.)[8]

These findings are worrying because when clients in therapy are encouraged to remember what happened in childhood they are often advised to go through old photo albums to aid their memories. We might expect this to jog true memories as much as false ones, but we now know that when people are asked to remember past experiences they are very open to suggestion. If a therapist suggests that certain people may have either abused or been abused, then seeing photos of these people may be enough to help them construct compelling but completely false memories in line with the therapists' suggestions.

Even without suggestion, retrospective accounts of childhood experiences can be wildly inaccurate. Researchers once asked over a thousand 18-year-old men and women, who had all been assessed every two years since childhood, about how they had been living at least 10 years previously. Their accounts were often very different from information given in the records of the time, and this was most likely when they concerned more sensitive matters, such as family conflicts and behaviour problems, the very things that therapists might one day be interested in learning about.[9] A later study came up with similar results. 73 boys were interviewed when they were 14 years old, asking them about themselves and their home circumstances. Contact was made with most of them a full 34 years later, when they were again asked about themselves at age 14. There was little agreement between the two accounts, no better than would occur by chance, and the authors warned against placing any reliance on adult memories when assessing childhood circumstances, saying that these should be seen as 'existential reconstructions' rather than reliable reports.[10]

Memories from early childhood are known to be particularly unreliable, but these are often the memories of most interest to the searching psychotherapist. Although many adults, if asked to recall their earliest memory, will be happy to talk about experiences they had when they were babies or toddlers, developmental psychologists tell us that these are very unlikely to be accurate memories. They are more likely to reflect experiences that were learnt about later. The early years of childhood are said to be characterised by 'childhood amnesia', which can last until the child is seven years old. This does not mean that young children are amnesic, rather that their memories cannot be retrieved at a later date. Infants are able to use memory from soon after birth, but their early non-verbal memories are very different from later biographical memories, which depend upon language and also on brain development. The brain structures (the hippocampus and the pre-frontal cortex) necessary for the establishment of long-term, narrative memories are not fully developed until the age of three or four. Thus the earliest memories that adults can retrieve will usually be from the fourth year of life.[11] The early pre-verbal memories are thought to be lost when children acquire language and develop a different style of encoding and retrieving memories.[12] Adults may know about things that happened in their earlier years, but that will be because they have been told about them, not because they remembered them at the time.[13]

The British Psychological Society recently published some guidelines on memory for use in the courts by expert witnesses.[14] This was thought necessary because there was now so much new knowledge about memory, based on many years of scientific research, that ran counter to some commonly held beliefs. These guidelines warned that any adult memories of childhood events before the age of seven years should be viewed with caution, as the accuracy of these memories 'cannot be established in the absence of independent corroborating evidence'. Memories which dated back to the age of three or less should definitely 'not be accepted as memories' without this evidence.

The fact that so many adults believe that they can remember their infancy (some have even claimed to remember being born) is further evidence of our wonderful imaginative capacity to tell ourselves stories about our past lives. Many people are now telling these stories to their therapists. Accounts of abuse during infancy are of special interest to therapists who treat dissociative disorders. These therapists believe that severe dissociative disorders can *only* be caused by prolonged, severe abuse that occurs during the first few years of life, well within the period of childhood amnesia. Like Freud, they expect their clients to have no memories of abuse when they start therapy, but when new abuse memories later emerge they believe them to be a reflection of what really happened long ago. Because of these beliefs, therapists who diagnose and treat dissociative disorders are especially liable to evoke fantasies and false memories. They have a theory about these disorders which leads them to undertake lengthy, coercive searches for extremely severe trauma. They usually find it, which is why their therapy is especially dangerous and is an important concern of this book.

Is it possible to forget childhood abuse?

Many therapists insist that it is necessary to search for childhood trauma rather than simply asking about it, because people may lose all memory for this trauma but still be suffering from its long-term effects. There has been much debate about how well we remember traumatic events, and it does appear that these are sometimes forgotten. In one well-known study, Linda Williams identified 129 women who were known to have been sexually abused as children. She interviewed them 17 years later, asking them about various past experiences, including abuse in general, but with no specific reference to the recorded instance. She found that 38% of these women failed to mention this instance, though many of them did mention other experiences of abuse. Failure to mention the abuse was associated with being younger at the time of the abuse, being subjected to force and to knowing the abuser. Williams interpreted not mentioning the known instance of abuse as not remembering it. She concluded: 'long periods with no memory of abuse should not be regarded as evidence that the abuse did not occur'.[15]

A later study also showed that not all people who are known to have been sexually abused as children will mention the fact at a later date. This time, out of 175 men and women, a smaller proportion, 19% , failed to mention abuse that was known to have occurred 20 years previously. Once again, not mentioning the abuse was related to being younger when it had occurred, but this time people were more likely to mention the abuse if it had been severe. Unlike Williams, these researchers did not assume that failure to mention the abuse necessarily meant that it had been totally forgotten.[16] To get a clearer idea of what might be involved in mentioning or not mentioning past abuse, the same team in a later study questioned those of their subjects who had previously mentioned their abuse, and asked them if there had ever been a time when they had forgotten about it. 15% of them said that this was so. This temporary forgetting was mainly reported by women who had suffered more severe forms of abuse, and the reason most often given was the wish not to think about it. Most of these people thought that their previous amnesia for the abuse had only been partial, in that if someone had asked them directly about it, they might then have been able to remember. However, five people said that, at this time, they would have been completely unable to remember the abuse. All of these people had later recovered their memories at some point in childhood.[17]

Remembering is an active process and memories do seem to come and go depending on how much we work on them. It seems that they can sometimes be pushed to the back of the mind without completely disappearing. Thus non-disclosure of abuse does not always mean that it has been completely forgotten, as memories can be both partial and transient. Most of the people in the above studies did remember the abuse they had suffered, but we should note that this was abuse that had been detected at the time, sometimes leading to criminal prosecutions.

Unfortunately, for perhaps a majority of its victims, sexual abuse is a private, extremely embarrassing experience that they have no wish to share. We might expect that more victims of undiscovered abuse would lose their memories of it, or be unwilling to mention it at a later date. It has been found that many women having treatment for the consequences of childhood abuse do say that they had at times completely forgotten about this abuse.[18] This may sometimes reflect the fact that their therapy was focused on helping them to recover lost memories of abuse. Even so, it does seem to be possible for the victims of childhood abuse to lose all awareness of their sufferings, at least for a while. When the abuse occurs early in childhood, during the years of childhood amnesia, developmental psychologists tell us that the memory of it is likely to be lost for ever.[19]

Freud believed that unpleasant memories were often lost, but not necessarily for ever. He developed the concept of *repression*. This was a process by which people protected themselves from painful memories by losing all awareness of them, and somehow diverting them into their subconscious minds. For Freud these memories were not dead but dormant, so that their emotional charge might still be channelled into various physical or emotional complaints. This was when psychoanalysis was called for, to help the client gain access to subconscious memories and work on the problems that they posed.

This idea that dormant memories may cause later problems has been promoted by those therapists who diagnose and treat dissociative disorders. The concept of dissociation, similar in many ways to that of repression, was first developed by Pierre Janet, a contemporary of Freud, but was then revived, with some important changes, in the 1980s. At that time Freudian theory formed an important part of the training of most North American psychiatrists, and it is perhaps significant that this new interest in dissociation was started by a small group of North American psychiatrists. In Chapter 3 I will be describing how, over the past thirty years, they have encouraged many therapists worldwide to diagnose and treat Dissociative Disorders. They have spread the theory that dissociation is a process used by some people in traumatic situations to protect them from remembering. As with repression, the memories are diverted rather than lost. They linger on in a separate part of the mind, and in extreme cases this part assumes an identity of its own, so that there seems to be a different person holding the traumatic memories. According to this theory, this is how people develop multiple personalities. This strange phenomenon of one person apparently having a number of separate identities is said to be far more common than most people realise. It has been renamed Dissociative Identity Disorder (DID), and is now seen as one example of a dissociative disorder. Treatment for this is focused on gaining access to the painful memories, so that those affected can integrate their separate parts and become unified people again. Implicit in the theories of both repression and dissociation is the belief that memories of trauma can seem to be completely lost for many years but can later be recovered in psychotherapy.

The theory that traumatic experiences are processed in a different way from other experiences was further developed by the psychiatrist Bessel van der Kolk.[20] He is held in great esteem by those who treat dissociative disorders, as his theory explains how people can forget even the most severely traumatic events, experiences that we would expect to remain firmly lodged in their minds. It has been claimed that people with dissociative disorders have been able to forget suffering repeated physical and mental torture, multiple rapes and even giving birth during adolescence. Some explanation of their previous amnesia is clearly called for. Van der Kolk tells us that when people are subjected to extreme stress, either in wars, natural disasters or when being abused, their perceptions become narrowed, and they are unable to describe what is happening to them. Their memories for these events are thus non-verbal images, with no accompanying narrative about what was happening. They may later be experienced as flashbacks, nightmares, states of terror and even bodily changes, which can neither be explained nor controlled, but which contain the unchanging remnants of past traumatic experiences. These 'implicit memories' can apparently persist indefinitely, blocking the formation of any conscious narrative memories of the trauma that generated them. That is why people who have experienced severe or persistent trauma may not know why they suffer until they are helped, by psychotherapy, to transfer their implicit memories into explicit, verbal, narrative memories.

Van der Kolk's theory gives us an explanation for what is seen in the therapy clinic, but what it fails to explain is the inconvenient fact that outside the clinic, most victims of known traumas, such as war, accidents or natural disasters, do not lose memories of their harrowing experiences. Although he claims that people suffering from Post Traumatic Stress Disorder (PTSD), a condition that can follow known trauma, show evidence of this type of fragmentary memory, we now know that for these people it rarely persists.[21] Instead, they are usually plagued by persistent painful memories. Implicit traumatic memories appear not to block the formation of conscious narrative memories in these cases, so why should they block those of survivors of severe childhood abuse?

There have been many studies of the effects of trauma and chronic stress on memory and on brain function, which have been expertly summarised by the American psychologist Richard McNally. He stresses that, except when there has been observable brain damage, many of the memory deficits reported after trauma are only temporary, and that no neural abnormalities have been discovered in trauma victims that could explain amnesia for past experiences. He finds no evidence that the presence of nightmarish flashbacks and other uncontrollable phenomena of implicit traumatic memory can actually stop an explicit, narrative memory from being laid down.[22] Van der Kolk has therefore developed an elaborate theory to explain something that is reported only in the therapy clinic.

Although it seems unlikely that people will forget severe and persistent trauma, we have seen that some people do apparently forget the more typical childhood experiences of abuse. This is especially likely if it occurs at an early age, before the parts of the brain responsible for narrative memory have been fully developed.[23] What we do not know is what happens to these lost memories. The theories of repression, of dissociation and of traumatic memory all make the claim that these memories do not disappear completely. They may be lost to consciousness but they will be still be seething away somewhere, and can be harmful unless they are brought into consciousness by a skilled psychotherapist. However, it is worth reminding ourselves how little we do, in fact, remember of our childhood. We cannot recall more than a tiny fraction of all the experiences that we have in the course of our lives. Our memories mostly consist of those experiences we have chosen to think about. So it does seem possible that past experiences that are never thought about, even if traumatic, may in time cease to bother us at all, because they have just faded away completely and irretrievably.

Can recovered memories ever be true?

As mentioned before, some people with known histories of childhood abuse have reported that at times they lost their memories of this but that when these memories returned they appeared to be accurate.[24] The answer to the above question must therefore be 'yes'. It does seem to be possible for memories of significant events to come and go, and some recovered memories are likely to be true. However, memories that come back spontaneously, often emerging unexpectedly in a variety of situations, should perhaps be distinguished from those that result from an active attempt at retrieval during therapy. Some people call spontaneously emerging memories 'discontinuous' rather than recovered.

Ross Cheit, an American political scientist, once had the experience of spontaneously recalling his own previously forgotten abuse.[25] He later became incensed by claims that no recovered memories of sexual abuse had ever been proved to be true. In 1997 he launched 'The recovered memory project', its purpose being 'to collect and disseminate information relevant to the debate over whether traumatic events can be forgotten and then remembered later in life'. Over the years he has been collecting cases in which

15

discontinuous memories of abuse have apparently been corroborated. When updated in 2011, his archive, which can be seen on his website, contained 110 'corroborated cases of recovered memory'.[26] It is an impressive list, with cases derived from legal proceedings, clinical research and other sources. Most of them involve sexual abuse, though some involve murder. The instances of corroboration he most frequently cites are confessions by the perpetrator and evidence from other victims or from witnesses. He sometimes relies on court judgements, or even, in some of the clinical cases, the clients' unchecked claims of corroboration, as evidence that the memories were accurate. We can object that these cases are questionable and incomplete, but we must accept that his list does contain cases which strongly suggest that discontinuous memories can be accurate. Most of these cases seem to feature memories that had been regained spontaneously rather than recovered in therapy.

In one survey of people reporting that they had suffered childhood abuse but had once lost all memory of this, it was found that more than half of them had regained their memories during therapy rather than spontaneously.[27] It is clearly important to find out more about the accuracy of memories regained in these circumstances. A recent study by Elke Geraerts and colleagues has been rigorous in its attempt to do this.[28] They used newspaper advertisements to contact people with both continuous and with discontinuous memories of childhood sexual abuse. Some of these people had regained their memories in therapy, some had regained them spontaneously. They then asked their subjects detailed questions about their memories of abuse. Those with discontinuous memories were asked about the extent of their memory loss and the circumstances in which they regained their memories. They were also systematically asked whether their memories of abuse were supported by any corroborative evidence. All claims of corroboration were then independently assessed by two different members of the research team, who did not know whether the memories had been continuous or discontinuous. Convincing corroboration was established for the abuse of 45% of the 71 people with continuous memories, and for 37% of the 41 people with discontinuous memories, regained without the aid of any therapy. The types of corroboration (others abused by the same perpetrator, others learning of the abuse, confession by the perpetrator) were similar for the two groups. However, none of the 16 people who had regained their abuse memories in therapy could provide any convincing corroboration for these memories.

Since being in therapy had apparently led these people to remember instances of abuse that could not be corroborated, the researchers wondered whether their therapy had been explicitly directed to unearthing new abuse memories. They asked all those who had regained their memories how surprised they had been by what they discovered. There was a significant difference between those regaining abuse memories in therapy and those who did this spontaneously. Those who gained their memories spontaneously were far more surprised by them. The researchers then found that those who were surprised at the emergence of the memory were more likely to have some corroborative evidence for that memory. There were no differences in the types of abuse reported by those who remembered it in therapy and those who remembered it spontaneously. The differences between the two groups, both in the corroboration of their abuse and in their surprise at remembering it, did seem to be firmly linked to the experience of therapy.

The same team of researchers wondered whether a heightened susceptibility to false recall was a general characteristic of people who gained new memories of child sexual abuse, or whether it was confined to those who recalled these memories during therapy.[29] They tested this susceptibility with a verbal memory test, comparing those who had regained their memories spontaneously with those who regained them in therapy. On this test there was a clear differrence: errors were found to be more common among those who had recalled memories of child sexual abuse in therapy. Their tendency to false recall was not shared by people who had recalled experiences of abuse spontaneously. These findings further support the theory that the experience of suggestive therapy can be a crucial factor in the emergence of false memories of abuse.

We should not assume, however, that because someone recovers an abuse memory during therapy then it must be a false memory. It is always very difficult to know whether these memories are true or not; they concern events that happened in private a long time ago. The necessary corroborative evidence is difficult to trace and not many therapists show much interest in looking for it. We find a refreshing exception to this in the work of the clinical psychologist Constance Dalenberg.[30] She had some clients, all women, who had recovered new memories of abuse during their therapy. Perhaps because she had an academic background and knew about the unreliability of past memories, she was concerned to know how accurate these were. After they had completed therapy, she selected 17 of these clients, all of whom had accused their fathers of sexual or physical abuse. She presented them with a list of potentially verifiable abuse related 'facts' that had been reported during therapy. She then took the unusual step of interviewing their fathers, questioning them about the same 'facts'. She invited both fathers and daughters to look for evidence that would either confirm or refute these memories. They were able to find some confirming evidence in 70% of cases. This evidence was then independently scrutinised by six raters, chosen for their divergent views about false memories. They considered that this evidence was trustworthy in three quarters of these cases. Thus a significant proportion of the new memories of this selected group of clients did appear to be corroborated, most frequently by a confession from the father. When they compared the new memories recovered in therapy with the memories that had been there continuously, they found that a similar proportion of both were supported by the evidence. Dalenberg makes the point that, since all memories are subject to distortion, it is illogical to expect that continuous memories must be accurate and recovered memories must be false; both can be either true or false.

This is a remarkable study in many ways. Unlike many therapists, Dalenberg was prepared to put her work to the test, to accept that some new memories might be false and to encourage her clients to look for evidence rather than simply trusting their memories. They were encouraged to go back to their families, where their memories might be rigorously tested, and even to question their alleged abusers. She took the unusual step of encouraging family reconciliation and reported that most of the father-daughter pairs reported an improved relationship once the true facts had been established. That so many of these memories recovered in therapy turned out to be true may well be due to way she had conducted therapy. She had been careful to avoid using many of the techniques which she considered 'risky' but which are popular with therapists who search for new memories. She never suggested that clients showed any symptoms of past abuse, and she never used guided imagery or hypnosis or recommended self-help survivor literature. Also, she had completed all therapy within 10 to 25 months, rather than allowing it to last for many years. She has shown us that psychotherapy for the victims of child sexual abuse does not have to involve false memories, family break-up or long-term dependence on the therapist. We will see in the following chapters that when therapists start searching for a hidden background of sexual abuse, all these things are only too likely to happen.

An alternative approach

We have seen that people who suffer sexual abuse during childhood may always remember it, may forget all about it or may have memories that come and go. It is impossible to know how many fall into each category. We have also seen that when anyone remembers something for the first time, this recovered memory may be true, may be distorted or it may be completely false. All distant memories are unreliable and we are all open to suggestion. That is why we have to tolerate uncertainty whenever we are dealing with the past. Unfortunately, when people go into therapy looking for answers to their problems, and when therapists are eager to find those answers, this uncertainty is the last thing that they want.

Most of us know the comfort that can come from being given a firm diagnosis of a medical condition: 'so that's what's causing it!'. We are grateful to doctors who do this, and we assume that they reach their conclusions by looking at what is happening in our bodies *now*. Physical problems may be revealed by observable physical signs. Mental problems do not reveal themselves in the same way, and we cannot see into each others' minds. Finding out what is wrong now is hard enough; working out what caused it in the past is perhaps better not attempted. Many psychotherapists, especially if they have trained as psychiatrists or clinical psychologists, now take this view. They work by watching and listening to their clients, observing their behaviour and the way they tackle their present problems. They hope they will be able to encourage these clients to adopt better strategies or try out new ways of thinking. This is the basis of cognitive behavioural therapy (CBT), a means of working with people that is based on experiment rather than theory, and is firmly based in the present. It can be contrasted to the psychodynamic approach adopted by those therapists who search for child sexual abuse. They look behind the presenting problem to ask what caused it, and this inevitably takes them back to the past. CBT avoids some of the damaging side effects that can result from psychodynamic psychotherapy. It may be less exciting but it is certainly a lot safer. Moreover, its effects have been tested in some rigorous outcome studies, showing that it can have some benefit for people with a wide range of problems.[31]

References – 1. The difficulty of knowing about the past

1 Freyd J.J. et al (2005). The Science of Sexual Abuse. *Science*, 308, 501.

2 Herman J.L. and Hirschman L. (1981). *Father-Daughter Incest.* Cambridge: Harvard University Press.

3 Masson J. (1992) *The Assault on Truth: Freud and Child Sexual Abuse.* London: Harper Collins.

4 Webster R. (1995) *Why Freud was Wrong.* London: Harper Collins, p. 512.

5 Freud S.E. *The Aetiology of Hysteria*, standard edition p. 204, quoted by Webster, ibid, p. 202.

6 Neisser U. and Harsch N. (1992). Phantom flashbulbs: false recollections of hearing the news about *Challenger.* In E.Winograd and U.Neisser (Eds). *Affect and Accuracy in Recall: Studies of "flashbulb" memories.* Cambridge: Cambridge University Press, pp. 9-13.

7 Porter S., Yuille J.C. and Lehman D.R. (1999). The nature of real, implanted, and fabricated memories for emotional childhood events: implications for the recovered memory debate. *Law and Human Behaviour*, 23, 517-537.

8 Lindsay D.S. et al (2004). True photographs and false memories. *Psychological Science,* 15, 149-154.

9 Henry B. et al (1994). On the "remembrance of things past": a longitudinal evaluation of the retrospective method. *Psychological Assessment*, 6 (2), 92-101.

10 Offer D. et al (2000). The altering of reported experiences. *Journal of the American Academy of Child and Adolescent Psychology,* 39 (6), 735-741.

11 McNally R.J. (2005). *Remembering Trauma.* London: Harvard University Press, pp. 43-48.

12 White S.H. and Pillemer D.B. (1979). Childhood amnesia and the development of a socially accessible memory system. In J.F. Kihlstrom and F.J. Evans (Eds). *Functional Disorders of Memory.* New York: Laurence Erlbaum Associates, pp. 29-73.

13 Eacott M.J. and Crawley R.A. (1998). The offset of childhood amnesia: memory of events that occurred before age 3. *Journal of Experimental Psychology: General*, 127, 22-33.

14 British Psychological Society (2010). Adult memory for childhood. Guidelines on memory and the Law: Recommendations from the Scientific Study of Human Memory. Leicester: BPS.

15 Williams L.M. (1994). Recall of childhood trauma: a prospective study of women's memories of child sexual abuse. *Journal of Consulting and Clinical Psychology*, 62, 1167-1176.

16 Goodman G.S. et al (2003). A prospective study of memory for child sexual abuse: new findings relevant to the repressed memory controversy. *Psychological Science*, 14, 113-118.

17 Ghetti S. et al (2006). What can subjective forgetting tell us about memory for childhood trauma? *Memory and Cognition*, 34 (5), 1011-1025.

18 Herman J.L. and Schatzow E. (1987). Recovery and verification of memories of childhood sexual trauma. *Psychoanalytuc Psychology*, 4 (1), 1-14.

19 Eacott M.J. and Crawley R.A. (1998). The offset of childhood amnesia: memory of events that occurred before age 3. *Journal of Experimental Psychology: General*, 127, 22-33.

20 Van der Kolk B.A. and Fisler R. (1996). Dissociation and the fragmentary nature of traumatic memories: overview. *British Journal of Psychotherapy*, 12 (3), 352-363.

21 McNally R.J. (2005). *Remembering Trauma*. London: Harvard University Press, p. 156.

22 Ibid p. 182.

23 Conway M.A. and Holmes E.A. (2010). Guidelines on memory and the law. Recommendations from the scientific study of human memory. *British Psychological Society: report from the research board.* Pp.1-2.

24 Ghetti S. et al (2006). What can subjective forgetting tell us about memory for childhood trauma? *Memory and Cognition*, 34 (5), 1011-1025.

25 Pendergrast M. (1996). *Victims of Memory*. London: Harper Collins, pp. 72-73.

26 http://blogs.brown.edu/recoveredmemory/ (Accessed August 2013. For Ross Cheit's list follow links >recovered memory project >case archive).

27 Feldman-Summers S. and Pope K. (1994). The experience of "forgetting" childhood abuse: a national survey of psychologists. *Journal of Consulting and Clinical Psychology*, 62, 636-639.

28 Geraerts E. et al (2007). The reality of recovered memories: corroborating continuous and discontinuous memories of childhood sexual abuse. *Psychological Science*, 18 (7), 564-567.

29 Geraerts E. et al (2008). Cognitive mechanisms underlying recovered-memory experiences of childhood sexual abuse. *Psychological Science*, 20 (1), 92-98.

30 Dalenberg C. (1996). Accuracy, timing and circumstances of disclosure in therapy of recovered and continuous memories of abuse. *The Journal of Psychiatry and Law*, 24, 229-275.

31 Butler A.C. et al (2006). The empirical staus of cognitive-behavioural therapy: a review of meta-analyses. *Clinical Psychology Review*, 26 (1) 17-31.

2. THE CONSEQUENCES OF CHILD SEXUAL ABUSE

We have seen that a growing awareness of child sexual abuse and some of its serious consequences has led many therapists to ask their clients about possible histories of abuse. Those who believe that traumatic memories can be repressed or dissociated may feel that asking is not always enough, and a certain amount of probing is called for, to search for any hidden memories. This is especially likely to happen when therapists believe they can detect certain 'signs' or 'symptoms' of abuse. In an influential book first published in 1989, Liz Hall and Siobhan Lloyd advised all 'helpers' of women who came to them with any current problems to routinely ask about their family and social history, and to follow this up with more searching questions when a combination of certain 'clues to child sexual abuse' were noted. They provided a list of these clues, of which the first three were as follows:

Combination of long-term effects (especially sexual problems, perceptual disturbances, fear of men or avoidance of relationships with men, self mutilation).
Previous psychiatric history and several different diagnoses and still not much better.
No memories of childhood / over-positive descriptions of childhood.[1]

They also suggested the wording for further questions:

'You have been describing a number of difficulties that are often found in women who report that they have been sexually abused as children. I wonder if this has ever happened to you.'
'The problems that you are describing suggest to me that something very unpleasant may have happened to you as a child. Were you ever abused physically?' (wait for answer) 'Sexually?'[2]

During the past 30 years we have been hearing more and more that a variety of adult problems can be seen as pointers to previous sexual abuse. We see this suggested in many of the self-help books that have been written for 'survivors' of child sexual abuse. The readers of one of these are invited to consult a 34 item 'Incest survivors after-effects checklist'. These 'after-effects' include so many common problems that most people must surely discover that they suffer from some of them. They include: depression, phobias, low self-esteem, anger problems, eating disorders, fear of the dark, high risk taking and also inability to take risks. Also present on the checklist is 'Denial, no awareness at all'.[3]

We need to know whether there are any links between adult problems and child sexual abuse that can justify the suggestive questioning that some people recommend. Is it feasible to suspect that someone has been abused solely on account of his or her present symptoms? Many therapists claim that it is. They usually back up their claim by telling us how many of their clients with these symptoms have been discovered to have a history of sexual abuse. However, these discoveries usually occur during therapy which is aimed at confirming the therapist's initial suspicions. So that when Dr. William Rader, a respected expert on eating disorders, tells us that approximately 85% of his clients have been sexually or physically abused, we must bear in mind that he recommends that treatment for eating disorders should include the uncovering of any hidden traumas.[4] Self-harming behaviour is another adult problem that many therapists have linked to childhood abuse. It has even been described as 'a manifestation of sexual abuse'.[5] However, it is when we come to the dissociative disorders that the most confident and insistent claims are made about links with childhood abuse. The respected Government-supported mental health charity known as Mind (formerly the National Association for Mental Health) informs us on its website, and also in a pamphlet updated in 2011, that a history of childhood trauma is 'almost always the case' for people with moderate to severe dissociative symptoms.[6]

The strongest claims of a link between adult disorders and

childhood abuse seem to be based on the testimony of clients undergoing recovered memory therapy, a form of therapy which encourages them to think back to childhood and consider the possibility of abuse. This abuse is often discovered for the first time during therapy. The reports of abuse that are 'almost always the case' in dissociated clients must therefore be seen, in part, as a response to therapy. This does not, in itself, invalidate these reports, but it raises our suspicions, since therapists are so good at finding what they are looking for. We need to use other methods to investigate the links between adult disorders and childhood abuse. One good method is to look at things the other way round, observing the children rather than the adults.

The impact of sexual abuse on children

Children who are known to have been abused can be followed up into adulthood, and their progress compared with that of a similar group who are not thought to have been abused. Prospective studies like this have an advantage over the more common retrospective studies of adults because they do not need to rely on adult memories of something that happened a long time ago. However, they also have an important limitation in that they can only deal with abuse that has been discovered. Sadly, the sexual abuse of children usually goes undetected at the time. Young children may have little understanding of what is being done to them and, for a variety of reasons, will not wish to report it.[7,8] The consequences of this undisclosed abuse may therefore be somewhat different from that of abuse that has been discovered, and there is no way this can be studied prospectively.

In 1993, a review of 45 studies of the impact of known sexual abuse on children was published.[9] Unfortunately none of these studies followed up the children into adulthood, but together they provided useful information on their initial responses, and gave widely differing estimates of psychological harm, with most of them reporting that children who were known to have been abused were more likely than other children to suffer from a variety of problems.

These varied in different studies, and covered a wide range including anxiety, depression, learning problems, aggression, hyperactivity and sexualised behaviour. Interestingly, no signs of dissociation seemed to be noticed. However, when children with known abuse were compared with children who were having treatment for psychological problems but were not thought to have been abused, the two groups were found to have very similar symptoms and these were in fact less common in the abused group. Thus the symptoms found in sexually abused children were not generally different from those found in other troubled children. Only one, sexualised behaviour, was found to be specific to the sexually abused children. About a third of sexually abused children showed no subsequent symptoms of distress, and many of those who did initially have symptoms soon lost them. Most of those studies that followed up the children for up to two years reported a lessening of their symptoms over time. The authors of this review seemed strangely sceptical about news of this apparent recovery from trauma, and suggested that although some symptoms might be transient 'this does not necessarily mean that the underlying trauma is resolved'.

It can be argued that for some children there is no 'underlying trauma' to be resolved. In an investigation into what actually happens when children are sexually abused, it was found that the majority of children were abused by someone they knew and that they had often been 'groomed' over a period of time and encouraged to regard the relationship as mutual.[10] One might expect that for a young child these experiences would be confusing or disturbing rather than traumatic since they would not, at that age, understand the significance of what was being done. Indeed several studies have questioned whether children are inevitably harmed by sexual abuse. David Finkelhor, a tireless researcher and campaigner for abused children, had earlier concluded from his study of their responses to abuse that many of them did not appear to have been harmed by their experiences.[11] A more recent review which looked back at 20 years of research also found that there was no evidence that most children known to have been sexually abused showed signs or symptoms of trauma. The studies reported in this review also contradicted the earlier finding that abused children were more likely to show sexualised behaviour. The researcher concluded, 'There is no sign or symptom that characterises the majority of abused children.'[12]

In a study which relied on retrospective reports of childhood sexual abuse, but adopted the unusual procedure of asking people who remembered their abuse how they had felt about it at the time that it was happening, Susan Clancy found that fewer than 10% of her sample said they had found the abuse traumatic.[13] These results are strikingly different from what we find in samples of clinic clients. Clancy had used newspaper advertisements to recruit 200 men and women who remembered being sexually abused as children. The types of abuse they had suffered, ranging from non-contact approaches to sexual intercourse, were similar to those that have been reported elsewhere and did not appear to be any less severe. These individuals had been on average about ten years old when they were abused.

The experiences of these men and women matched what was found by other authors,[14] and also some larger population studies of child sexual abuse in the US, in that they were usually abused by someone they already knew, and in most cases no force had been used to ensure their compliance. Most of them said that they had not found their abuse traumatic at the time.[15,16] However, almost all of them said that they did feel they had been damaged by it. They reported symptoms of Post Traumatic Stress Disorder, depression, drug and alcohol abuse and sexual problems. They made the important point that these were problems that they had developed later, when they were older and realised the significance of what had been done to them. Clancy tells us how, by encouraging them to talk about how they had felt at the time, she gained insight into a rarely revealed child's perception of sexual abuse. She was forced to overcome her own revulsion at what had been done to these children and realise that for them it was very different, as they did not understand what was going on. When asked to describe their feelings, most of them said they had been 'confused'.[17]

As children, these people had mostly, in their own words,

"participated", "consented" or "allowed it", though some of them had sensed that it was wrong and most of them did not want to tell anyone about it. They had been seduced rather than assaulted, and it was their remembered compliance that contributed to their distress when they later came to reinterpret what had happened to them. Then they recognised for the first time that they had been exploited and betrayed, often by people whom they had loved and respected. It was at this stage that the damaging consequences of their abuse started to make themselves felt, and they felt guilty, contaminated and insecure. Clancy argues that widespread emphasis on the traumatic nature of sexual abuse increases this distress by ignoring the reality of what the child has experienced.

Among many mental health professionals any abused client is now seen as a 'survivor', reinforcing the view that they have suffered trauma. The trauma view of child sexual abuse is now well entrenched, and we see it at its most extreme in the pronouncements made by those promoting the dissociative disorders. They repeatedly focus on a trauma that is so severe that the normal functioning of memory is disrupted and the victim has to seek protection in an altered state of mind. This bears no relation at all to the experiences of abuse reported by Clancy's respondents. It is of course possible that people diagnosed with dissociative disorders have suffered different types of abuse, but it seems just as likely that the different experiences they report result from the type of therapy they encounter as adults.

Consequences of child sexual abuse for adults

Studies of adults with a known history of childhood sexual abuse are unfortunately rare, and usually focus exclusively on women. Two recent studies to some extent fill this gap. The first was carried out in the United States by Allan Horwitz and colleagues.[18] They identified 640 men and women who had documented histories of childhood abuse or neglect in the 1970s, and they interviewed them 20 years later, comparing them with a control group from the same population. They found that men and women who had suffered sexual abuse in childhood were more likely to suffer from mood or personality disorders than people in the control group. The women, but not the men, were also more likely to have alcohol problems. However, they also noted that these people seemed to have been socially disadvantaged from the start and had suffered more stressful life events than those in the control group. This led them to conclude that, when this was taken into account, 'childhood victimisation had little direct impact on lifetime mental health outcome'.

A more recent Australian study came to rather different conclusions.[19] The authors also identified people with histories of documented abuse, focusing on all serious child sexual abuse cases reported between 1950 and 1991 in the state of Victoria. The sexually abused children in their sample were on average nine years old when first identified, and most were thought to have suffered penetrative sexual abuse. These samples were larger: 1,612 previously abused men and women and 3,139,745 control subjects from the same population with no known history of sexual abuse. (This huge figure represents the total population of Victoria born between 1950 and 1991). With samples this size, the researchers could not interview their subjects, but had to get their information from official records of contacts that these people later had with public mental health services in Victoria. They found that 12.4% of the abused group but only 3.6% of the comparison group had later contact with public mental health services. A wide range of psychiatric and behavioural disorders had been diagnosed in both groups, with the abused group showing increased rates of mood and anxiety disorders.

These researchers claimed that their findings 'demonstrated a clear association between child sexual abuse validated at the time and serious disturbances in mental health in both childhood and adult life'. However, their figures only recorded whether or not a contact had been made with mental health services, and one explanation could be that more help was offered to those children who were known to have suffered serious sexual abuse. Of the 200 people who had been sexually abused and were later seen by mental health services, 40% had no recorded diagnosis (compared with 26% in the control group). It is possible that instead of having a 'serious disturbance in mental health' they were just being assessed after their trauma, since it is often assumed that all abused children should be offered some therapy. We do not know whether they got better with time, and it is a great pity that this study had to rely on past records and could give us no information on the current mental state of people with histories of abuse. It should perhaps also be noted that a large majority (88%) of those men and women who had suffered serious sexual abuse in childhood had no further recorded contact with mental health services.

Instead of following up cases of abuse that were documented at the time, most studies of the long-term consequences of child sexual abuse have relied on reports of this abuse that were recalled later by adults. In these studies reported abuse has been linked, not only to mental disorder, but to a surprising number of physical health problems. In a retrospective study of over a thousand elderly men and women, it was found that those who reported childhood sexual abuse (12% of the sample) were more likely, if they were men, to suffer from thyroid disease, and if they were women, to suffer from arthritis or breast cancer.[20] The rates of many other disorders, including diabetes, asthma, migraine and obesity, were similar in both groups. In women the increased incidence of both arthritis and breast cancer was especially marked when they reported repeated sexual assaults. These women were four times more likely to have arthritis or breast cancer than women without such histories. This is a striking result, but before we assume that these disorders were the long-term consequences of earlier abuse, we need to know more about other factors, such as poverty or a disturbed home background, which might have affected this small group of women. The 23 women who had been repeatedly sexually assaulted made up only 2.7% of the total sample of women, and most of the women who succumbed to arthritis or breast cancer in later life did not report any childhood sexual abuse. The same was true of most of the men with thyroid disease. Clearly there are many other reasons why some people get these diseases.

31

Child abuse has in other studies been linked to adult problems of obesity, headaches, chronic pelvic pain, psychogenic seizures, gastrointestinal disorders, and Chronic Fatigue Syndrome.[21-23] However, the researchers who carried out most of these studies stressed that if we want to know about the specific effects of child sexual abuse we should never look at it in isolation. Sexually abused children are especially likely to suffer other forms of ill-treatment, such as neglect or physical abuse, and to come from disturbed family backgrounds. These have been called 'confounding variables' and they may have a greater influence on later outcomes than sexual abuse itself. Many studies have failed to find any link between child sexual abuse and any particular adult disorder, including dissociation.[24-26] Even when there does appear to be a link with a specific mental health problem, it has been argued that, because so many of these confounding variables are involved, it is unwise to assume that any one factor, such as sexual abuse, is responsible for the later problems.[27-29] This has not prevented some writers from making extreme claims. Thus, it was asserted in 2005 that although child abuse (both physical and sexual) could not be linked to any one disorder it had been found to have 'a causal role in most adult disorders'.[30] This contradicts the findings of a host of careful studies in which *all* the relevant factors were examined.

Despite these findings there have been a couple of studies which found, after taking these confounding variables into account, that there still appeared to be some specific link between child sexual abuse and later mental health problems. In one of these a sample of more than a thousand female twins obtained through a twin registry in the US was studied.[31] The authors interviewed these women on several occasions, asking about their family backgrounds, and in some cases also interviewing their parents. In addition they carried out repeated diagnostic interviews for several mental disorders and gained information on childhood sexual abuse from mailed questionnaires. 30% of their subjects reported some form of childhood sexual abuse, and for 8.4% this had involved attempted or completed intercourse. Those who reported abuse were more likely to be diagnosed with at least one mental disorder, and this association between abuse and disorder was 'dose related' in that it was far stronger among those with the most serious abuse. By gaining detailed family information and looking at pairs of twins in which only one had been abused but both might have grown up in a similar environment, these researchers were aiming to separate out any specific effects of abuse from the other risk factors. When these factors were taken into account the association between abuse and most later disorders was weakened but it remained significant, especially for those whose abuse had been most intrusive.

A more recent study came to a similar conclusion.[32] This time both men and women were included and made up a large unselected sample of young adults who had been followed up from birth in New Zealand. The researchers questioned their subjects about childhood physical and sexual abuse and carried out repeated diagnostic interviews for several mental disorders. They found that those reporting either child sexual abuse or child physical abuse were more likely to suffer from major depression, anxiety disorder, anti-social personality disorder, drug or alcohol dependence and suicidal thoughts or attempts. Because they had detailed knowledge of the family backgrounds of their subjects, they were able to assess the effects of possible confounding factors such as parental education, living standards, parental attachment, drug and alcohol use and family disruption. After allowing for these, there was no longer a significant link between physical abuse and later problems, but the link between sexual abuse and later problems, though weakened, was still highly significant. Moreover, as in the previous study, it was said to be dose related in that those whose abuse had been more serious (involving attempted or completed penetration) were the most likely to have later problems.

These two careful studies provide evidence that child sexual abuse can make some people more vulnerable to a range of later disorders. Their conclusions differ from those of many others, in that they suggest that this vulnerability cannot be wholly explained as the result of other disadvantages suffered by abused children. Thus it does seem possible that child sexual abuse can sometimes be identified as an important risk factor for a range of later problems in some people. However, none of these problems or disorders is specific to past abuse. People with no history of sexual abuse also suffer from them, and no specific post-abuse symptom or syndrome has been identified.

Child sexual abuse and psychosis

Most of the investigations into the consequences of child sexual abuse have looked at relatively common mental health problems rather than the rarer and more serious disorder of schizophrenia. This may be because most psychiatrists now believe that schizophrenia is largely genetic in origin. Despite this, a high proportion of psychiatric hospital in-patients have been found to report abuse, and it is likely that some of them will have a diagnosis of schizophrenia. Rates of child sexual abuse reported by hospital in-patients with psychotic or schizophrenic symptoms have been found, in various studies, to range from 32% to 78%.[33] However, it is in hospital that we are particularly likely to find the casualties of a range of adverse childhood experiences, so these studies (and)=? may not tell us much about what happens in the population at large.

A systematic study of a large community sample (4045 men and women) in the Netherlands identified almost 1% with psychotic symptoms.[34] A far greater proportion had reported some form of childhood abuse (physical, sexual or emotional), thus showing that most of those reporting abuse had not gone on to develop psychotic symptoms. However, the risk of developing psychotic symptoms, though slight, was found to be three times greater in the group who had reported abuse. Once again this risk appeared to increase with the severity of the abuse, so that those reporting the most frequent abuse were estimated to be 30 times more likely to develop serious psychotic symptoms requiring special care. It must be stressed that only seven individuals (0.17% of the total sample) fell into this category, and because the numbers were so small the researchers did not feel justified in comparing the effects of the various forms of reported abuse. They did, however, suggest that early adversities could lead to psychological and biological changes that might increase vulnerability to psychosis.

A British study which also used a large community-based sample produced similar findings but came to rather more cautious conclusions.[35] Diagnostic interviews were conducted, noting the occurrence of not only psychotic disorders but also the more common neurotic disorders and drug and alcohol dependence. The authors also asked about a range of adverse childhood experiences, including physical assault, disturbances at home or at school and sexual abuse. They found that these adverse childhood experiences tended to be clustered together and also that many people had more than one disorder in adulthood. People suffering from any adult disorder reported adverse experiences more frequently than did those who had no disorder, and the small minority (less than 1%) who had a psychotic disorder were especially likely to report these experiences. However, these researchers were unwilling to assume that it was the adverse experiences that had caused the later disorders. They thought it possible that both the adverse experiences and the later problems simply reflected a pre-existing vulnerability to these problems. Thus certain children might, from the start, be more at risk both of abuse and of later problems. Although sexual abuse could be identified as the experience that was most clearly linked to several adult disorders, they insisted that this did not mean that it had any specific role in causing any adult disorder, including schizophrenia.

For some time researchers have noted that children who later develop schizophrenia often show early oddities of behaviour.[36,37] This was investigated by Mary Cannon and colleagues in a study which was especially valuable because it was prospective and followed up a 'birth cohort' of over a thousand people in New Zealand born at the same time.[38] They were assessed every other year from birth until they were 11, and then again when they were 26 years old. Those who had developed a psychiatric disorder at this stage were likely to have shown a variety of emotional, social and cognitive difficulties as children. Some childhood difficulties were noted only in those who were found at age 26 to have developed schizophrenia (1% of the sample) or similar psychotic symptoms (a further 2.7%). These individuals were more likely to have shown developmental impairments in their language, motor skills, cognitive and social abilities from as young as three years old. They were also more likely to have already reported some psychotic symptoms at age 11. Early environmental factors such as birth difficulties or maternal inadequacies could not entirely account for these early impairments, and the researchers thought it likely that they 'reflect the expression of schizophrenia-susceptibility genes'.

In the above study no attempt was made to look for any evidence of abuse. Its findings are, however, relevant to claims that abuse can cause schizophrenia. People who develop schizophrenia are likely to have been somewhat handicapped from their early years onwards, so it is difficult to be sure that any one factor, such as sexual abuse, caused their condition. Alternatively it could have been the emergence of their condition that led to the abuse, by making them specially vulnerable. Paedophiles tend to select their victims carefully; the child has to be alone and unlikely to tell other people. This is one reason why handicapped, unsociable or neglected children have been found to be specially at risk.[39] Here we have another confounding factor which makes the unravelling of cause and effect so very difficult. We do now have evidence that child sexual abuse is an important risk factor for many adult disorders, including schizophrenia, but it is clearly not the only one.

In all the above studies the researchers were meticulous in looking, not just at child sexual abuse, but at a range of experiences and situations that might influence the later development of their subjects. They were aware of the mantra 'correlation is not causation', so that when they did find links between child sexual abuse and adult disorders they did not assume that the abuse had caused the disorder. They used statistical procedures to measure the relative influence of the other confounding variables. When these were taken into account the abuse-disorder links were always weakened. However, in some studies the link remained statistically significant, with the strongest links being found in cases of the most intrusive and persistent abuse.

Recovery from Child Sexual Abuse

In most of the above studies the victims of child sexual abuse were not asked how they themselves felt about it once they had reached adulthood. We have seen that, as a group, they were at increased risk of developing a range of later disorders though the majority of them did not succumb. It is important to know how a representative sample of victims think they have been affected. To discover this it is necessary to carry out random population surveys, so that those who experienced child sexual abuse can be questioned about this and also compared with those who escaped this fate.

Several of these surveys have been carried out and their findings have been usefully collated in two 'meta-analyses'. A meta-analysis is a method of pooling the results of comparable studies. This is thought to iron out any irregular results and give a general picture that is more reliable than the results of any one study. The first of these included seven large studies that had been carried out in the US, Canada, the UK and Spain on random population samples.[40] Many thousands of people had been contacted and those who reported childhood sexual abuse asked how it had affected them at the time and later. In five of the studies some measures of personal adjustment were included, so that those who had suffered child sexual abuse could be compared with those who had not. The percentages of respondents who had been sexually abused as children varied considerably between studies, but averaged out at 11% for men and 19% for women. There were striking differences between the men and women in their assessments of the negative effects of the abuse and also in the way that their personal adjustment compared with those who had not reported abuse. Less than half of the abused men said they had been negatively affected by the abuse, and although, on average, they seemed less well adjusted than those who had not been abused, this difference was very slight. A majority of the women reported some negative effects of the abuse, and their personal adjustment ratings were more noticeably affected. However, most of these women denied that they had suffered any lasting harm.

In order to obtain more detailed information about reactions to child sexual abuse the researchers then conducted a larger analysis of 59 studies in which subjects had been asked about how they had been affected by their experiences of sexual abuse; they were also rated for their present adjustment.[41] The thousands of subjects involved in this meta-analysis were all US college students, so these were no longer representative population studies. Since college students probably represent a relatively successful section of the population, we might expect them to have better chances of recovery. However, when compared with the previous population samples, they were found to be remarkably similar both in their experiences of abuse and in their later reactions to it. Once again there was a marked difference between the men and the women, with negative effects being reported by only a third of men but by nearly three quarters of women. The personal adjustment ratings of those men and women who had been abused were lower than those of their peers, but this difference was very slight for the men. In these studies the family backgrounds had been assessed, and those who had been sexually abused were often found to come from poorer, more disorganised families. Once again we have a confounding variable that complicates the picture. When statistical tests were done to measure the relative importance of family background and of sexual abuse in determining later adjustment, family background was found to have a far stronger influence.

These researchers claimed that their results contradicted the widely held assumption that child sexual abuse typically causes harm. It did appear to cause lasting harm in some cases but not in the typical case, and only a minority of men had suffered any negative effects. The women had been more seriously affected, but most of them denied any long-term damage to their lives. This good news caused no great stir in academic circles, where perhaps it was not totally unexpected, as it was in line with several earlier findings.[42,43]

Several months later, however, when members of a wider public got wind of these findings they reacted with outrage. This painstaking work, carried out by Bruce Rind, Philip Tromovitch and

Robert Bauserman was now seen as a national scandal. Protests started when the National Association for the Recovery and Treatment of Homosexuality (NARTH) claimed that this study had legitimised paedophilia, which they considered to be a cause of homosexuality. The study was next denounced in the press and on a TV chat show, where it was attacked as 'junk science'. It aroused the indignation of several Republican members of Congress, and eventually, a year after publication, it even reached the attention of the US government. In July 1999 the United States House of Representatives voted 355-0 with 13 abstentions to pass a resolution which proclaimed the study to be 'seriously flawed'. Apparently fewer than 10 of these politicians had taken the trouble to read this study, and none of them was prepared to question whether, as politicians, they had any right to criticise academic research. The resolution condemned 'all suggestions in the article… that indicate that sexual relations between adults and "willing" children are less harmful than believed'. It also called for further investigations to research the effects of child sexual abuse, using 'the best methodology'.[44] By this they presumably meant methodology that could be trusted to come up with more agreeable results.

The American Psychological Association (APA), who had published the paper, were asked to repudiate it. Having found no flaws in its methodology, they refused to do this, though they did later put out a statement saying the child sexual abuse was harmful and wrong. In response to pressure they eventually agreed to re-examine the paper, but could find no errors in the way the research had been conducted or in the conclusions that were reached. Seven years later a further analysis of similar studies was independently carried out, and this confirmed the findings of the original meta-analysis.[45]

By reporting the good news that child sexual abuse does not inevitably cause lasting damage, the authors of this study had clashed with a widespread public feeling that in condemning child sexual abuse as wrong we must also stress how harmful it is. The authors themselves had asserted that it was wrong and they did not call for any change in the law. It was unfortunate that their findings might provide some emotional support for paedophiles who wanted to justify their behaviour, but they certainly would not affect the legal position of these people. This episode reminds us that there are some things we are not supposed to say, even if they are backed up by evidence. It is also a reminder of how the disturbing subject of sex between adults and children can make us quite irrational. Adult-child sex can never be justified because it involves exploitation and it violates some of our most strongly held values about childhood and about civilised behaviour. It is wrong in itself, irrespective of whether it is harmful. Most of us are specially revolted by the idea of sexual contact between adults and very young children, yet these are the victims who may be least likely to suffer any lasting harm since they are the least likely to understand what is being done to them or to remember it afterwards. We have many reasons for referring to sex with children as abuse, and for condemning it, but we should be relieved to discover that it is not always distressing for the children at the time, and that it does not necessarily leave any lasting damage.

Perhaps we become confused about child sexual abuse because we are using the one term to cover so many different activities, some of which may be far more harmful than others. Yet it is often assumed that all victims of sexual abuse should be offered therapy, either while they are children or when they are adults. As adults they may be encouraged to believe that any current problems may be the result of the earlier abuse and it is only by 'disclosing' to the therapist what happened to them that they will resolve their difficulties. Again and again, men and women who were abused as children are now being told that they must have been damaged by it. They may also have been damaged by abuse that they cannot now remember. Women are especially likely to be encouraged to undergo therapy or to consult a self-help book which tells them that their present difficulties probably result from their abuse. In 1988 Ellen Bass and Laura Davies wrote the most influential of these self-help books, *The Courage to Heal*.[46] This has been sold by the millions all over the world, and is now in its third edition. I will be commenting, in Chapter 7, on some of the changes that have been introduced during its 20 year history. What remains unchanged is its categorical claim that all sexual abuse, even when it involve no physical contact, is damaging and can be blamed for almost any present difficulty.

The long-term effects of child sexual abuse can be so pervasive that it's sometimes hard to pinpoint exactly how the abuse affected you. It permeates everything: your sense of self, your intimate relationships, your sexuality, your parenting, your work life, even your sanity... Many survivors have been too busy surviving to notice the way they were hurt by the abuse. But you cannot heal until you acknowledge the impact of the abuse.[47]

Bass and Davies invite survivors to embark on a healing journey, and tell them that they cannot do this on their own, they will need 'good resources and skilled support' for a process that will last for many years.

Categorising all child sexual abuse as damaging may be in line with public sentiment, but does it help its many victims? Or does it insult some of them by emphasising their helplessness and giving them new doubts about themselves, and about the possible causes of their current problems? We have seen that child sexual abuse can have harmful effects, and some of its victims may need help in dealing with these. However, there may be many more who have found their own ways of recovering. We may never know whether these people would have benefited from therapy. What we do know is that therapy itself sometimes has serious costs. In the following chapters I will be looking at the problems that can arise when anyone who is even suspected of having an abuse history is persuaded that they need long-term psychotherapy.

References – 2. The consequences of child sexual abuse

1   Hall L. and Lloyd S. (1989). *Surviving Child Sexual Abuse: a handbook for helping women challenge their past.* London: The Falmer Press, p. 92.
2   Ibid p. 93.
3   Blume, E.S. (1990). *Secret Survivors: Uncovering Incest and its After-effects in Women.* New York: Ballantyne. Pp. xxvii-xxx.
4   Rader W.C. (1992). Incest and Eating Disorders. *Professional Counsellor,* 6 (4), 16.
5   Cavanaugh R.M. (2002). Self mutilation as a manifestation of Child Sexual Abuse in adolescent girls. *Pediatric Adolescent Gynecology,* 15, 97-100.
6   Mind. www.mind.org.uk/help/information_and_advice. (Accessed August 2013. Follow links > mental health A-Z > Dissociative Disorders > causes).
7   Finkelhor D. et al (1990). Sexual abuse in a national survey of adult men and women: prevalence, characteristics, and risk factors. *Child Abuse and Neglect,* 14, 19-28.
8   Paine M.L. and Hanson D.J. (2002). Factors influencing children to self-disclose sexual abuse. *Clinical Psychology Review,* 22, 271-295.
9   Kendall-Tackett K.A., Meyer Williams L. and Finkelhor D. (1993). Impact of sexual abuse on children: a review and synthesis of recent empirical studies. *Psychological Bulletin,* 113 (1), 164-180.
10 Conte J. and Berliner L. (1988). The impact of sexual abuse on children: empirical findings. In L. Walker (Ed.) *Handbook on sexual abuse of children.* New York: Springer Publishing.
11 Finkelhor D. (1979). *Sexually Victimised Children.* New York: Free Press.
12 Hagan M. (2003). Faith in the model and resistance to research. *Clinical Psychology: Science and Practice.* 10 (3), 344-348.
13 Clancy S.A. (2009). *The Trauma Myth.* New York: Basic Books.

14 Berliner L. and Conte J. (1990). The process of victimisation: the victim's perspective. *Child Abuse and Neglect*, 14 (1), 29-40.

15 Finkelhor D. (1979) ibid.

16 Vogeltanz N.D., Wilsnack S.D. and Harris T.R. (1999). Prevalence and risk factors for childhood sexual abuse in women: national survey findings. *Child Abuse and Neglect*, 23, 579-592.

17 Clancy S. (2009) ibid p.38.

18 Horwitz A.V. et al (2001). Impact of child sexual abuse on adult mental health: a prospective study. *Journal of Health and Social Behaviour*, 42, 184-201.

19 Spataro J. et al (2004). Impact of child sexual abuse on mental health : prospective study in males and females. *British Journal of Psychiatry*, 184, 416-421.

20 Stein M. and Barrett-Connor E. (2000). Sexual Assault and Physical health: findings from a population-based study of older adults. *Psychosomatic Medicine*, 62, 838-843.

21 Alvarez J. et al (2007). The relationship between child sexual abuse and adult obesity among Californian women. *American Journal of Preventive Medicine*, 33 (1), 28-33.

22 Heim C.A. et al (2006). Early adverse experiences and risk for Chronic Fatigue Syndrome: results for a population based study. *Archives of general Psychiatry*, 63, 1258-1266.

23 Paras M.L. et al (2009). Sexual abuse and lifetime diagnosis of somatic disorders. *Journal of the American Medical Association*, 302 (5), 550-561.

24 Beitchman J.H. et al (1992). A review of the long term effects of child sexual abuse. *Child Abuse and Neglect*, 16 (1), 101-118.

25 Dong M. et al (2003). The relationship of exposure to child sexual abuse and other forms of abuse, neglect and household dysfunction. *Child Abuse and Neglect*, 27, 625-639.

26 Grief Green J. et al (2010). Childhood adversities and adult psychiatric disorder in the national comorbidity survey replication 1. *Archives of General Psychiatry*, 67 (2), 113-123.

27 Bushnell J.A., Wells J.E. and Oakley Browne M.A. (1992). Long-term effects of intrafamilial sexual abuse in childhood. *Acta Psychiatrica Scandinavia*, 85 (2), 136-142.

28 Felitti V.J. et al (1998). The relationship of adult health status to childhood abuse and household dysfunction. *American Journal of Preventive Medicine,* 14 (4), 245-258.

29 Edwards V.J. et al (2003). Relationship between multiple forms of childhood maltreatment and adult mental health in community respondents: results from the adverse childhood experiences study. *American Journal of Psychiatry,* 160 (8), 1453-1460.

30 Read J. et al (2005). Childhood Trauma, psychosis and schizophrenia: a literature review with theoretical and clinical implications. *Acta Psychiatrica Scandinavia,* 112, 330-350.

31 Kendler K.S. et al (2000). Childhood sexual abuse and adult psychiatric and substance use disorders in women. *Archives of General Psychiatry,* 57, 953-959.

32 Fergusson D.M., Boden J.M. and Horwood L.J. (2008). Exposure to childhood sexual and physical abuse and adjustment in early adulthood. *Child Abuse and Neglect,* 32, 607-619.

33 Read J. et al (2005) ibid.

34 Janssen I. et al (2004). Childhood abuse as a risk factor for psychotic experiences. *Acta Psychiatrica Scandinavia,* 109, 38-45.

35 Bebbington P.E. et al (2004). Psychosis, victimisation and childhood disadvantage. *British Journal of Psychiatry,* 185, 220-226.

36 Done J. et al (1994). Childhood antecedents of schizophrenia and affective illness: social adjustment at ages 7 and 11. *British Medical Journal,* 309, 699-703.

37 Bergman A.J., Wolfson M.A. and Walker E.F. (1997). Neuromotor functioning and behaviour problems in children at risk of psychopathology. *Journal of Abnormal Child Psychology,* 25, 229-237.

38 Cannon M. et al (2002). Evidence for early childhood, pan-developmental impairment specific to schizophreniform disorder: results from a longitudinal birth cohort. *Archives of General Psychiatry,* 59, 449-456.

39 Sullivan P.M. and Knutson J.F. (2000). Maltreatment and disabilities: a population based epidemiological study. *Child Abuse and Neglect,* 24, 1257-1273.

40 Rind B. and Tromovitch P. (1997). A meta-analytic review of findings from national samples on psychological correlates of child sexual abuse. *Journal of Sex Research*, 34, (3), 237-255.

41 Rind B., Tromovitch P. and Bauserman R. (1998). A meta-analytic examination of assumed properties of child sexual abuse using college samples. *Psychological Bulletin*, 124, 22-53.

42 Constantine L.L. (1981) Effects of early sexual experience: a review and synthesis of research. In L.L. Constantine and F.M. Martinson (Eds), *Children and Sex: new findings, new perspectives*. Boston: Little Brown and Co.

43 Browne A. and Finkelhor D. (1986). Initial and long term effects: a review of the research. In D. Finkelhor, *A Sourcebook on Child Sexual Abuse*. Beverley Hills: Sage.

44 Rind B., Bauserman R. and Tromovitch P. (2000). Science versus orthodoxy: anatomy of the congressional condemnation of a scientific article and reflections on remedies for future ideological attacks. *Applied and Preventive Psychology*, 9, 211-225.

45 Ulrich H.M., Randolph M. and Acheson S. (2006). A replication of the Meta-Analytic Examination of Child Sexual Abuse by Rind, Tromovitch and Bauserman 1998. *The Scientific Review of Mental Health Practice*, 4 (2), 37-51.

46 Bass E. and Davis L. (1988). *The Courage to Heal*. New York: Harper.

47 Bass E and Davis L, (2008). *The Courage to Heal*. New York: Harper. p. 3.

3. THE STRANGE HISTORY OF THE DISSOCIATIVE DISORDERS

We have seen that the many careful studies of the consequences of child sexual abuse give us a mixed picture. Long-term damage is certainly not inevitable, and when it does occur, it has sometimes been thought to result from the adverse family circumstances that can accompany it as much as from the abuse itself. Some researchers have found that the abuse itself increases the risk of its victims developing some later disorder, but the symptoms of these disorders cannot be seen as indicators of child sexual abuse since they are mostly quite common and are also suffered by people with no abuse history. No specific post-abuse syndrome has therefore been identified from this research. Despite this, there are people who still believe that such a syndrome does exist, and for some of them there is one condition that is a sure sign of severe early trauma. It is called Dissociative Identity Disorder, one of a class of ailments known as the dissociative disorders. It is argued that the only reason that the symptoms of these disorders were not detected in any of the studies of children or adults known to have been sexually abused is that the researchers failed to look for them. Because these manifestations of dissociation are hard to identify, the researchers either missed them altogether or mistook them for evidence of other disorders. Those who would like to see dissociative disorders more widely recognised claim that many people have for years been misdiagnosed with conditions such as depression, borderline personality disorder, anxiety disorders, schizophrenia and even some physical ailments such as chronic pelvic pain, when they were really suffering from an underlying dissociative disorder.[1]

So what are these elusive symptoms? Wikipedia tells us [2]

Dissociative disorders can be defined as conditions that involve disruptions or breakdowns of memory, awareness, identity and/or perception. People with dissociative disorders use dissociation, a defence mechanism, pathologically and involuntarily. Dissociative disorders are thought to be primarily caused by psychological trauma.

This does not tell us much about what symptoms to look out for, though it does tell us how they are caused. In fact the dissociative disorders seem to be defined as much by what causes them in the first place as by their presenting symptoms. To understand more we need to look at their history.

The dissociative disorders were not officially recognised until 1980, when they were first included in the Diagnostic and Statistical Manual of Mental Disorders (DSM-III), which psychiatrists in the United States and Canada use to classify their patients. Inclusion in the DSM is very important in North America, since health insurance can only be claimed for disorders which are listed. In 1980 DSM-III described five dissociative disorders: Dissociative Amnesia, Dissociative Fugue, Depersonalisation Disorder, Multiple Personality Disorder and Dissociative Disorder Not Otherwise Specified.

The inclusion of Multiple Personality Disorder raised a few eyebrows. This had previously been seen by most clinicians as far too rare and weird to be a believable diagnosis. Many others dismissed it altogether as an iatrogenic disorder generated in susceptible people by the interest of the doctor.[3-5] However, once multiple personality was included in the 1980 DSM-III, no amount of scepticism was able to stop a few North American psychiatrists claiming that it was not rare at all, that it might even be as common as schizophrenia. They now claimed that they had personally encountered many cases, and that its previous apparent rarity had simply been due to ignorance.[6] Before 1980 there were said to be only 200 cases of multiple personality in the entire world literature, but four years later more than 1000 documented cases had been claimed in the United States alone.[7] In an attempt to rid it of its former freakish connotations, multiple personality disorder in the 1994 DSM-IV was renamed 'Dissociative Identity Disorder', the most severe of the five dissociative disorders.

The reason for this keen interest in Multiple Personality/Dissociative Identity Disorder lay in the sinister new significance that it had acquired as being 'trauma-related'. This new understanding was broadcast around the world, so that, as we have seen, a UK mental health charity now endorses the trauma-related view, not just of Dissociative Identity Disorder but of 'moderate to severe dissociative symptoms'.[8]

Previous studies of Multiple Personality Disorder

Before 1980 the phenomenon of multiple personality was seen as both rare and mysterious. Multiple personalities had been noted throughout history and, at different times and in different places, had been seen as evidence of reincarnation, spirit possession or magical powers.[9] In the late 19th and early 20th centuries growing interest in hypnosis led to a new fascination with multiple personalities and some less supernatural explanations. There were some celebrated cases, such as Miss Beauchamp, whose story was told in a book written by her psychiatrist, Morton Prince.[10] She was a strict, anxious and inhibited young woman who suffered from headaches and lassitude. Under hypnosis she revealed a completely different character called Sally, who was extraverted, mischievous and flirtatious, much to the delight of her psychiatrist. In her normal waking state Miss Beauchamp was unaware of Sally's existence, but Sally apparently knew all about Miss Beauchamp and popped out from time to time to play tricks on her. This contrast between the different personalities was seen in several of the reported cases of that time, and sometimes featured as a partial explanation for what was happening. The alternative personality could offer an escape from current restrictions or problems. Past traumas did sometimes get a mention but were not usually thought to have caused the dissociation.

One of the contributors to the study of multiple personality at this time was Pierre Janet (1859 – 1947), a French psychologist who also had a medical degree. He is of special interest here because he coined the term *dissociation* and is held in great respect by many of the therapists who currently promote its trauma-related significance.

They claim to be following his theories. I find this surprising because the picture he presents of multiple personality and of dissociation in general seems so different from theirs.

Janet worked at the Salpêtrière Hospital in Paris with the celebrated neurologist Jean Martin Charcot, and later with Charcot's pupil, Sigmund Freud. At this time there was a growing interest in bizarre varieties of behaviour, including the 'Conversion Hysterias', in which people became blind, paralysed or otherwise disabled, with no apparent physical cause. The term 'hysteria' had originally been applied only to women, since this condition, which was characterised by a state of mental excitation and distress, was thought to be caused by a disorder in the uterus. Nearly all of Janet's patients, like nearly all of today's dissociated clients, were women of child-bearing age. Janet likened their dissociation to hypnosis. He used the term 'somnambulism' to describe both the hypnotic and the dissociated states of mind, in which patients were detached from their usual perceptions and capacities, and were highly suggestible. When these states were protracted and complicated, they could give rise to 'double existences, double personalities'. He was interested in the remarkable cases of dual personality presented by some of his fellow clinicians, and was well aware of Morton Price's 'Miss Beauchamp' and similar cases. He saw them as rare curiosities, but insisted that it was possible for there to be even rarer cases of multiple personality. He wrote about these 'complicated cases' with not just two personalities but 'as many as nine or ten'. However, he warned:

> In these complex cases a new influence makes itself felt which complicates matters a great deal. I mean the influence of the observer himself, who, in the end, knows his subject too well and is too well known to him. Whatever precautions one may take, the ideas of the observer in the end influence the development of the somnambulism of the subject, and give it an artificial complication.[11]

For Janet, suggestibility was an important characteristic, not only in multiple personalities, but in all manifestations of hysteria. It was a major feature of hypnosis, and it could be used therapeutically, but there was always this danger that 'the ideas of the observer' could have an undue influence. Janet's observation that dissociated patients often end up reflecting back their therapists concerns rather than their own does not appear to have occurred to many of the present promoters of the trauma-related view of dissociation.

An even more important way in which Janet's ideas differed from those currently being promoted is his understanding of the possible causes of dissociation. For Janet, dissociation could just be a constitutional characteristic of the individual, or it could be brought about by a variety of unpleasant experiences, usually very frightening. He gave examples of being run over, seeing a dead body in the street or watching one's mother die. In *The Major Symptoms of Hysteria*, which, unlike most of his works, was written in English, he used the word 'accidents' for these happenings. When talking of hysterical paralyses he noted that these accidents might be very slight in themselves, though accompanied by violent emotions and 'disturbances of the imagination'.[12] Dissociation usually followed an emotional shock, but Janet had no interest in looking for these shocks in early childhood. For Janet dissociation was not a necessary defence against overwhelming childhood trauma, but was a pathological response to more recent shocks, and it did not help the sufferer get over the bad experiences. Although dissociated patients might have periods of amnesia, they would also have intrusive thoughts of real or imagined terrors, and these would be cut off from more purposeful ways of thinking.

Janet, unlike his contemporary Freud, never founded a school of psychotherapy and seems to have had little later influence. Most of us, however, have had our ideas influenced to some extent by Freud, and for much of the 20th century Freudian theory and practice formed part of the training of psychiatrists in North America. As I mentioned in Chapter 1, Freud believed that most adult problems could be traced to unconscious conflicts in early childhood. He had great faith in his theories and, unlike Janet, never seemed to be aware that when he found what he expected to see, this might be because he had imposed his own ideas upon his patients. Perhaps this was one of the reasons he was so much more influential than Janet. The belief that dissociative disorders are almost always due to severe childhood trauma, can, in my opinion, be traced back to Freudian theory and practice. It is a belief that was born when one psychiatrist decided to conduct the first ever psychoanalysis of someone with multiple personality disorder.

The creation of Sybil

Cornelia Wilbur was a 37-year-old psychiatrist working in Omaha, Nebraska when she was first consulted by a 22-year-old student who was later to be known as Sybil. Sybil was suffering from headaches and memory lapses, and in that first session Wilbur decided to psychoanalyse her. However, it was not until many years later that treatment was able to start because Sybil's mother had intervened by hiding her appointment card. Her mother confessed to this crime on her deathbed, and Sybil then became determined to undertake the psychoanalysis. She had to save up for five years and move halfway across the US to New York in order to do this. Once there, she was immediately welcomed by Wilbur, and together they embarked on the lengthy analysis that gave us the first ever account of the way early childhood trauma could lead to the formation of multiple personality disorder.

During the following 11 years Sybil spurned the advances of several suitors and centred her life around her therapy. This diverged from the classic rules of psychoanalysis, which require the analyst to function like a blank screen on which the patient can project her free associations. Wilbur played an active role; she sometimes used hypnosis and drugs, and she often made herself available outside office hours. The therapy was intensive and lengthy, involving 2354 office appointments as well as many other personal contacts.[13] In the course of this treatment Sybil was said to manifest 16 alternative personalities, and through them to recall and describe a variety of cruel and bizarre abuses inflicted on her by her mother. These included being repeatedly beaten and tied up, and even suspended from the ceiling and having cold water injected into her bladder.

51

Having described these traumas, through her 16 alternative personalities, Sybil was eventually able to become reintegrated and regain employment, though she always remained dependent to some degree on Wilbur, and the two of them remained close friends until Wilbur's death in 1992.

Wilbur had apparently been excited at the prospect of carrying out the first ever psychoanalysis of a multiple personality, and was eager to publish her findings; but no professional, peer reviewed journal would accept her story. She then approached her journalist friend Flora Schreiber, and together they collaborated to turn her treatment records into the book *Sybil*.[14] It was therefore Schreiber who was responsible for telling us 'The true and extraordinary story of a woman possessed by sixteen separate personalities'. This was an immediate best-seller, and was made into an acclaimed film in 1976. It was even filmed again in 2006, though with less success this time.

It is certainly an extraordinary story, but does it reveal the truth about Sybil's childhood? Wilbur had to work very hard to unearth tales of maternal cruelty. She regularly used both hypnosis and sodium pentothal to elicit Sybil's alternative personalities. She recorded what Sybil said while she was under the influence, and then played this back to the alert Sybil. Schreiber describes how Wilbur was guided by her expectations, based on Freudian theory, to build upon what these 'personalities' were telling her, and also perhaps to shape their testimony.

> She knew that it would be necessary to treat each of the selves as a person in her own right and to winnow away at the reserve of Sybil, the waking self, otherwise the total Sybil Dorsett would never get well... The pivotal question was *why* had Sybil become a multiple personality?... The doctor believed however that Sybil's condition stemmed from some childhood trauma, though at this stage she couldn't be certain.[15]

Sybil's alternative personalities then provided the doctor with the stories that she needed to turn theory into fact. They spoke of the expected childhood traumas, all inflicted by Sybil's mother. There was no need to look for corroboration; Wilbur could work out what had happened, and Schreiber was able to describe, for the first time, how dissociation can help a child survive overwhelming trauma.

> Normal at birth, Sybil had fought back until she was about two and a half, by which time the fight had been literally beaten out of her. She had sought rescue from without until, finally recognising that rescue would be denied, she resorted to finding rescue within. First there was the rescue of creating a pretend world inhabited by a loving mother of fantasy but... being a multiple personality was the ultimate rescue.[16]

Wilbur never gave any account of how she was able to reconstruct Sybil's early years with such confidence. Schreiber's second-hand account of Wilbur's theorising has, however, come to be accepted as an accurate history of Sybil's childhood, and it is this story which was believed, not just by an enthralled public, but by a number of experienced and influential psychiatrists. We are still seeing the effects of this today.

At one stage during her therapy Sybil denied that she had multiple personalities. She wrote Wilbur a long letter, of which an excerpt is included in Schreiber's book.

> I'm not going to tell you that there isn't anything wrong. We both know there is. But it's not what I have led you to believe. I do not have any multiple personalities. I do not even have a "double" to help me out. I am all of them. I have been essentially lying in my pretence of them. The dissociations are not the problem because they do not actually exist, but there is something wrong or I would not resort to pretending like that. And you might ask me about my mother. The extreme things I told you about her were not true. My mother was more than a little nervous. At times she was flighty, clearly overanxious, but she did love me. My parents were better than a lot of parents are. [17]

Shreiber then tells us how Wilbur invoked the Freudian concept of denial to explain this lapse. Denial occurs when patients find that the new truths, revealed by treatment, are too painful to bear. It can even be a sign that treatment is really getting somewhere. Wilbur was later able to persuade Sybil to accept what her personalities and her therapist were telling her.

There is little mention in Shreiber's book of Herbert Spiegel. He was a fellow psychiatrist and colleague who gave advice and took over Sybil's treatment when Wilbur was unavailable. Spiegel also saw Sybil independently, as he had discovered that she was highly hypnotisable, and he used her in his demonstrations of hypnosis to medical students. In an interview with Mikkel Borch-Jacobson, given 22 years after the publication of *Sybil*, he gave us a completely new insight into what lay behind Sybil's denial of having multiple personalities.

> One day during our regression studies, Sybil said "Well, do you want me to be Helen?" And I said "What do you mean?" And she said "Well, when I'm with Dr Wilbur, she wants me to be Helen." I said "who's Helen?" "Well, that's a name Dr Wilbur gave me for this feeling"… That's when I realised that Connie was helping her identify aspects of her life, or perspectives, that she then called by name. By naming them this way she was reifying a memory of some kind and converting it into 'personality'.[18]

He was asked why there was hardly any mention of his role as assistant therapist in Schreiber's book, and provided a very revealing explanation.

> I think they [Schreiber and Wilbur] were both angry with me because I refused to collaborate with them on the book. Wilbur had decided she was going to make the Sybil case into a book, because she couldn't get it published in professional journals. So she engaged Schreiber, who was a professional writer, and they both came to see me to ask if I wanted to be

a co-author with them. That was the original proposal: since I had all this information about the case, would I join in with them?... But toward the end of our discussion, they said they would be calling her a "multiple personality". I said, "but she's not a multiple personality!" I think she was a wonderful hysterical patient with role confusion, which is typical of high hysterics. It was hysteria... I could change Sybil's state of awareness just by regressing her to this and that, but that didn't make her a multiple personality. It didn't mean that a personality was enduring, or was taking charge of her life. So I told Wilbur and Schreiber that it would not be accurate to call Sybil a multiple personality, and that it was not consistent with what I knew about her. Schreiber then got in a huff. She was sitting right in that chair there, and she said, "But if we don't call it a multiple personality we don't have a book! The publishers want it to be that, otherwise it won't sell![19]

It seems from Spiegel's conversation with Mikkel Borch-Jacobsen that labelling Sybil a remarkable case of multiple personality was initially a commercial decision, and a very shrewd one! The book did sell. By 1975 it had been a best-seller for six months and was still selling at 40,000 to 50,000 copies per month. All three protagonists, Wilbur, Schreiber and Sybil, remained close friends and shared in the royalties. When Wilbur later left New York to take up a teaching post in Lexington, at the University of Kentucky, Sybil also moved there in order to be near her. Spiegel had no regrets at distancing himself from their project, and said he was embarrassed by the 'whole new wave of hysteria' which followed publication of the book .

This wave of hysteria seems even more embarrassing now that the records kept by Schrieber while writing her book have become available. Thanks to an exhaustive examination of them by Debbie Nathan we now know a lot more about how this book came to be written.[20] We learn that Schreiber herself had serious doubts about the truth of Sybil's revelations about her childhood. This led her to make her own investigations. Against Wilbur's wishes she visited Sybil's home town to look for some corroboration from Sybil's remaining family members, neighbours and her doctor. Her records show that this quest for supporting evidence drew a complete blank. They also reveal that she was disturbed by some discrepancies between Wilbur's accounts of therapy and accounts that Sybil had written in her therapy journal. However, she had agreed to write this book which she correctly predicted would become a best-seller and greatly benefit all three protagonists.

Sybil's legacy

While Wilbur was treating Sybil in her New York clinic, she was not alone in her interest in Multiple Personality Disorder. Other psychiatrists and psychologists had regretted that this condition had fallen out of fashion since the 1930s, and was now rarely diagnosed. They attributed this to the emergence of a new disease concept which was being used to explain a wide range of mental disturbances. This was schizophrenia, which literally means 'split mind' and was said to be an organic illness with a very poor prognosis. Organic psychiatry was gaining ground, and for some psychiatrists this must have jarred with the psychodynamic theories derived from Freud that were part of their training. I believe that this is an important factor which ignited a new enthusiasm for Multiple Personality Disorder (MPD) and which started a campaign by a small group of American psychiatrists, some of whom were colleagues of Wilbur, to get this strange condition officially recognised as a disorder requiring treatment. They argued that many people with MPD were being misdiagnosed as schizophrenics. It is interesting that, according to Spiegel, Wilbur had initially considered Sybil to be schizophrenic.[21] It is due to the tireless activities of a small group of clinicians (which included Bennet Braun, Frank Putnam, George Greaves, Robert Kluft and Ralph Allison), rather then any stirrings in mainstream psychiatry, that MPD gained its first recognition as a psychiatric disorder in the 1980 DSM-III .[22]

These clinicians had all greeted the publication of Sybil with uncritical delight. According to Greaves 'the case of Sybil firmly linked Multiple Personality Disorder with child abuse'. He claimed that

Wilbur 'went to great lengths' to validate Sybil's testimony, and that she interviewed 'her parents'.[23] We now know this to be a complete fabrication. Sybil's mother had, of course, been dead long before the therapy started. We learn from Nathan's account that it was Schreiber who visited Sybil's childhood home but failed to find the evidence she was looking for.[24] We shall probably never know what really happened to Sybil when she was a little girl. Since her true identity became known, shortly before her death in 1998, and before Nathan's recent researches, others have made similar investigations into her past, some wishing to validate her story and others to debunk it.[25] The evidence is inconclusive. Sybil's mother was certainly rather odd, and according to her medical records she had once been diagnosed with 'asthenia', which would probably now be termed depression. There is no evidence that she was ever, as Wilbur had supposed, schizophrenic.[26] Her father said he did not know of any abuse and the neighbours noticed nothing strange, but that does not mean that nothing went on. Sybil herself never repudiated the story in the book, but, of course, it was not in her interest to do so.

Wilbur went on to diagnose further cases of MPD, as did other members of her group. Greaves claimed that he knew of 50 cases diagnosed during the 1970s, though there had only been 14 known cases between 1944 and 1969. He was soon outdone by Braun, who estimated that 500 cases had been diagnosed by 1979. According to him, this number increased to 1,000 by 1983 and 5,000 by 1986.[27] All these new cases were said to be trauma-related, firmly linked to child abuse. Within a short span of time MPD had gone from being both rare and mysterious to being a common psychiatric disorder with a known cause. But was this common psychiatric disorder really the same thing as the previous mysterious phenomenon?

Two earlier surveys of reported cases of multiple personality give us a picture of how differently this phenomenon was seen before *Sybil*. In 1944, an exhaustive search through the world literature looking for cases of multiple personality had only come up with 76 cases, half of them from the nineteenth century.[28] Then in 1962, J.P. Sutcliffe and Jean Jones presented more detailed accounts of 16 'notable cases', most of which had been included in the earlier sample.[29] They found that first dissociation was often said to occur shortly after some trauma, sometimes in adolescence, but usually in adulthood, and suggested that brain damage might be a factor here. In many other cases they suggested that the enactment of an alternative personality served the function of enabling people to overcome their customary inhibitions (for example, when Morton Price's prim and proper Miss Beauchamp became the lively, flirtatious Sally). It could also be a way of avoiding current difficulties.

Like Janet, Sutcliffe and Jones noticed that therapists often seemed to shape the emerging dissociations, and that cases with the most 'luxuriant growth' were usually the products of long-term hypnotherapy. All the therapists had accepted the reality of these other personalities, had given them names and discussed them with their patients. They admitted, in accounts of their cases, that the transformations had impressed them, and that they were fascinated with a startling phenomenon. Those therapists who looked for conflicting aspects of their patients' personalities or used techniques such as hypnosis or automatic writing were especially likely to encounter multiple personalities, while others might never come across them. However, these researchers were unwilling to dismiss multiple personalities as entirely iatrogenic. Multiple personalities would be more likely to appear if the individual was susceptible and had been exposed to some precipitating factor, such as a severe shock or conflict. It is striking that none of these earlier therapists apparently looked beyond this precipitating trauma to anything that might have happened in early childhood. Most alternative personalities were not seen until treatment was underway, and no conjectures were made about any earlier function they might have had.

Perhaps the most important distinction between alternative personalities before and after *Sybil* is that before *Sybil* they were assumed to represent the fantasy life of the host personality. They might give insights into his or her present state of mind, but were not otherwise seen as reliable informants. After *Sybil* we find that alternative personalities suddenly become the repositories of truth. They are often assumed to be accurate re-enactments of the host personality as a child, and it is to them that the therapist turns to find the truth of what happened long ago. For more than thirty years therapists treating MPD and DID have assumed that any new identities emerging during treatment can provide a believable, first-hand account of childhood experiences because they have been there since childhood. Nobody noticed these alternative identities at the time, but they must have been there because that is what the theory demands.

Alter selves usually manifest themselves in early childhood, as early as age 2½ and typically by age 6 or 8.[30]

MPD develops when an overwhelmed child who cannot flee or fight, takes flight inwardly and creates an alternative self structure and psychological reality within which and/or by virtue of which emotional survival is facilitated.[31]

DID is a little girl pretending that the abuse is happening to somebody else[32]

It is widely agreed that a diagnosis of DID is *prima facie* evidence of early trauma, because only severe disruption before the sense of self as an individual is formed can provide such severe dissociative symptoms.[33]

Assessing the evidence of trauma

The link between Dissociative Disorders and severe early child abuse is now treated as a given by those promoting these disorders.

As many as 99% of people who develop dissociative disorders have documented histories of repetitive, overwhelming and often life threatening trauma at a sensitive developmental stage of childhood.[34]

The websites of many organisations, including an NHS hospital, are now telling us the same thing: a history of childhood trauma or abuse is 'almost universal' for those with dissociative disorders. [35,36]

What we are not told is how we can be so sure about this. The therapists are convinced by the shocking reports of sexual abuse they hear from their clients. In conversations with them I have noticed how powerfully they are affected by this, and how sincerely they believe them and want to help. Told about horrifying and repulsive activities, often by someone who seems to have regressed to the young age when she suffered this abuse, they ask 'Why would she put herself through all this if it wasn't true?' These therapists see no need to look for corroboration, and feel that they would be betraying their clients if they did so.

Nevertheless, to convince a wider public about 'documented histories' of child abuse some external corroboration needs to be available. Sometimes this is said to exist, but we are not usually given sufficient information to enable us to judge its reliability. In one study of clients treated over a five-year period the therapist reported that just over half had 'instances of confirmed abuse', but he also confessed that in most cases he accepted what his clients had told him about this corroboration, and did not check it himself.[37] In a more systematic study of 90 clients in a unit for dissociative disorders it was claimed that 'nearly all participants who reported physical and sexual abuse and who attempted corroboration were able to find some kind of verification'. But since less than a quarter of them actually made this attempt, we are left wondering about the rest of the sample, and also what 'some kind of verification' really involved.[38]

Since child sexual abuse is a regrettably common occurrence it is indeed likely that some people with DID will have been abused; but in most cases we cannot be certain what really happened long ago, or whether this has any bearing on their current state of mind. We do know that anyone having therapy for a disorder that is thought to result from childhood abuse is likely to be influenced by their therapist's expectations. So if we want to obtain uncontaminated testimony from people with dissociative symptoms, we have to leave the therapy clinic and question unselected samples of people who have not yet been diagnosed with DID. They will probably be unaware that they have a dissociative disorder and will therefore not have been influenced by any therapist into thinking they have been sexually abused. A self-administered questionnaire which lists the symptoms of DID has been useful here. This is the Dissociative Experiences Scale (DES), which identifies people at risk of having DID; it will be fully described in the next chapter.

There have been several studies aimed at discovering whether people who get high scores on the DES (indicating many dissociative experiences) are especially likely to report childhood abuse. In one of the first, which used a community sample of more that a thousand women in New Zealand, subjects completed the DES, and were asked whether they had experienced sexual or physical abuse during childhood.[39] They were also questioned about any current psychiatric problems. The small proportion of these women who obtained high DES scores were found to be more likely than the rest of the sample to report sexual and physical abuse. They were also more likely to report current psychiatric symptoms. At first sight this study appears to show the expected relationship between childhood abuse and dissociation, but because both were also related to current psychiatric illness the researchers felt unable to make any firm conclusions about which was most relevant. On the contrary, they claimed that their results 'call into question the hypothesised direct effects of childhood sexual abuse on dissociation'. They made the point that previous studies looking only at samples of women in treatment had probably overestimated the link between abuse and dissociation because abused women would be more likely to seek treatment, and the treatment would be likely to increase their level of dissociation.

A further community study, also in New Zealand, looked not only at the link between childhood sexual abuse and dissociation, but also at the ways in which women coped with problems and used psychiatric services.[40] These women were interviewed and assessed, using several different questionnaires including the DES. Those who reported child sexual abuse were compared with those who did not. There were no differences between the groups in their average DES scores, but they did differ significantly on several other measures. Those reporting child sexual abuse were more likely to have sought professional help within the past year, and to show immature ways of coping with difficulties. Once again, the various measures used were interrelated, and it was not possible to tease out any causal relationships between them. There was no suggestion of any relationship between dissociative symptoms and a history of child sexual or physical abuse, but dissociation was found to be related to psychiatric disorder and recent requests for help. These researchers concluded that women who were sexually abused as children but are not in treatment are not likely to show abnormally high levels of dissociation, though they may have other psychological problems.

In both the above studies, dissociative symptoms were shown to be associated with other psychological disorders. A high level of such symptoms has often been found in people who are having psychological treatment. A sample of men and women admitted to a psychiatric hospital in the Netherlands were given the DES and interviewed about various adverse childhood experiences such as separation, bad parenting, physical and sexual abuse.[41] Almost a fifth of them gained DES scores that were suggestive of dissociative disorders, and there was a weak relationship between dissociative symptoms and reports of both physical and sexual abuse. But the single factor that was found to be most closely related to dissociation was having a mother who was a heavy drinker. These researchers suggested that recent traumatic experiences and the stress of being admitted to hospital might be just as important in provoking dissociative symptoms as anything that happened during these patients' childhoods.

Theory has it that people with DID have been using dissociation as a defence ever since they were traumatised as young children, though they may be unaware of this before they enter therapy. There does not appear to be any evidence to support this idea. Dissociative symptoms have not featured in surveys of abused or traumatised children,[42] and a recent review has revealed that only a very small number of cases of childhood DID have been discovered during the past 30 years, in contrast to the hundreds of thousands of adult DID cases that have been seen during this time.[43]

If we want to find out whether abused children are at risk of developing DID we need to look at prospective studies in which children who are known to have been abused are followed up into adulthood and then assessed to see whether they show symptoms of DID. Once again, because this disorder only becomes apparent once treatment is underway, researchers have had to rely on questionnaire responses that are said to identify people at risk of developing DID. Two such prospective studies have now been completed, both of which used the DES. In the first of these a large sample of children from low income families in the US were studied over a period of 20 years.[44] Some of them were known to have suffered physical and sexual abuse during this time. When they were 19 years old, they completed the DES. It was found that high dissociation scores at this age were associated with poor attachment to their early caregivers, who had been judged to be remote. This had been noticed during the first two years of their lives. However, these high dissociation scores were not associated with any of the episodes of physical or sexual abuse that were also known to have occurred. A later study, using very similar methods, produced remarkably similar results.[45] Once again, family interactions were observed, and problems noted over many years. When the children had reached about 19 years, those contacted were given the DES, and high dissociation scores at this time were again found to be associated with deficiencies in the quality of early care, especially with lack of maternal involvement. However, as in the previous study, some documented early occurrences of physical and sexual abuse were not associated with any increase in later dissociation scores, a finding that clearly surprised the researchers.

Some people are now suggesting that it is a lack of secure attachment to mothers or other caregivers in early life that might be crucial in leading to later dissociative symptoms. They have drawn upon the work of John Bowlby, which demonstrated the importance of this early attachment.[46] This has led them to give an interesting tweak to their original theory about the origins of dissociation: 'infant attachment disorganisation is in itself a dissociative process, and predisposes the individual to respond with pathological dissociation to later traumas and life stressors.'[47] This speculation involves a significant departure from the 'overwhelming trauma' which was originally supposed to set the whole process in motion. A poor relationship with early caregivers may well be damaging, but this is not what people with DID have been talking about to their therapists. Their stories always seem to involve sexual abuse, which is usually both severe and persistent. It was to protect themselves from full awareness of this trauma that they were thought to need to use the defence of dissociation.

Thus, the supposed link between dissociation and early childhood abuse is not supported by any reliable experimental evidence. Retrospective studies that rely on adult reports of childhood abuse have shown, at best, only an indirect association, with high DES scores being related as much to adult problems as to childhood abuse. Prospective studies, in which the early abuse was verified, have shown no link at all between this and later DES scores. A shortcoming in the above studies was that they did not include people with a definite diagnosis of DID, but only dealt with self-reported dissociative symptoms, indicated by high questionnaire scores. Nevertheless, an association between dissociation score and childhood abuse was expected but was not found. Members of the public who gained high scores have given accounts of their childhood that are very different from those of people being treated for DID. The notion that DID has its origin in childhood trauma appears to have the status of a strongly held faith rather than a scientific theory.

References – 3. The strange history of the Dissociative Disorders

★ All webpages could be accessed in August 2013

1   Steinberg M. and Schnall M. (2001). *The Stranger in the Mirror.* New York: Harper.
2   en.wikipedia.org/wiki/Dissociative_disorder
3   Merskey H. (1992). The manufacture of personalities: the production of multiple personality disorder. *British Journal of Psychiatry*, 160, 327-340.
4   Piper A. (1994). Multiple Personality Disorder. *British Journal of Psychiatry*, 164, 600-612.
5   Seltzer A. (1994). Multiple personality: a psychiatric misadventure. *Canadian Journal of Psychiatry, 39,* 442-445.
6   Ross C.A. (1991). Clinical presentations of Multiple Personality Disorder. *Psychiatric Clinics of North America*, 14, 605-629.
7   Braun B.G. (1984). Foreward. *Psychiatric Clinics of North America*, 7, 1-2.
8   Mind. www.mind.org.uk (Follow links > information and advice > mental health A-Z > dissociative disorders > causes).
9   Ellenberger H. (1970). *The Discovery of the Unconscious: the history and evolution of dynamic psychiatry.* New York: Basic Books.
10 Prince M. (1906). *The Dissociation of a Personality.* New York: Longmans, Green and Co.
11 Janet P. (1907). *The Major Symptoms of Hysteria.* London: Macmillan and Co, p. 85.
12 Ibid. p. 139.
13 Greaves G.B. (1980). Multiple Personality 165 years after Mary Reynolds. *Journal of Nervous and Mental Diseases*, 168, 577-596.
14 Schreiber R. (1973). *Sybil.* Chicago: Regnery.
15 Ibid p. 75.
16 Ibid p. 185.
17 Ibid p. 74.

18 Borch-Jacobsen M. (1997). Sybil – The making of a disease: an interview with Dr. Herbert Spiegel. *New York Review of Books.* New York, April 24.

19 Ibid.

20 Nathan D. (2011). *Sybil Exposed: the extraordinary story behind the famous multiple personality case.* New York: Free Press.

21 Borch-Jacobsen M. (1997) ibid.

22 Ross C.A. (1989) *Multiple Personality Disorder: Diagnosis, Clinical Features and Treatment.* New York: Wiley, p. 45.

23 Greaves GB (1993). A History of Dissociative Identity Disorder. Chapter 19 *in* RP Kluft and CG Fine (Eds.), *Clinical Perspectives on Multiple Personality.* New York: American Psychiatric Press.

24 Nathan D. (2011). ibid pp.161-166.

25 Rieber R.W. (2006). *The Bifurcation of the Self.* New York: Springer, p. 129.

26 Nathan D. (2011) ibid p. 116.

27 Ross C.A.(1989) ibid p. 45.

28 Taylor W.S. and Martin M.F. (1944). Multiple Personality. *Journal of Abnormal and Social Psychology,* 39, 281-300.

29 Sutcliffe J.P. and Jones J. (1962). Personal identity, multiple personality, and hypnosis. *The International Journal of Clinical and Experimental Hypnosis,* X, 4, 231-269.

30 Greaves G.B. (1980). ibid.

31 Kluft R.P. (1991). Clinical presentations of multiple personality disorder. *Psychiatric Clinics of North America* 14, 103-110.

32 Ross C.A. (1997). *Dissociative Identity Disorder: Diagnosis, Clinical Features and Treatment of Multiple Personality.* New York: Wiley, p. 92.

33 Galton G. (2008). Some clinical implications of believing or not believing the patient. *In* Sachs A. and Galton G. (Eds.) *Forensic Aspects of Dissociative Identity Disorder.* London: Karnac, p. 118.

34 Sidran Institute. www.sidran.org (Follow links > resources > what is a dissociative disorder?)

35 Great Ormond Street Hospital. www.gosh.nhs.uk (Follow links >medical conditions>dissociative disorders> more information).

36 Mind, ibid.

37 Kluft R.P. (1993). The confirmation and disconfirmation of memories of abuse in Dissociative Identity Disorder patients: a naturalistic study. *Dissociation*, 8, 253-258.

38 Chu J.A. et al (1999). Memories of childhood abuse: dissociation, amnesia and corroboration. *American Journal of Psychiatry*, 156, 749-755.

39 Mulder R.T. et al (1998). Relationship between dissociation, childhood sexual abuse, and mental illness in a general population sample. *American Journal of Psychiatry*, 115, 806-811.

40 Romans S.E. et al (1999). Psychological defence styles in women who report child sexual abuse: a controlled community study. *American Journal of Psychiatry*, 156, 1080-1085.

41 Draijer N. and Langeland W. (1999). Childhood trauma and perceived parental dysfunction in the etiology of dissociative symptoms in psychiatric patients. *American Journal of Psychiatry*, 156, 379-385.

42 Kendall-Tackett K.A., Meyer Williams L. and Finkelhor D. (1993). Impact of sexual abuse on children: a review and synthesis of recent studies. *Psychological Bulletin*, 113 (1), 164-180.

43 Boysen G. (2011). The scientific status of childhood dissociative identity disorder: a review of published research. *Psychotherapy Psychosomatics*, 80, 329-334.

44 Ogawa J.R. et al (1997). Development and the fragmented self: longitudinal study of dissociative symptomatology in a non-clinical sample. *Developmental Psychopathology*, 9 (4), 855-879.

45 Dutra L. et al (2009). Quality of early care and childhood trauma: a prospective study of developmental pathways to dissociation. *Journal of Nervous and Mental Disease*, 197, 383-390.

46 Bowlby J. (1982). *Attachment and Loss: Attachment*. London: Basic Books.

47 Liotti G. (2006). A model of dissociation based on attachment theory and research. *Journal of Trauma and Dissociation*, 7(4), 55-73.

4. DIAGNOSING DISSOCIATIVE DISORDERS

Since 1994, when DSM-IV was drafted, and Multiple Personality Disorder was renamed Dissociative Identity Disorder (DID), we have been told that DID is just one of a range of dissociative disorders. The others include Dissociative Amnesia, Dissociative Fugue and Depersonalisation Disorder. We hear very little about the first two of these disorders and their supposed causes. More interest has recently been shown in Depersonalisation Disorder, with the suggestion that this too may be linked to childhood trauma.[1] However, the most severe of these disorders (and apparently the most interesting) is still said to be Dissociative Identity Disorder. We are told that this is the condition that has often been overlooked by researchers and therapists because they did not recognise its elusive symptoms. In this chapter I will be describing some of the questionnaires and guided interview schedules that have been devised to help them in this task.

Despite the attention that has been given to DID, and the many aids devised for its diagnosis, we find that this is not the most commonly detected dissociative disorder. This distinction goes to Dissociative Disorder Not Otherwise Specified (DDNOS), which has been described as 'a lesser form of DID'.[2,3] It was originally defined as 'dissociative presentations that do not meet the full criteria for any other dissociative disorder'.[4] This curiously negative disorder has symptoms which are not sufficient to indicate DID, yet they are apparently thought to be sufficient to indicate the same history of severe early childhood abuse. The justification for this has never been explained. This has the effect of casting the diagnostic net far wider with the alarming result that DDNOS has been claimed to affect 10% of the population.[5]

The International Society for Trauma and Dissociation has published authoritative guidelines for the treatment of dissociative disorders and these fail to differentiate between DID and DDNOS.[6] Sometimes a further fudge is introduced by using the term 'complex dissociation', which presumably covers both DID and DDNOS. In most of the recent literature promoting the treatment of dissociative disorders, the other dissociative disorders of amnesia, fugue and depersonalisation are largely ignored, but the catch-all diagnosis of DDNOS gets similar attention to DID, and no distinction is made in the recommended treatment.

The difficulties of psychiatric diagnosis

Psychiatrists usually classify mental disorders in terms of the symptoms that tend to go together and respond to certain types of treatment, but there is often so much overlap between the symptoms of different disorders that the decision about which disorder best fits any particular set of symptoms is extremely difficult. It is for this reason that the American Psychiatric Association in 1952 first published their classification system, the DSM, which is now internationally recognised and used in many other countries. In the UK the preferred classification system for psychiatrists is a section (Mental and Behavioural Problems) of the International Classification of Diseases and Related Health Problems (ICD), published in 1992 by the World Health Organisation. Both systems have been through many revisions, so that by 2010 DSM-IV and ICD-10 were the current versions in use as aids to psychiatric diagnosis.

The use of classification systems can never rule out error, especially when they deal with psychological complaints since these are difficult to describe objectively and are subject to many different interpretations. In an effort to standardise psychiatric diagnosis, various structured interviews and questionnaires have been introduced. These can help clinicians decide which of several diagnoses is most appropriate or whether none really fits their client's problems. It is, however, impossible to rule out personal preference and changing diagnostic fashions. Clinicians will always be more likely to diagnose a disorder if they believe they can treat it, and the incidence of some disorders seems to increase when new remedies are found. One example of this is the recent dramatic increase in reported cases of bipolar disorder. This diagnostic shift has been attributed to the development and marketing of new drugs, said to be 'mood stabilising' and effective in treating this disorder.[7] It is worth remembering therefore that the campaign to promote the diagnosis of dissociative disorders has been led, from the start, by psychiatrists who have developed and practised their own new form of psychotherapy for its treatment.

For a variety of reasons, diagnosis will always be something of a hit or miss affair, and we have to find some way of monitoring the frequency of both the hits and the misses. When a clinician gets a hit, diagnosing a disorder in someone who really does turn out to have it, we call it a true positive, and when they miss, failing to diagnose the disorder in someone who has it, we call it a false negative. A correct decision that a disorder is not present gives a true negative, and the diagnosis of a disorder in someone who does not have it is a false positive. When diagnostic methods produce few false positive results they are said to be specific, and when they produce few false negative results they are said to be sensitive, and there is always a trade-off between specificity and sensitivity. When any diagnostic method narrows its focus and becomes more specific there is an increased chance that it will miss some cases and produce false negatives. When it widens its scope to become more sensitive there is an increased chance of it including people who do not have the disorder thus giving them false positive diagnoses.

In encouraging clinicians to diagnose disorders which were previously overlooked, the promoters of dissociative disorders are asking them to be more sensitive: to enquire about complaints not previously seen as symptoms of any disorder, and also to consider symptoms previously thought to indicate other disorders. This increases the risk of false positive diagnosis, so that clinicians have to be extra vigilant, making sure their enquiries are also specific to this particular disorder. They also need to find some means of distinguishing between the true and false positive diagnoses. But how do you tell whether a disorder of the mind is really present or not? In physical medicine a laboratory test often determines whether or not the disorder is present. A bacillus grown from a sputum sample can give indisputable evidence of tuberculosis. In psychiatry, however, there are usually no clear markers, and we are left with clinical opinion as the only yardstick.

Diagnosis in the absence of specific symptoms

The task of diagnosing dissociative disorders is especially difficult because of the lack of presenting symptoms. Ever since clinicians were first encouraged to consider diagnosing MPD they were warned that this can be difficult because it is often a 'covert' disorder. Most of those affected are unaware that they have multiple personalities and are unlikely to show any obvious signs of their disorder.

A clinician will not find MPD if he or she is not willing to look for it.[8]

The irreducible core of MPD is a persistent form of intrapsychic structure rather than overt behavioural manifestations.[9]

Now that the disorder is known as DID the difficulties seem to get worse, because the net has been widened to include DDNOS, with symptoms that are even less obvious than those of DID. It is hard to see how these can ever be detected, since even with DID people may not at first show any obvious signs of dissociation. A supervisor in the Advanced Psychotherapy Training Programme in Washington DC urges, however, that absence of symptoms should never stand in the way of a suspicion of DID.

In my experience, only one of about every 10 DID patients I meet has the classic symptoms… If that's what you look for then you will miss a lot of DID… Please ask your patients about trauma. With the patient who is an "atypical" depressed or bipolar patient, has panic attacks, an eating disorder that can't be classified, may have been called schizophrenic years ago, but clearly is not, or is simply unresponsive to exhaustive psychopharmacologic and psychotherapeutic efforts, think DID. Don't expect to notice changes between alter personalities in an initial interview.[10]

Until recently the website for Dissociation Australia, an organisation established in 2004, gave a similar warning:

> Individuals suffering from the dissociative disorders rarely present with the symptoms that define the various disorders.[11]

Clinicians are advised to see any symptoms of other known psychiatric disorders as secondary to the 'underlying' dissociative disorder that has yet to manifest itself.

> Although individuals with dissociative disorders may present with symptoms which mimic psychosis and may endorse items on the SCL-90 [a measure of psychiatric distress] associated with psychosis, clinicians should be aware that elevated polysymptomatic profiles may reflect underlying dissociative rather than psychotic spectrum disorders.[12]

Since the time when MPD was first included in the DSM III and became more frequently diagnosed, those making this diagnosis have noted that their clients may have symptoms that would usually point to a completely different disorder. In 1987, Robert Kluft suggested that because many of the established 'first rank' symptoms of schizophrenia, including hallucinations and delusions, were so often seen in MPD, these should now be seen as 'a valuable diagnostic clue to multiple personality disorder'.[13] This willingness to enlist the symptoms of other disorders to aid the diagnosis of a disorder whose own symptoms remain hidden has continued to this day. The symptoms of depression, bipolar disorder, anxiety, borderline personality disorder, self-harming and substance abuse have all been invoked as pointers to an underlying dissociative disorder. It has been claimed that clients typically spend many years being misdiagnosed with these disorders and receiving inappropriate treatment, because clinicians do not know how to recognise the elusive dissociative disorders.

Diagnostic tools: 1.The Dissociative Experiences Scale

Several aids have been developed to help clinicians with the task of diagnosing dissociative disorders. Asking clients to fill in a questionnaire is one method. This tells the client which symptoms are being looked for and then asks whether or not they have been experienced. There have been several such questionnaires, but only two will be discussed here. The most widely used questionnaire was one of the first to be developed. This is the Dissociative Experiences Scale (DES), introduced by Eve Bernstein and Frank Putnam in 1986; it is reproduced in full in the appendix. It contains 28 questions, chosen by clinicians to represent what they imagined their dissociated clients experienced. They all have the same format, as seen below:

Some people have the experience of finding themselves in a place and having no idea how they got there. Circle a number to show what percentage of the time this happens to you.

Some people sometimes have the experience of feeling that other people, objects, and the world around them are not real. Circle a number to show what percentage of the time this happens to you.

Some people find that in one situation they may act so differently compared with another situation that they feel almost as though they were different people. Circle a number to show what percentage of the time this happens to you.[14]

Earlier versions of this questionnaire asked the respondent to mark a line at a point to indicate the frequency with which they experience the given symptom. Percentages were later used because this made scoring easier. The overall DES score in this case is the sum of the percentages for each question divided by 28, the number of questions. Thus possible scores range from 0 to 100. The higher the score, the more likely that it will indicate DID. In unselected populations the average score will usually be around 10, since some of the questions deal with things experienced by many people. As Figure 1 shows, the distribution of scores in the general population is usually very skewed, with most people gaining low scores and very few gaining the higher scores. There is a gradual decrease in frequency as the scores get higher. This suggests that dissociation, as

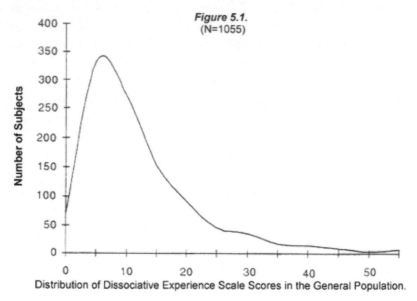

Figure 5.1.
(N=1055)

Distribution of Dissociative Experience Scale Scores in the General Population.

Figure 1 (from www.rossinst.com)

measured by the DES, varies along a continuum, and that people may be more or less dissociated but they cannot be clearly sorted into two separate categories: those with a dissociative disorder and those without. It is therefore difficult to decide where to draw the line between 'normal' dissociation reported by ordinary people and the pathological dissociation that suggests DID. There has been much disagreement about how high a DES score should be to suggest a dissociative disorder. Originally a cut-off score of 30 was proposed, which would have high specificity and a low risk of false positive diagnoses. However, as we will see later, far lower cut-off scores have been recommended in order to detect all those who might be 'at risk' of having a dissociative disorder.[15]

The distribution of DES scores in the general population suggests that people with high dissociation scores differ from the rest of us in degree only, rather than forming a recognisably separate category. This has never been the view of the promoters of dissociation, since they claim that the cause of serious dissociative disorders is something that does put people into a separate category. They have either suffered early and severe child abuse or they have not. Although child abuse varies along a continuum, from mild or brief ill-treatment to sustained destructive cruelty, it is only the more severe and long-lasting forms of child abuse that are said to lead to dissociative disorders. People with DID are thus assumed to have suffered in a categorically different way from most other people and to have employed a 'pathological' form of dissociation to cope with this.[16]

To justify this view of DID it is necessary to identify this pathological dissociation, which is assumed to be distinct from normal dissociation. In an ingenious study, Niels Waller, Frank Putnam and Eve Carson claimed to have achieved this. They examined the DES responses of 228 adults who had been diagnosed with DID and compared them with 228 'normal controls'. They then used three sophisticated computer programs (taxonomic procedures) to identify which of the 28 DES items did clearly differentiate between these two groups, by being hardly ever endorsed by the normal control subjects. They found eight items (numbers 3, 5, 7, 8, 12, 13, 22 and 27) which were thus assumed to measure pathological rather than normal dissociation. These items related to amnesia, to feelings of depersonalisation and derealisation and to identity confusion, but not to the more normal feelings of absorption, which is the tendency to alter consciousness by narrowing or expanding focus of attention, thus blurring the boundary between self and world. They claimed that they had established by these means that the dissociation found in people with DID is different in kind from 'normal dissociation' and that it can be identified by using the eight item form of the DES, which they called the DES-T.[17]

Several later studies have questioned this claim that pathological dissociation can be distinguished from normal dissociation. When a large community sample of people completed the DES and a battery of other self-report measures of psychopathology and imaginative involvement, those who scored highly on items dealing with 'pathological' dissociation also endorsed many items dealing with 'normal' dissociation, and high scores on both were related to other measures of psychological distress. They were also associated with high levels of imaginative involvement, i.e. fantasy proneness, absorption and daydreaming immersion.[18] Similar results have been reported from another large non-clinical sample, this time college students, who were given the DES and a personality questionnaire (the Minnesota Multiphasic Personality Inventory). Once again, high scores on the DES were associated with scores on the personality questionnaire that suggested general psychological disturbance, and scores for pathological dissociation were highly correlated with scores for normal dissociation.[19]

A more complex study compared the scores of six different groups of subjects on the various versions of the DES, and on a measure of fantasy proneness, the Creative Experiences Questionnaire. The six groups in this study included students, healthy adult women, people with schizophrenia, with borderline personality disorder and with mood disorder, and women who reported a history of child sexual abuse. Their scores on all tests were highly inter-correlated and DES-T scores suggested that a substantial minority might have a dissociative disorder. The authors warned that use of this subscale could therefore produce many false positives and lead to serious over-diagnosis of DID.[20]

If the DES, or any of its subscales, does not identify a specific category of pathological dissociation, what does it measure? People with high DES scores have repeatedly been found to have other psychological problems .[21-24] In particular, they appear to be more prone to fantasising. When given a questionnaire asking about their use of daydreaming and imaginative fantasies (the Creative Experiences Questionnaire), those with high DES scores are more likely to respond positively.[25,26] High DES scores have also been associated with suggestibility and errors on memory tests, especially false recognition of things not seen before.[27]

A remarkable feature of the DES is the way all the questions are phrased in the same way. Respondents are repeatedly told of an experience which happens to some people and asked 'how often' it happens to them. As its promoters state: 'the questions are framed in a normative way that does not stigmatise the respondent for positive responses.'[28] One could argue that positive responses are actually encouraged by this format. It has long been known that people answering questionnaires tend to show an 'acquiescence bias'. This means that they are more likely to agree than to disagree with questions that are asked, and that they will match their questionnaire responses to what they think is expected of them. For that reason compilers often include questions that invite disagreement to test the genuineness of any positive responses.[29,30] There is a noticeable lack of any such safeguards in the DES. This is especially worrying since, as we have seen, those who gain high scores have been found, in other tests, to be suggestible and fantasy prone. Could high DES scores simply reflect the way some suggestible, imaginative and fantasy-prone individuals respond to the task of filling in a questionnaire?

It has been suggested that people who gain high DES scores are, of course, likely to be psychologically disturbed and fantasy prone because they have a disorder that was caused by severe childhood trauma. However it is also plausible that some psychologically disturbed people might give positive DES responses scores in order to be given a dissociative disorder diagnosis. Ever since dramatic cases of multiple personality have been observed, there have been suspicions that this was sometimes voluntary play-acting rather than an unavoidable condition. Thigpen and Cleckley, who achieved fame with the case later known as 'The Three Faces of Eve', also warned that any observed alternative personalities might be examples of 'pseudo- or quasi-dissociation that helps the patient gain attention or maintain an acceptable self image.'[31] Even those who have campaigned for increased recognition of dissociative disorders have admitted that this can land them with some new problems. Robert Kluft was one of the first to admit that clinicians could sometimes be generating the very condition they were supposed to be treating (iatrogenesis). He has been quoted as warning, in 1989, that alternate personalities may be created to please the therapist, to prolong the therapy or to express the client's memories or thoughts.[32]

Several studies have demonstrated that when ordinary people are asked to respond to the DES in a way they imagine to be typical of people with DID, they find it very easy to simulate typical DID responses.[33,34] Clinicians now stress that the DES should be used only as an initial screening technique to indicate whether someone is 'at risk' of having DID. However, what they may be most 'at risk' of is *imagining* themselves to have this intriguing disorder. It is easy to see how use of the DES or any other self-report questionnaire can lead to many more people being diagnosed with DID and other dissociative disorders.

2. The Somatoform Dissociation Questionnaire

This self-report questionnaire was developed by Ellert Nijenhuis 10 years after the DES and has been used in research and as a means of identifying clients with dissociative disorders.[35] It is of interest here because it shows us how broadly some people are able to define dissociation. Nijenhuis suggests that dissociation can manifest itself not only in the psychological symptoms of amnesia, depersonalisation, derealisation and identity fragmentation, but also in many dysfunctional physical symptoms, such as chronic pain, insomnia, paralysis and anaesthesia. His 20 item Somatoform Dissociation Questionnaire (SDQ) identifies these symptoms. Individuals are invited to indicate, on a five-point scale, the extent to which these and other experiences apply to them, and they are also asked whether there is a known physical cause for them.

My body, or a part of it, feels numb.
I have pain while urinating
I cannot see for a while (as if I am blind)
I cannot speak (or only with great effort) or I can only whisper
I cannot sleep for nights on end, but remain very active during daytime

Nijenhuis justifies his belief that these diverse experiences are dissociative by referring back to Janet's work and also by observing that 'patients with dissociative disorders report many somatoform symptoms and may meet DSM-IV criteria for somatic dissociation and conversion disorder'. His extension of the concept of dissociation seems to depend largely on his clinical observations and his belief in body memories.

Pain symptoms and sexual dysfunction are not described as conversion symptoms, yet according to clinical observation they can represent definitive dissociative phenomena. For instance, localised pain may be dependent on the reactivation of a traumatic memory that was previously dissociated and manifests as a physical pain in a particular body part.[36]

Though he claims that dissociation and 'so called conversion symptoms' share the same underlying process, Nijenhuis concedes that independent studies have shown only a moderate correlation between his SDQ and the DES. This leads him to conclude that these are 'not completely overlapping' measures. Dissociative disorders now seem to have increasingly fuzzy boundaries, and the use of the SDQ as an additional screening tool to detect them seems likely to have a marked net-widening effect and draw in many more potential dissociative clients.

3. Structured Clinical Interviews

For those who are eager to promote the diagnosis of dissociative disorders, the risk of missing some cases with false negatives is seen as a more serious problem than the risk of false positive diagnoses.

> Self-report formats may be problematic for the diagnosis of the dissociative disorders, since patients with dissociative disorders are often reluctant to describe, or may be entirely unaware of symptoms such as amnesia or identity alteration and therefore unable to complete an accurate self-report.[37]

These authors propose that clients may be unwilling to disclose their symptoms unless they get some personal encouragement. If the suggestions in a questionnaire fail to prompt some recognition of the covert problems, then perhaps face-to-face contact in a clinical interview will be effective. A structured interview contains set questions that can be followed up with supplementary queries and clarifications when appropriate. It thus allows more flexibility than a self-report questionnaire.

There have been two widely used structured interviews for dissociative disorders. The first to be developed, by Colin Ross and colleagues, was the Dissociative Disorders Interview Schedule (DDIS). This has 131 main questions, with many possible supplementary enquiries. In addition to asking about dissociative symptoms (for example: 'have you ever felt like there are two or more very different personalities within yourself, each of which is dominant at a particular time?') it asks about 'related' symptoms of depression, borderline personality disorder and schizophrenia, and also about an 'associated' history of childhood sexual or physical abuse. Since positive responses on all these things can count towards the diagnosis of a dissociative disorder, this makes it a sensitive test, with a reduced chance that any alternative diagnosis will be suggested, thus very much increasing the chance of false positives. It should also be noted that by treating an assumed cause of dissociation (child abuse) as one of its symptoms, the link between the two becomes stealthily reinforced. After testing this measure on 80 psychiatric inpatients, the developers of the DDIS satisfied themselves that it did detect all those who had dissociative disorders, and proceeded to promote its use in estimating the prevalence of dissociative disorders.[38]

The DDIS has a fixed format with closed questions that do not allow respondents to use their own words. The developers of a later structured interview tried to improve on this by allowing more flexibility, so that the interviewer could check on the severity and significance of any revealed symptoms. The Structured Clinical Interview for Dissociative Disorders (SCID-D) was launched in 1990 by Marlene Steinberg and colleagues.[39] It contains 200 questions, designed to evaluate the dissociative symptoms of amnesia, depersonalisation, derealisation, identity confusion and identity alteration. It has a format similar to the DES in that subjects are first told that other people have experienced certain symptoms, and then asked about their own experiences.

> Some people have had experiences that feel very real to them, but are very hard to explain to other people. Now, I'm going to ask you about some of these experiences.
> Have you ever had the feeling that you were a stranger to yourself?

Each time there is a positive response supplementary questions are asked, e.g. 'When was that? What was the experience like?' Thus the interview can be completed in 15 minutes if few symptoms are reported, but can take up to five hours when a number of dissociative symptoms are endorsed and then explored with further questions. Steinberg and her colleagues admit that in allowing this flexibility they had to abandon some of the features of structured interviews that are said to make them more reliable. This was necessary 'because of the complex nature of dissociative symptoms'.[40] Thus repeated questioning about specific symptoms was allowed and inconsistent responses could be disregarded.

At the end of what appears to be an exhaustive search for symptoms of the five dissociative disorders, responses are scored according to their severity on a four-point scale: giving possible scores ranging from 5 to 20. In the initial trial of this measure it was found to differentiate between people previously diagnosed with DID, psychiatric outpatients and 'normal' controls. Steinberg and her colleagues were thus satisfied that they now had a reliable way of detecting all dissociative disorders, though once again their main objective seems to have been to be able to detect cases of DID.

Like many others who encourage the diagnosis of dissociation, these researchers have ignored the possibility of false positives because they are so eager to eliminate any false negatives. In a later paper they compared their SCID-D with the DES, for its ability to detect 'patients at high risk for dissociative disorders', and seemed pleased to report that SCID-D could pick out many more of these patients.[41] They thought that the usual DES cut-off score of 30 made this diagnostic tool too specific and failed to identify many who were later identified as dissociative by using SCID-D. They therefore recommended that people with DES scores as low as 15 should be 'further evaluated with such diagnostic instruments as the SCID-D or by in-depth clinical follow-up'. We can see from Figure 1, above, that this would give us the daunting prospect of a substantial proportion of the population needing to undergo this quest for a diagnosis which has some very serious consequences. This prospect is made more worrying by the way that SCID-D is now being widely promoted as the 'gold standard' for diagnosing dissociative disorders.

Ten years after the launch of SCID-D, Marlene Steinberg and Maxine Schnall published a book for the general public which contained an abbreviated, do-it-yourself version of this assessment tool. *The Stranger in the Mirror* warned of the 'hidden epidemic' of dissociation. Potential readers were invited in with an intriguing promise:

> This book will give you a context for recognising symptoms of a condition that, through a conspiracy of silence, misunderstanding, and ignorance, has become the secret epidemic of our time. The material in its pages will finally shine a light on what could very well be the underlying cause of the anxiety, depression, manic-depression, panic attacks,

ADHD, OCD, or even schizophrenia that you or a loved one may have been diagnosed with mistakenly. Based on a recent study *over 30 million people, or 14% of the general public, experience "substantial" dissociative symptoms.* You may be one of the millions whose symptoms have been undetected and untreated because you couldn't identify them to report them to a therapist or were not asked about them. This may be the reason you feel stuck in life or are wandering lost in therapeutic circles, not making any significant headway or achieving long-lasting improvement.[42]

The italics are in the original, and no reference is given for the alarming statistics that are quoted. We have already seen how the symptoms of some disorders (e.g. self-harm and anorexia) have mistakenly been thought to be pointers to childhood abuse. Here the connection is less direct but more inclusive: these disorders, and many others, may be pointers to dissociation, which itself is definitely related to child abuse.

Readers of *The Stranger in the Mirror* are invited to complete five questionnaires, each containing between 12 and 15 questions, all taken from SCID-D. These are considered diagnostic of the five dissociative disorders. They all describe certain experiences and then ask about how often the reader has had them. Supplementary questions ask how disturbing the experiences were found to be. Scoring instructions are given, so that responses can be allocated to one of three categories: no disorder, mild disorder or moderate to severe disorder. Any reader finding themselves in the third category for any of the five disorders is advised to see a professional who has been trained to administer the full SCID-D. At the end of each of these five chapters they get the same reassuring message:

Should an experienced clinician find that you have a dissociative disorder, you have a treatable illness with a very good prognosis for recovery. Your illness is widely shared by others who coped with trauma by using the self-protective defence of dissociation. [43]

The diagnosis of a dissociative disorder here seems to be held out as a reward for the discontented reader who is looking for a reason for his or her difficulties. There is no warning that the recognised treatment takes many years, is intensive and disturbing or that the 'very good prognosis' has yet to be demonstrated (further details of the treatment and its outcomes will be given in the next two chapters). The reader is also not warned that this treatment will leave them with new disturbing memories which are likely to alienate them permanently from their families.

Estimating the Prevalence of Dissociative Disorder

To demonstrate that dissociation really is one of the most common mental disorders, much effort has been spent trying to get an estimate of its prevalence. Very difficult, when nobody seems to know that they have it, unless they are diagnosed by someone who specialises in these disorders. Three of the diagnostic tools described above (DES, DDIS and SCID-D) have, however, been used in attempts to demonstrate that, once you start looking for them, people with dissociative disorders can be found in many different populations and in many different countries. The results of some of these prevalence studies are shown in Table 1. It must be remembered that they have mainly measured positive responses to interview or questionnaire items, rather than observed signs of any disorder. The strikingly wide variations in the reported prevalence rates are due partly to the different populations studied, with psychiatric patients generally showing highest prevalence. There are further inconsistencies which may reflect the different methods used, and also perhaps the different intentions of some of the researchers. In many studies the DES was used to screen the population under review. The structured interviews, DDIS or SCID-D, were sometimes then given only to sub-groups, with results extrapolated to make them representative of the whole group. In one study however, this method was rejected. It was suggested that all those who had completed the DES should also have a structured interview, since use of the DES alone can result in an underestimate of the prevalence of dissociative disorders. The researchers pointed out that if they had only interviewed people with a DES score above the accepted cut-off point, they would have missed 46% of their positive diagnoses. They made the rather alarming suggestion that the structured interview is a better diagnostic tool because it yields 'more accurate, higher prevalence rates'.[44]

Table 1: Prevalence of dissociative disorders

Authors	N	Population	Method	% Dissociative disorder	% DDNOS	% DID
Ross, Joshi, Currie (1990)[45]	1055	General, Canada	DDIS	12		1
Ross et al (1991)[46]	345	College students US	DDIS	11		6.3
Saxe et al (1993)[47]	110	Female psychiatric inpatients US	DDIS	15		3.6
Latz, Kramer, Hughes (1995)[48]	173	Female psychiatric in-patients US	DDIS	46		12
Tutkun et al (2000)[49]	150	Psychiatric outpatients Turkey	DDIS	12		5.4
Friedl, Draijer (2000a)[50]	122	Psychiatric inpatients Netherlands	SCID-D	8	6.6	2
Ross, Duffy, Ellason (2002)[51]	50	Psychiatric inpatients US	DDIS SCID-D	40.8 44.5		7.5 9.1
Foote et al (2006)[52]	82	Psychiatric outpatients US	DDIS	29	9	6
Dorahy et al (2006)[53]	20	Psychiatric outpatients N. Ireland	DDIS	65	25	6
Sar, Akyuz, Dogan (2007)[54]	628	General, female Turkey	DDIS SCID-D	18.3	8.3	1.1

In most of these studies the subjects were said to be randomly selected, and samples of psychiatric patients were often from consecutive hospital admissions. The small sample of Northern Ireland outpatients was exceptional, as it consisted only of 'complex psychiatric patients', nearly all of them women, who had been unsuccessfully treated for psychiatric complaints over many years. This alone could explain the exceptionally high prevalence of dissociative disorders that was found. It may also be significant that all the psychiatric staff participating in this study were first encouraged, before they made their assessments, to read a selection of 'key papers' written by those promoting the diagnosis of dissociative disorders. The researchers admitted that their intention in this study was to show that in Northern Ireland, as elsewhere, there were plenty of clients with dissociative disorders waiting to be discovered. Perhaps their study was an attempt to redress an earlier imbalance, since in a previous review of prevalence studies, it had been noted that the reported prevalence of dissociative disorders was likely to be five times higher when studies were done in the US rather than anywhere else.[55]

We see in Table 1 that prevalence of dissociative disorders in general is always found to be very much higher than that of DID, and that in the four studies which mentioned the prevalence of DDNOS, this was also more frequently diagnosed than DID. As already mentioned, DDNOS is said to be the dissociative disorder most frequently seen in clinical practice. Since both its assumed cause and its recommended treatment seem to be just the same as for DID, the use of this vague diagnosis must greatly increase the number of people who qualify for the type of treatment that used to be reserved for DID.

Interpreting inner confusion : believing is seeing

All four of the diagnostic tests mentioned above (DES, SDQ, DDIS and SCID-D) are said to have been validated by the clinical judgement of a psychiatrist or psychologist experienced in the treatment of dissociative disorders. This means that scores are measured against the opinions of a clinician who has previously examined the people tested and decided on their correct diagnoses. The greater the agreement between this expert judgement and the scores on the test, the more valid the test is thought to be, with fewer false positives or false negatives. Yet we have seen that the experts themselves may disagree about the significance of various scores, and we look in vain for any clear evidence that tells us whether or not this disorder really is present. Because it is a state of mind rather than a state of the body, there are no laboratory tests that can detect pathological dissociation. How can we be sure that the expert clinician has not produced his own false positives and negatives?

When they consider the possibility of a dissociative disorder, clinicians are looking for something that is covert, which they can find only through lengthy probing, with detailed enquiries about subjective mental states. There is ample scope here for both misinterpretation and suggestion. Even in a first interview it is possible for investigation to slide gradually into persuasion. The director of a dissociative disorders treatment clinic programme in North Carolina suggests some very persuasive methods for detecting signs of 'alter' personalities during the assessment stage.

It may happen that an alter personality will reveal itself to you during this [assessment] program, but more likely it will not. So you may have to elicit an alter... You can begin with indirect questioning such as "have you ever felt like another part of you does things that you can't control?" If she gives positive or ambiguous responses ask for specific examples. You are trying to develop a picture of what the alter personality is like... At this point you may ask the host personality "Does this set of feelings have a name?"... "Can I talk to the part that is taking these long drives in the country?" [56]

However much he tries, the clinician cannot avoid being influenced by the confirmation bias that affects us all. We are all primed to find evidence that supports our theories and to miss those inconvenient facts that refute them. That is how believing becomes seeing, and the process may be irreversible.

Many people have suggested that *all* diagnoses of DID and DDNOS are false positives and that these disorders are no more than unhelpful concepts in the minds of overzealous therapists.[57-59] If that is so, we would not expect the therapists' clients to respond well to the treatment they offer for these disorders. Yet the therapists claim that these clients, who have usually been unsuccessfully treated for years for other disorders, only start to improve after they get the correct diagnosis of DID or DDNOS followed by the appropriate treatment. We need to know what this 'improvement' really means. Do they become integrated and lose their alternative personalities? Do they recover from the symptoms of the other disorders, which were said to have been misdiagnosed? Perhaps the proof of the diagnosis of DID or DDNOS lies in the client's response to treatment. In the following two chapters I will be looking at this treatment and at the way clients respond to it.

References – 4. Diagnosing Dissociative Disorders

* Unless otherwise stated, all webpages were accessible in August 2013.

1 Simeon D. et al (2001). The role of interpersonal trauma in depersonalisation disorder. *American Journal of Psychiatry*, 458 (7), 1027-1033.

2 Chu J.A. et al (2010). Guidelines for treating dissociative identity disorder in adults: third revision. *Journal of Trauma and Dissociation*, 12, 115-187.

3 Van der Hart O., Nijenhuis E.R.S. and Steele K. (2006). *The Haunted Self.* New York: Norton, p. 26.

4 American Psychiatric Association (1994). Diagnostic and Statistical Manual of Mental Disorders-IV. New York: APA.

5 Boon S., Steele K. and van der Hart O. (2011). *Coping with Trauma-Related Dissociation*. London: WW Norton and Co.

6 Chu J.A., et al (2011). Guidelines for treating dissociative identity disorder in adults: third revision. *Journal of Trauma and Dissociation*, 12, 115-187.

7 Borch-Jacobsen M. (2010). Which came first, the condition or the drug? *London Review of Books,* October, pp. 31-33.

8 Putnam F.W. (1989). *Diagnosis and treatment of Multiple Personality.* New York: Guildford Press, p. vii.

9 Kluft R.P. (1991). Clinical Presentations of Multiple Personality Disorder. *Psychiatric Clinics of North America*, 14, 605-629.

10 Chefetz R.A. (2000). Disorder in the therapist's view of the self: working with the person with Dissociative Identity Disorder. *Psychoanalytic Enquiry*, 20 (2), 305-329.

11 Dissociation Australia www.dissociationaustralia@yahoogroups.com (Accessed during 2010).

12 Steinberg M. et al (2005). SCI-90 Symptom patterns: indicators of dissociative disorders. *Bulletin of the Menninger Clinic*, 69 (3), 237-249.

13 Kluft R.P. (1987). First rank symptoms as a diagnostic clue to multiple personality disorder. *American Journal of Psychiatry*, 144, 293-298.

14 Bernstein E.M. and Putnam F.W. (1986). Development, reliability and validity of a dissociation scale. *Journal of Nervous and Mental Disease*, 174, 727-735.

15 Steinberg M., Rounsaville S. and Cichetti D.V. (1991). Detection of dissociative disorders in psychiatric patients by a screening instrument and a structured diagnostic interview. *American Journal of Psychiatry*, 148, 1050-1054.

16 Van der Hart et al (2006). ibid.

17 Waller N.G., Putnam F.W. and Carlson E.B. (1996). Types of Dissociation and Dissociative Types: a taxonic analysis of dissociative experiences. *Psychological Methods*, 1 (3), 300-321.

18 Levin R. and Spei E. (2004). Relationship of Purported Measures of Pathological and Nonpathological Dissociation to Self-reported Psychological Distress and Fantasy Immersion. *Assessment*, 11 (2), 160-168.

19 Merrit R.D. and You S. (2008). Is there really a dissociative taxon on the dissociative experiences scale? *Journal of Personality Assessment*, 90 (2), 201-203

20 Giesbrecht T., Merckelbach H. and Geraerts E. (2007). The Dissociative Experiences Taxon is related to Fantasy Proneness. *The Journal of Nervous and Mental Disease*, 194 (9), 769-772.

21 Mulder R.T. et al (1999). Relationships between dissociation, child sexual abuse, child physical abuse and mental illness in a general population sample. *American Journal of Psychiatry*, 155, 806-811.

22 Roman S.E. et al (1999). Psychological defence styles in women who report child sexual abuse: a controlled community study. *American Journal of Psychiatry*, 156, 1089-1085.

23 Levin R.and Spei E. (2004). ibid.

24 Merritt R.D. and You S. (2008). ibid.

25 Rauschenberg S.L. and Lynn S.J. (1995). Fantasy proneness, DSM-III-R axis I psychopathology, and dissociation. *Journal of Abnormal Psychology*, 104, 373-380.

26 Merckelbach H. et al (2000). Dissociative experiences, response bias, and fantasy proneness in college students. *Personality and Individual Differences,* 28, 49-58.

27 Ost J., Fellows B. and Bull R. (1997). Individual differences and the suggestibility of human memory. *Contemporary Hypnosis,* 14 (2), 132-137.

28 Ross Institute. www.rossinst.com/dissociative_experiences _scale.html

29 Martin J. (1964). Acquiescence: measurement and theory. *British Journal of Social and Clinical Psychology,* 3, 216-225.

30 Javeline D. (1999). Response Effects in polite cultures: a test of acquiescence in Kazakhstan. *Public Opinion Quarterly,* 63 (1), 1-28.

31 Thigpen C.H. and Cleckley H.M. (1984). On the incidence of multiple personality disorder. *International Journal of Clinical and Experimental Hypnosis,* 32, 63-66.

32 Goff D.C. and Sims C.A. (1993). Has Multiple Personality remained constant over time? A comparison of past and recent cases. *The Journal of Nervous and Mental Disease,* 181, 595-600.

33 Gilbertson A.D. et al (1992). Susceptibility of common self-report measures of dissociation to malingering. *Dissociation,* 5 (4), 216-220.

34 Brand B.L. et al (2006). Assessment of genuine and simulated dissociative disorder on the structured interview of reported symptoms. *Journal of Trauma and Dissociation,* 7(1), 63-85.

35 Nijenhuis E.R.S. et al (1996). The development and the psychometric characteristics of the Somatoform Dissociation Questionnaire. *Journal of Mental Disease,* 184, 688-694.

36 Nijenhuis E.R.S. (2000). Somatoform Dissociation: major symptoms of dissociative disorders. *Journal of Trauma and Dissociation,* 1 (4), 7-32.

37 Steinberg M., Rounsaville S. and Cicchetti D.V. (1990). The Structured Clinical Interview for DSM-III-R Dissociative Disorders: preliminary report on a new diagnostic instrument. *American journal of Psychiatry,* 147 (1), 76-82.

38 Ross C.A. et al (1989). The Dissociative Disorders Interview Schedule: a structured interview. *Dissociation,* II (3), 169-181.

39 Steinberg M. et al (1990), ibid.

40 Ibid.
41 Steinberg M., Rounsaville B. and Cicchetti D. (1991). Detection of dissociative disorders in psychiatric patients by a screening instrument and a structured diagnostic interview. *American Journal of Psychiatry*, 148, 1050-1054.
42 Steinberg M. and Schall M. (2001) *The Stranger in the Mirror*. New York: Harper, p xvi-xvii.
43 Ibid pp. 51, 67, 81, 99, 117.
44 Foote B. et al (2006). Prevalence of Dissociative Disorders in Psychiatric Patients. *American Journal of Psychiatry*, 163, 623-629.
45 Ross C.A., Joshi S. and Currie R. (1990). Dissociative experiences in the general population. *American Journal of Psychiatry*, 147, 1547-1552.
46 Ross C.A. et al (1991). High and low dissociators in a college student population. *Dissociation*, 4. 147-151.
47 Saxe G.N. et al (1993). Dissociative disorders in psychiatric inpatients. *American Journal of Psychiatry*, 150, 1037-1042.
48 Latz T.T., Kramer S.I. and Hughes D.L. (1995). Multiple personality disorder among female inpatients in a state hospital. *American Journal of Psychiatry*, 152, 1343-1348.
49 Tutkun H. (2000). Frequency of dissociative disorders in psychiatric outpatients in Turkey. *Comprehensive Psychiatry*, 41 (3), 216-222.
50 Friedl M.C. and Draijer N. (2000a). Dissociative Disorders in Dutch Psychiatric Inpatients. *American Journal of Psychiatry*, 157, 1012-1013.
51 Ross C.A., Duffy C.M.M. and Ellason J.W. (2002). Prevalence, reliability and validity of dissociative disorders in an inpatient setting. *Journal of Trauma and Dissociation*, 3 (1), 7-17.
52 Foote B. et al (2006). Prevalence of Dissociative Disorders in Psychiatric Patients. *American Journal of Psychiatry*, 163, 623-629.
53 Dorahy M.J. et al (2006). Do Dissociative Disorders exist in Northern Ireland? Blind psychiatric – structured interview assessments of 20 complex psychiatric patients. *The European Journal of Psychiatry*, 20 (3), 172-182.
54 Sar V., Akyuz G. and Dogan O. (2007). Prevalence of dissociative

disorders among women in the general population. *Psychiatry Research,* 149 (1), 169-176.

55 Friedl M.C. and Draijer N. (2000b). Prevalence of Dissociative Disorders in Psychiatric Inpatients: the impact of study characteristics. *Acta Psychiatrica Scandinavia,* 102, 423-428.

56 Buie S.E., quoted in www.psycom.net/mchugh.html

57 Merskey H. (1992). The Manufacture of Personalities: the Production of Multiple Personality Disorder. *British Journal of Psychiatry,* 160, 327-340.

58 Piper A. (1997). *Hoax and Reality: The Bizarre World of Multiple Personality Disorder.* New York: Jason Aronson.

59 Merckelbach H., Devilly G.J. and Rassin E. (2002). Alters in dissociative identity disorder: metaphors or genuine entities? *Clinical Psychology Review,* 22, 481-492.

5. THERAPY

It is now easy to find guidance on how to treat dissociative disorders.[1,2] In addition to many textbooks we have detailed guidelines that have been drawn up by an organisation that has been promoting their diagnosis and treatment ever since the 1980s. This was when the publication of *Sybil* sparked both a new interest in treating Multiple Personality Disorder (MPD) and the discovery that it was far more common than anyone had ever realised. The psychiatrists who were then treating MPD became highly organised, and in 1984 they founded the International Society for the Study of Multiple Personality and Dissociation.[3] This has now become the International Society for the Study of Trauma and Dissociation (ISST-D). It is worldwide but still based in the US, and, as a visit to its website (www.isst-d.org) reveals, it is very active, running conferences, promoting research and also providing guidelines for the treatment of the dissociative disorders.

Treatment guidelines from the experts

The ISST-D have produced comprehensive guidelines drawn up by 34 of their members. These were updated in 2011 and now run to 72 pages. In them we learn that the recommended treatment for DID and DDNOS is unlike any other psychiatric treatment in that it does not seek primarily to relieve the presenting symptoms. It is likely to exacerbate them, but this is necessary in order for the clients (here described as patients) eventually to get better. Therapists are advised that they must be prepared to help patients to become aware of their alternative identities and must themselves engage with them.

Clinicians must accept that successful treatment of DID almost always requires interacting and communicating with the alternative identites.[4]

94

This is a radical form of psychotherapy. It involves giving patients a completely new life history: changing the past as well as the present. For this reason it is both lengthy and intensive, and therapists are advised to divide it into three phases: 1. Establishing safety, stabilisation and symptom reduction. 2. Confronting traumatic memories. 3. Identity integration and rehabilitation. During the first phase the patient is made more aware of her different identities and of their 'adaptive role' in holding the traumatic memories. (Since the overwhelming proportion of DID patients are women I will be using feminine pronouns from now on to avoid the cumbersome use of he or she.) Once the patient feels safe with the therapist and accepts that she has these parts or identities that know more than she does about her past, she is ready for the next phase of treatment. It is during this second phase that traumatic memories have to be brought into consciousness. Most therapists seem to have adopted Van der Kolk's theory about traumatic memory (described in Chapter 1), which explains why patients may at first have no conscious memories of abuse.[5] These traumatic memories are said to be processed differently from the usual verbal memories. They are experienced as disconnected images, bodily sensations or dream fragments, which the therapist can reach by talking to the dissociated identities of the client. In this way they are gradually transformed into verbal narrative memories, so that the patient, for the first time, learns something of the trauma that she has experienced.

Work in this phase involves remembering, tolerating, processing, and integrating overwhelming past events. This work involves the process of *abreaction* – the release of strong emotions in connection with an experience or perception… specific interventions for DID patients involve working with alternative identities that experience themselves as holding the traumatic memories… As the various elements of a traumatic memory emerge, they are explored rather than being re-dissociated or rapidly contained… Over time, and often with repeated iterations, the material in these memories is transformed from traumatic memory to what is generally termed *narrative memory*... the patient gives the traumatising event a place in... her personal autobiography. Sometimes it is this realisation process that the DID patient fears most, resulting in... her avoiding the synthesis of traumatic memories at all costs. (Original italics)[6]

Therapists are warned about 'symptom exacerbation' at this stage. Various techniques may be used to relieve the distress of the patient, such as cognitive therapy, eye movement desensitisation and reprocessing (EMDR) or drug treatment. Hypnosis is specially recommended as a 'facilitator of psychotherapy' that can not only calm the patient but help her face the remembered trauma. In any case 'some form of hypnosis inevitably takes place in therapeutic work with this highly hypnotisable group of patients'. Visualisation and regression techniques are both said to be helpful 'when recollecting past events'. The ISST-D are aware that many people believe that these practices always increase the likelihood of false memories. However, while noting that there are 'current controversies' about this, they argue that memory distortion under hypnosis is a problem only when suggestive or misleading questions are asked.

Therapists are warned that they will encounter 'denial' during this second phase of treatment. This is an expected aspect of therapy, reflecting the client's unwillingness to face unpleasant truths. We saw that Sybil herself expressed denial at one stage during her therapy, but her therapist helped her to overcome this. Today's therapists are advised to do likewise. We find an ingenious explanation for the fact that denial is so common in an online newsletter from a US based Christian organisation for counsellors and mental health professionals. This reminds us that all dissociation was originally a product of denial, when it was used by the child to deny what was happening. Therefore therapists must tackle this head-on, working through much distress in the process.

Giving up denial can be a process for the survivor, passing through progressive stages. Often in the beginning the whole idea of being multiple may be denied. When the reality of the split-off parts is finally accepted, the reality of some, or all, of the trauma may be denied. Perhaps abuse by one perpetrator is accepted but not by another, or the memories of sexual abuse are finally accepted but not those involving anything Satanic...

Changing this perspective will involve identifying, challenging and correcting many false beliefs. It will also mean coming face to face with horrendous emotions and deep-seated identity issues. The truth is that becoming whole requires tremendous motivation, ego strength, and courage on the part of the survivor.[7]

When therapist and client are satisfied that all the traumatic memories have been brought into consciousness, the client is ready for the third phase of treatment. This is when she needs help in facing the prospect of living with her grim new reality, with new memories that are accessible at all times. The dissociated identities of the patient, which were previously the essential informants about abuse, are now no longer needed. Apparently they do sometimes just fade away spontaneously at this stage, but this is not what usually happens. Most patients seem to be reluctant to lose their separate parts. They may no longer be needed by the therapist, but after many years, these alternative identities become valued companions for the patient, and she will be unwilling to let them go. She may be afraid of facing her new reality in a unified state of mind. That is why ISST-D have to admit that 'even after undergoing considerable treatment a considerable number of DID patients may not be able to achieve final fusion and/or will not see fusion as desirable'.[8]

This 'considerable treatment' will most often take the form of one-to-one outpatient psychotherapy, though brief inpatient treatment may sometimes be necessary during crises. The recommended frequency of sessions is at least once a week, with twice or three times a week usually preferred. The conventional 50 minute session may be too short, and 'many therapists find 75-90 minutes better'. The ISST-D is strangely uninformative about how long this extremely intensive therapy is expected to last. We have to look to an earlier version of these guidelines to remedy this important omission. Here we learn that, despite early reports that treatment could be completed in two to three years, patients are now expected to require three to five years or more. It is also suggested that for particularly disturbed patients 'incremental improvement may continue for as long as two decades of treatment or more'.[9]

What these guidelines tell us is that treatment for DID and DDNOS is very intensive, distressing, lasts a long time and does not usually result in the loss of the alternative identities that were supposed to be the reason for treatment in the first place. In most cases these identities were not apparent before treatment started, so we could say that they are gained rather than lost during treatment. During their treatment clients also gain the knowledge that they have suffered years of severe abuse, usually at the hands of their parents. Their present lives and also their past lives have thus become changed beyond all recognition.

This treatment for DID and DDNOS is said to be justified because once the client learns about the trauma that caused her present problems, she will find it easier to overcome them. Many therapists seem untroubled at the persistence of the dissociative identities and see their aim in treatment to be the improved mood and day-to-day functioning of their clients. This is a sign that the treatment is working. In the next chapter we will be looking at these possible benefits of treatment.

The experience of therapy

The treatment recommended for dissociative disorders clearly involves many years of hard work for both client and therapist. For the client it is also acutely painful, as nightmarish fragments of feelings not only have to be repeatedly experienced but also given new meaning. Bad dreams must be remorselessly turned into bad reality. We have seen that this recovered memory therapy has not been restricted to clients with dissociative disorders. It has been widely used whenever therapists have suspected that their clients have been abused, are now unaware of this fact and need to become aware before they can get better. Clients will be encouraged to build on fleeting images and bodily sensations until they begin to feel like memories. The only difference with dissociated clients is that the therapist can do this work with the alternative personalities rather than the mature host personality. These 'alters', 'parts' or 'identities' are trusted to piece together the fragments and get at the truth.

As mentioned above, therapists may encounter denial at any stage during therapy. The clients fight against believing what the therapists are suggesting and may recover new memories only to insist later that they made them all up. This process has been described by some of those who eventually repudiated all that they learned from recovered memory therapy:

> There were so many instances where I would say… this is not true, this didn't happen, I'm making this up. It's sprinkled throughout my medical notes throughout those six and a half years. I would say it to a doctor, I would say it to a nurse, and no one ever followed up on that. No one. The doctor disregarded it every time I said it.[10]

> Why did I write down accusations about abuse that I knew had not happened, why did I blacken my father's name again, knowing perfectly well that none of it had ever happened? I don't know; I just don't know. Was it part of the illness? I don't know. Was I just seeking attention? I don't know. Why did no one ever just stop me and say "You are lying, you know none of it happened"… Whatever I said was simply noted, sometimes commented upon but never contradicted or even questioned.[11]

> I wanted to get well so bad I would have done just about anything… It was his way or no way. I had doubts all the

time, but I was told that this was my denial, my not wanting to get well. I believed the therapist. After all, who was I to question someone who was supposed to know everything. I looked at him as a god who could do no wrong.[12]

Recovered memory therapists do not usually tell us much about the mounting distress of their clients as they discover unforeseen horrors in their pasts. Once again we are more likely to learn about this from the rare cases in which the distress of their clients becomes so intense, and the nature of their outpourings so unbelievable, that they finally turn their backs on this type of work. Mark Pendergrast was able to interview such a therapist, whom he calls Robin Newsome, and in the following excerpt she gives us some insight about how recovered memory therapy can work, even when the client is not apparently dissociated.

One day Sally came to see me after getting the image of a little girl sitting in a pool of blood. All the details of when, where and who were unclear. I had her close her eyes and led her through guided imagery, asking my typical questions. "How old are you? What are you wearing? What time of year is it? What happens next?" With my prompting she began to retrieve little bits of memory. In the end she saw her father penetrating her when she was three. At the end of the session Sally asked, "Can this possibly be true?" She had always felt so close to her Dad… She had no memory of him sexually abusing her before this image. I gave her the classic line: "Sally, there would be no way for you to have invented this much detail unless it really happened". After that first memory she started having others…

By this time I had witnessed many clients recovering repressed memories, and I totally believed them. If you saw the emotion, you too would have no reason to doubt. The images were punctuated over and over again by the anguish, tears, contorted face, clenched fists, and rage that was expressed in hitting and kicking and ripping and gnashing of teeth… We honestly believed the images that came into their heads were the horrifying records of true events.[13]

Robin Newsome later came to doubt these beliefs and was horrified to realise the damage that she had done. We will meet her again in the next chapter, describing Sally's further deterioration. Meanwhile it is important to note that she had done no more than use the standard techniques that for many years have been recommended for recovered memory therapy.

A survey of fifteen women with DID

The notes that therapists keep while treating their clients throw a useful light on their methods. We do not normally see these notes, but several years ago I was authorised to carry out an investigation in the NHS hospital where I worked into the previous outpatient treatment that people with DID had received there. This enabled me to examine the treatment notes of the three therapists who had undertaken most of the treatment of DID clients. They were all experienced female clinical psychologists, and they had, between them, seen 15 women with DID. The following extracts from their notes show how they, like the therapist above, used the standard techniques for recovering traumatic memories. They made frequent use of dreams, 'body memories' and 'flashbacks' to guide their clients. They also worked predominately with the dissociated 'parts' of the client. Each of the following three women, whose names have been changed, was seen by a different therapist.

Angela, age 42, was referred by her GP because she seemed mildly depressed and tired, and also suffered non-specific abdominal pains. On her first appointment she said that her symptoms had become worse after the death of her father, and she also spoke of recurrent nightmares she had had about being sexually abused as a child. After a month her therapist wrote:

Nightmares and flashbacks are worse if anything – is waking as a child and lashing out before managing to find herself.

101

Screaming, curling up, terrified. Flashbacks of movements under the bed and hand under the covers. Wonders if she made it up – reassured her on this. Did a lot of disclosure today. I was pushing quite a bit, and I think she found it difficult… Lent *Outgrowing the Pain* [a self-help book for survivors of sexual abuse].

[next day] A difficult night… as soon as she closed her eyes everything came flooding back… Didn't want to come back here but feels she has to … Guilt and shame at having the flashbacks – as if I want to relive it.

Angela was still in treatment nearly two years later, and by now her memories had moved on:

Fed back content of recent memories… knowledge comes and goes for Angela, knows things but cannot grasp them. Opportunity to mention ritual abuse arose. I explained what I thought – she had some hints (eg snuff videos, media coverage – so it could have happened to me) + [husband] was sure. She accepted it…

[Two months later] 8 year old disclosures – I pushed her harder – successful disclosures of the degradations, sexual abuse by women and men. Some names … Frantic if I mention Mum and Dad but good arguments for saying they were not involved.

A year later Angela did believe that her mother was involved, but she also began to question the ritual abuse memories, saying that they didn't belong to her. She was, however, 'reassured' by her therapist that other people were talking about ritual abuse and saying similar things to what she was describing. No further doubts were apparently expressed.

[Four months later] Long session 2 ¾ hours. Hard to get

them started but then personalities came out spontaneously… Body harness put on to prevent body marking. Beaten, kicked. Tied to board then to cross. Man, then woman raped. Man raped anally. Dildo penis, like banana sewn on, made to do it to woman. Put head into bath dirty water. Dressed in no clothes or boy's clothes.

Three years after this disclosure, and nearly six years after starting therapy, Angela and her therapist both felt that she was getting better. She seemed to have become used to her horrific memories, and was talking of joining a survivors' group. She was discharged. Her GP thought that she was in worse shape than before treatment, and later referred her for further psychotherapy.

Jennifer age 28 was referred by her GP for treatment of 'psychosomatic complaints'. Her therapist noticed signs of dissociation during her ninth appointment, when she 'seemed to be talking to a more aggressive person'. A few weeks later Jennifer had accepted the idea of dissociation and said she found it helpful. Her first mention of sexual abuse came four weeks later:

Thinks P, who claims to be her father, could have abused her, because he was often around when she was little.

[Two weeks later] Work with 6 year old – afraid of mother – still having nightmares…. "Horrible" new memory – but won't tell. When I began to guess, she got v anxious and cries that she didn't want to talk about it. I gave her a hug and reassured her – she said it was about sexual matters but was not normal.

[Six months later] 15 year old's memories of being terrified in grandfather's bed. Grandfather worse than mother. Wanted to know about the memories of sexual abuse. Pleased with her breakthrough and wanted books to read. Arranged for her to read *Sybil* next week.

[One year later] Katie told her she and Anne had been abused as children by grandfather. Jennifer had been shocked and wondered why so many people in her family were abusers or abused. We made a chart… most men and grandma were abusers and surrounded girls who were abused.

Jennifer became increasingly disturbed during the following months, and had to be briefly admitted to hospital under a section of the mental health act. She was described as regressed, and acting like a six year old. When her therapy finally ended, after just over three years, she was thought to be much calmer and able to manage on her own, although 'probably still regressed'. Her GP thought that the therapy had been helpful, but did later refer her for more psychiatric treatment.

Pat, age 30, had already told her GP that she had been sexually abused by her father, and was referred because she was 'at breaking point and not coping well'.

[First appointment] She began by acknowledging she had very little memory of her childhood and problems at the time. She found it difficult to think back and make sense of the past times.

[Next session] Pat talked in more detail about the abuse. She had particular memories that she disclosed of being abused in her father's delivery van. As she began to disclose this, the fog lifted on the whole memory… she knows that the abuse started long before she was 12, but still cannot say when it was. She remembers telling her mother but also remembers that her mother abused her as well when she was 14…

[Eight months later] Pat had written a letter revealing the presence of at least two further personalities. I gave her this to read and explained that she may be MPD. She had a number of features that are suggestive of a multiple personality. She often misses time and particularly recently. She feels she hears conversations in her head. She often meets people who seem to know her, and there is some suggestion that there may be personalities who took over the sexual role… She felt that the therapeutic work would never end. She then started to dissociate rather than face the things we were saying…

[Next session] Once we started talking about our conversation re MPD, a lot of things began to happen. She thought she would be able to get in touch with personalities by telephone! This immediately brought out the 13 year old who spoke through Pat. 5+ personalities – baby, 6 yrs, 9 yrs, 12 yrs, 13 yrs + several personalities older than this.

[One month later] She wanted to continue to explore her multiplicity… She was able to go back and talk about things that happened when she was a very young girl but then blocked. At that point a very small child personality took over. This was a three year old who was able to disclose sexual abuse by a woman who was looking after Pat whilst her mother was in hospital having her brother, and also the beginning of sexual abuse by her father. Even at this young age it was severe. Pat returned to herself and took the news fairly well that she had been abused from such an early age. It didn't surprise her at all.

Pat surprised her therapist four months later by saying that she was concerned about becoming too attached to her, and therefore wanted to stop treatment for the time being. She had been seen for eighteen months only, making this by far the shortest treatment that any of these women had received.

These three women all gained many new memories of persistent and severe abuse during therapy, and this was true of all the 15 women with DID whose treatment notes were seen. Nine of them had reported some sexual abuse before starting therapy, but the abuse that they had remembered by the end of therapy was always far more severe than anything they had been aware of before. At the start of therapy most of the women who reported abuse mentioned only one abuser, but by the end of therapy all of the women said they had been abused by at least five people, in some cases very many more. Initially all abusers were said to be male. By the end of therapy eight women said they had been sexually abused by women as well as men, six by their mothers. The abuse reported at the start of therapy was sexual in eight cases and physical in one; but all women went on to report both sexual and physical abuse, and in four cases this included the grotesque horrors of ritual abuse. By the end of therapy all the women believed that they had been abused from the time they were four years old, sometimes well before that, when they were babies. Eight women said that the abuse had continued beyond the age of 16, and three claimed that it was still going on during the course of therapy. None of the three therapists seemed to have problems in accepting these often bizarre revelations as accounts of true happenings.

This amazing expansion of memory was achieved by working intensively with all clients, often seeing them more than once a week and allowing additional telephone contact, and sometimes involving co-therapists for further support. During this time all clients were encouraged to work on their memories between sessions, by recording their feelings in journals, drawing pictures and noting their dreams. They were given self-help survivor literature to read, including *The Courage to Heal,* the best-selling book that has become notorious for its misleading statements about the nature of memory and for suggesting that a whole range of common problems could be caused by sexual abuse.[14] Clients were also introduced to fellow survivors, especially when they were having difficulty accepting this new status for themselves.

There was continuous pressure to discover new memories, since the therapists believed that it was only by unearthing all of them that 'healing' could take place. Many of these 15 women did apparently have great difficulty believing their new memories, and they sometimes struggled desperately against the direction in which their therapy was leading them. However, there was no indication in any of the therapists' treatment notes that they ever accepted a client's objections. Disbelief would be referred to as 'denial', a sign that the memory was too painful to be faced, not that it was untrue. Eventually all clients seemed to become resigned to accepting their therapists' interpretations. Denial was overcome and clients were duly led to a drastic rewriting of their past histories. After five years of therapy Susan wrote an anguished letter to her therapist:

> I am still having problems accepting what my mother did. I need you to tell me over and over again that this really did happen. It is me the adult that can't believe it did happen. I just can't at this moment. I might feel different after seeing you on Thursday.

She did indeed feel different after Thursday, and her mother was acknowledged to be one of her abusers. Yet when she was finally discharged, after more than a year's further therapy, she was said to be still 'struggling with ambivalent feelings to mother'.

Another woman who struggled hard against new feelings towards her mother was Lucy, who believed when she started therapy at age 30, that she had had a normal childhood and that her problems of stress and anxiety were related to her current lifestyle. Lucy's story gives us an example of how far some therapists will go in encouraging and shaping the most bizarre and improbable beliefs. After just over two years of therapy Lucy had been persuaded that she had been brutally abused from infancy by a ritual abuse cult which had included both her parents. She had initially denied any experience of abuse, but began having new memories during her first few months of therapy, after she had been encouraged to get in touch with her 'inner child'. The therapist then saw evidence of several inner children and, after six months of therapy, was able to diagnose DID. Lucy had by now read *The Courage to Heal* and had begun to have suspicions about her father. After a further year she started having memories of having a baby, and also spoke of people in cloaks and masks. Her therapist noted: 'RA [ritual abuse] memories emerging', and in the following months Lucy reported increasingly gruesome scenes in which babies were killed and she was tortured, branded and repeatedly raped. She also came to believe that she had once given birth to a baby who was later killed. From now on she seemed increasingly reluctant to believe her new memories, and frequent notes were made of her 'denial' and efforts to block memories. She had accepted that her father had abused her from an early age and that she had suffered the most horrible ritual abuse, but she could not believe that her mother was in any way involved. She had earlier said she that she had been very close to her. This makes the therapist's record of her persistent efforts to overcome Lucy's denial particularly distressing to read, as, month after month, and at times with daily sessions, she records her efforts to overcome Lucy's denial:

Disbelief and denial v strong. …Not able to deal with much, but body memories strong v sore, esp vaginally and rectally. In danger of overload again. Prob build up to new memory.

[Two weeks later] Recognised that denial comes down to her being ordered to deny in memory form. Generally much calmer. Flashbacks eased. Some problems (less) in accepting Mum's involvement.

[Three months later] Acknowledged mother's collusion + abuse – close to acknowledging mother's abuse of her. Much less denial – seeing denial as defence against overwhelming anxiety.

When therapists work with ritually abused clients they can interpret their denial, not just as unwillingness to face unpleasant truths, but as the result of 'programming' by the cult: special training to make them doubt their memories or say ridiculous things. This gives the therapist leave to disregard anything their clients say that does not fit into their imagined scheme of things. Thus the therapist's hypothesis can never be disproved.

[Two weeks later] Worked on denial programming – Mother on fringe of RA group is current hypothesis, but definitely a denier and acted as a good cover-up for father's activities. Denial still v strong. Calmer when not denying. Gets v agitated when she denies.

[One week later] Denial – still frightened to face role of mother. Looked at levels of denial – programming. Encouraged her to look at methods of programming in rel. to denial.... Later spoke to another survivor Anne who confirmed some of these methods.

[Five days later] Denial less, followed by memory recall... Mother – girl killed – spoke in detail of horror of this incident. Frightened of being locked up. Much calmer afterward. Noticeable improvement following day. Denial lessening all the time – now got safe passage to healing – finding it helpful.

During this time Lucy's parents and other members of her family had made repeated appeals both to Lucy herself and to her therapist, asking for a chance to make contact and to refute these terrible new beliefs. This was not allowed. However, even if they had been able to point to evidence of Lucy's orthodox upbringing and regular school attendance leading to a university degree, this might not have changed anything. The therapist already knew some of these things, and they did not apparently dent her belief that Lucy's childhood and adolescence had been characterised by unremitting degradation and suffering. If she had bothered to check Lucy's medical record, as I did, she would also have learnt that a gynaecological examination had indicated that Lucy had still been a virgin when she was 19 years old. Would this inconvenient fact also have been discounted?

The therapy of these 15 women took place during the 1990s, before the present version of the ISST-D guidelines had been published. However, these therapists used methods similar to those currently recommended, and the only noticeable difference was that they started probing for memories at earlier stages of treatment and completed treatment within a shorter period of time. This therapy lasted on average three years six months, ranging from 18 months to nine and a half years. In some cases it would have lasted longer if two of the therapists had not left to work elsewhere. As we have seen, the ISST-D recommends at least three to five years of therapy, and suggests that it may take far longer. There are obvious costs to this therapy, especially in the clients' distress, so we need to know what is achieved during this time. The clients may feel that, knowing the worst about their early lives, they now have an explanation for any present difficulties. We need to know how much this helps them in their later lives.

References – 5. Therapy

★ All web pages were accessed in August 2013

1 Haddock, D.B. (2001). *The Dissociative Disorder Sourcebook*. New York: Mcgraw Hill.
2 Van der Hart O., Nijenhuis E.R.S. and Steele K. (2006). *The Haunted Self: structural dissociation and the treatment of chronic traumatisation*. New York: Norton and Co.
3 Pendergrast M. (1996). *Victims of Memory*. London: Harper Collins.
4 Chu J.A. et al (2011). Guidelines for Treating Dissociative Identity Disorder in Adults: third revision. *Journal of Trauma and Dissociation*, 12 (2), 115-187.
5 Van der Kolk B.A. and Fisler R. (1995). Dissociation and the Fragmentary nature of Traumatic Memories: overview and exploratory study. *Journal of Traumatic Stress*, 8 (4), 505-525.
6 Chu J.A. et al (2011), ibid, p. 142.
7 Restoration in Christ Ministries: www.rcm-usa.org/ (Follow links > Articles > Denial: the key to Resolution).
8 Chu J.A. et al (2011) ibid, p. 133.
9 Chu J.A. et al (2005). International Society for the Study of Dissociation: Guidelines for treating dissociative identity disorder in adults. *Journal of Trauma and Dissociation*, 6 (4), 69-149.
10 www.examiner.com/article/remembering-lies-interview-with-psychiatric-abuse-victim-Jeanette-bartha
11 Fairlie J. (2010). *Unbreakable Bonds (they know about you dad)*. London: Austin and McAuley. P. 322.
12 Lief H.I. and Fetkewicz J. (1999). Retractors of false memories: the evolution of pseudo memories. *Journal of Psychology and Law*, Fall, 411-435.
13 Pendergrast M. (1995). "First of all, Do no Harm": A recovered memory therapist repents. *The Skeptic*, 3 (4), 36-41.
14 Bass E. and Davies L. (1988). *The Courage to Heal: a Guide for Women Survivors of Child Sexual Abuse*. New York: Harper Perennial.

6. THE CONSEQUENCES OF THERAPY

Attempts to assess the benefits of treatment

Since the recommended therapy for dissociative disorders involves so many years of intensive and painful work, we need to know if it is worth it. Such therapy can only be justified if it can be shown to be effective. Do the clients eventually get better? There are now many textbooks and treatment guidelines telling us that they definitely do benefit from this treatment. What evidence do they have for this claim?

Proving that any treatment is effective is notoriously difficult. We know from the history of medicine that a clinician's conviction that he has benefited his patient is not enough. Doctors have in the past been wrongly convinced that they were reducing their patients' fevers by draining their blood, or curing their tuberculosis by exposing them to the open air. We now expect their clinical judgement to be backed up by some scientific evidence. This is why the randomised, controlled, double blind trial has become the gold standard for testing any new treatment in physical medicine. In such a trial patients are randomly selected for different procedures, and treatments are tested against each other, against an inert substance (a placebo) or against no intervention at all. In drug trials, neither the patient nor the person giving the drug and assessing its effects knows whether the subject is receiving the active drug or a placebo. This is the 'double blind', which lessens the possibility of personal convictions or hopes influencing the results of the trial. It is clear that we cannot reach these standards when assessing any form of psychotherapy since neither client nor therapist can be blind to the nature of the treatment being tested. Nevertheless it is possible to gain some measure of treatment effectiveness by trying to reduce bias. It helps if relatively objective pre and post treatment measures are used, if randomly selected groups of clients are compared, if attempts are made to replicate any findings and if the evaluation is carried out by researchers who have not in any way been involved in giving the treatment.

Clinicians who promote the psychotherapy of dissociative disorders have strong convictions that their methods work, and they have been at pains to convince people that these convictions are backed up by evidence. Thus, from the early days, when the disorder in question was called Multiple Personality Disorder (MPD), it was promoted as a severe mental disorder that responded well to the correct treatment. Clinicians were even warned that failure to diagnose MPD could result in their being sued for professional malpractice, and by 1988 it was asserted that

> Although authorities differ, evidence is becoming increasingly convincing that MPD patients have a good prognosis if properly diagnosed and treated. Equally important in terms of malpractice potential is the poor prognosis when not properly diagnosed and treated... The psychiatrist or therapist must be alert to the potential danger of a malpractice suit arising from failure to diagnose MPD.[1]

Malpractice suits did later start arriving, but they all came from clients who were complaining because they *were* given this diagnosis. Several clients in the US and Canada have now successfully sued their therapists for the damaging effects of being given this diagnosis and undergoing the recommended treatment. Bennett Braun, one of the pioneer promoters of MPD, suffered this fate, as did other well-known therapists such as Judith Peterson and Diane Humenansky.[2] However, even while this was going on, the enthusiasts were making repeated claims about the treatment's efficacy and cost-effectiveness. They have always suggested that before they get diagnosed most people with MPD will have undergone useless and expensive psychiatric treatment for many years, but that once they get the appropriate diagnosis and treatment they will at last get better.

In a Canadian sample of people with MPD, it was found that

they had previously spent an average of 6.8 years having psychiatric treatment, and before being diagnosed with MPD they had received on average three different diagnoses. This was taken as evidence that MPD treatment was 'exceptionally cost effective', and it was claimed that there were 'many case studies and some preliminary outcome data' to confirm this 'clinical impression'.[3]

In 1993 Colin Ross and Vikram Dua calculated the savings in Canadian dollars that might be made by diagnosing and treating someone with MPD ($84,900 over 10 years per client). This was based on an assumption that treatment would take an average of four years, but that the client, if untreated, would spend 10 years having other psychiatric treatment. They had extrapolated from a sample of just 15 women with MPD who seemed to complete their treatment unusually quickly. Nevertheless, they managed to be very upbeat about the implications of their work, and said that if their findings could be replicated and generalised, then psychotherapy of MPD would be shown to be 'the most cost-effective mental health intervention known'.[4]

To judge whether this confidence was justified, we can look at what the experts had to say 18 years later. Colin Ross was one of the 34 authors who produced, in 2011, the authoritative ISST-D treatment guidelines that were mentioned in Chapter 6. The section dealing with treatment outcome takes up less than one page out of the 72 in this document, and gives us very little further information. We learn that, more than 20 years after the first outcome studies, 'rigorous research is still in its infancy'. Most assessments of treatment outcome have been carried out by those who provided the treatment, and there have been no comparisons with any control groups. Also, it has been very difficult to assess the benefits of treatment that often lasts 10 years or more. Thus, after all these years, we are given 'preliminary evidence that treatment is effective in reducing a range of symptoms associated with Dissociative Identity Disorder'. In addition, a large, ongoing international study is said to show some benefit of treatment for DID and DDNOS because 'those further on in their treatment had fewer dissociative, posttraumatic and general psychiatric symptoms compared with patients early in their treatment'.[5] These conclusions seem very lame compared to the previous forecasts.

The authors of a recent review of outcome studies were clearly dismayed by the poor quality of existing research. They complained that not only were clinical observations about treatment response usually made by the person who had carried out the treatment, there were also no standardised measures, the follow-up periods were too brief, the samples of patients too small and not randomly selected and there was a high drop-out rate. They regretted that they still did not have the evidence they wanted, and urged 'we must do a better job in our efforts to gather evidence for effective treatment of DD' [Dissociative Disorders].[6]

These 'efforts to gather evidence' have all been made by people who want to promote the treatment of dissociative disorders. They have an urgent need to prove that their treatment works, because, as we learn from a recent editorial in the *Journal of Trauma and Dissociation*, the insurance companies that fund it in the US are getting increasingly restive. They have noticed that people with DID have been 'among the most expensive psychiatric patients to treat and had a high risk of early mortality'. This suggests that it is not just better outcome studies that are wanted, but better treatment. This editorial admits the need to develop 'better, empirically supported ways to effectively treat DID'.[7] The optimistic forecasts that were made so long ago now seem very wide of the mark. But today's message is not 'we got it wrong', but rather 'we must try harder to prove we were right'.

Attempts to assess some costs of treatment

The sceptics, who disapprove of this treatment of dissociation, have lost no time in criticising the methods of those who have conducted outcome studies but have not, as far as I know, carried out any such studies themselves.[8,9] That has always been one of the problems for such sceptics: they only have an outsider's view of what is going on and they do not have access to all the data. I was faced with this problem myself in my study (mentioned in the previous chapter) of 15 women who had been diagnosed with DID. I was fortunate in having access to their case notes and in being able to contact the GPs of most of them, but I was never able to meet the women themselves to assess their mental state, and to learn directly how they felt about their treatment. Nevertheless I did attempt some assessment of the effects of this treatment.[10]

As mentioned before, these women were aged between 28 and 42 at the start of treatment, and were in treatment for an average of just over three years, during which they all gained new memories of severe sexual and physical abuse. Their case notes revealed that most of them became extremely distressed during treatment and that eight of them had harmed themselves or threatened suicide. Of these, four made suicide attempts and had to be admitted to psychiatric hospital. Only a third of these 15 women had previously had repeated psychiatric treatment. Their psychiatric diagnoses had included Depression, Anxiety State, Hysteria, Personality Disorder, drug and alcohol dependence. A further three women had had brief outpatient psychiatric contact during this time, but the remaining seven women had had no contact at all with mental health services during the previous eight years. On examining their records approximately three years after they had completed treatment I found that one woman was lost to follow-up, having left the area, and of the remaining 14, all but one had further contact with mental health services. Six had been referred both to psychiatrists and to psychologists, the rest had been seen by either a psychiatrist, a psychologist or a community psychiatric nurse. These women thus made greater use of mental health services in the years following treatment than they had in the years before. When they began their treatment seven of these women had been in full-time work, but only one of them remained in work by the end of the treatment.

Most of these women were well known to their GPs, and were frequent attenders at their surgeries both before and after treatment. When the GPs were asked whether they thought the treatment had been helpful, their responses were very diverse. Three of them gave no opinion, and three said that they thought it had been helpful. A further three were very doubtful, saying that their patient claimed that it had been helpful, but that they were now worried by her condition. Two noted that there had been no improvement in their patient's condition and three said that their patients were definitely worse following the treatment. Most of the women continued to attend their GPs' surgeries frequently in the year following treatment, and some GPs commented on their increased need for help at this time. This was especially noticeable for the six women who had no apparent knowledge of any childhood sexual abuse before they started their treatment. They had consulted their GPs on average 12.4 times in the year preceding treatment, but in the year following the end of their treatment they made an average of 27 consultations. Now that they saw themselves, for the first time, as survivors of child sexual abuse they seemed to need more professional help rather than less. This small study has many limitations, but it does suggests that arguments in favour of the cost effectiveness of treatment for DID are based on hope rather than evidence. The recommended treatment is extremely costly, both in the time that it requires and the distress it inevitably causes, yet we still, after all these years, have no convincing evidence that it benefits its clients.

There is growing evidence that recovering memories of child abuse can be life-threatening as well as distressing, whether or not a diagnosis of dissociative disorder has been made. A young Scottish woman, Katrina Fairlie, was admitted to hospital with an eating disorder in 1994. There she was subjected to recovered memory therapy which caused her to experience the images of sexual abuse that confirmed the suspicions of the psychiatric staff. Her subsequent belief that she had been abused by her father had devastating effects on her and her family, which lasted for many years. After recognising that this belief was completely false, she has now, together with her father, written a shocking account of her inappropriate treatment and its consequences. In reading it, we can understand why the Tayside NHS Trust responsible was eventually persuaded to settle her claim for damages with a substantial out of court settlement.

117

Those who have been subjected to Recovered Memory Therapy (RMT) will know that you tend to continue to have the images that were created, long after the therapy has ceased. I was repeatedly told I was so ill that I might never get well enough to function as a normal person. Had I been prepared to listen and continue to allow the psychiatrists to keep me in therapy, I am convinced I would not have survived. During my time in their care in Murray Royal in Perth, a period of fifteen months, there were 66 incidents when I self harmed or attempted suicide. At least four of those attempts almost succeeded. Since discharging myself from their tender mercies, there has not been a single instance of either self harm or attempted suicide.[11]

The majority of compensation claims for damaging psychotherapy appear to come from people who have been diagnosed with DID or some other 'trauma-related' dissociative disorder. In the US and Canada there have been many such claims. Between 1991 and 1995 the Washington State Crime Victims Compensation Program apparently received 670 of them, of which just under half were approved. In 1996, Elizabeth Loftus reviewed 183 of the successful claims and then looked in detail at a sample of 30, taken at random from this group.[12] She found that all but one of these claimants was female. They tended to be well educated and all had been treated by a university educated therapist for at least three years; 26 of them had gained their first memory of child sexual abuse during this therapy. They all then gained many new horrific memories, and all but one of them eventually believed that they had been ritually abused. When Loftus looked at indicators of the mental state of these 30 people, comparing them before they gained their new memories and after, this is what she found:

Number thinking of suicide: Before 3 After 20
Number admitted to psychiatric hospital: Before 2 After 11
Number self harming: Before 1 After 8
Number in employment : Before 25 After 3

By the time these people had been in therapy for three years they had all broken away from their extended families. The compensation board accepted that they had been harmed by therapy and met their claims, at a total cost of $2,533,000. This was a very selective group of people who had presumably lost faith in their therapy and rejected the idea that recovering memories might eventually help them. It must also be noted that they had a financial interest in demonstrating that they had been harmed by therapy. However, similar changes, though less extreme, were seen in my small sample of more satisfied therapy clients. An increase in suicide attempts following treatment for DID has been noted elsewhere, and this may be what lies behind the findings of insurance companies that these clients have a high risk of early mortality.[13,14]

Two therapists count the costs

A graphic description of the deterioration of one recovered memory client, not at first diagnosed with DID, is provided by Robin Newsome, the therapist who, in the previous chapter, described how she encouraged her client Sally to start remembering that she had been abused. Once Sally started to have abuse memories she lost confidence, started having nightmares and gradually became unable to look after her children or keep house. She had now been convinced by Robin Newsome that the images she had had of sitting in a pool of blood as a little girl suggested that she had been abused, and that her father was involved. After confronting her father, who was said to be 'in denial' about the abuse, Sally had started to feel a little better, but then another round of memories caused further deterioration:

> Just when we would start to work on current issues, like her troubled marriage or the problem she was having with her younger son, boom! there would be another image. Then one day she came to me and said "I had this image that involved my mother... She remembered that her mother

119

had a miscarriage. Sally was seven years old; she found her mother in the kitchen dismembering the baby with a knife on a chopping block. When her mother saw her, she made her help. Sally remembered severing a tiny leg, and then she had to fry it and eat it. I was horrified. During the week after this session, I began to realise I was having a hard time believing this memory, I told myself it was so horrible that I probably didn't *want* to believe it.[15]

Robin Newsome blamed herself for this failure to believe Sally, but realised that her scepticism meant she could no longer continue to treat her. So Sally was referred to a counsellor at a Baptist church.

I later learned that after the first week or two of her new therapy, her counsellor suggested she might have multiple personality disorder. By her fourth session she had discovered three personalities. From that point on she developed more and more. I understand she now has 35 or so. She has been hospitalised at least five times. She has overdosed and cut herself again and again. After three years of weekly and sometimes twice weekly therapy with a counsellor and a psychiatrist, she shows no sign of improvement… Her new counsellor told Sally that things would have to get worse before they got better. He sure was right about that!

It takes enormous courage for any therapist to face up to the possibility that the work to which that they have been dedicating themselves over many years has been harmful rather than beneficial. We all look for evidence that reinforces our convictions and try to ignore or dismiss anything that suggests they may be false. For Robin Newsome, however, the shock of not being able to believe her client started an extremely painful process of questioning both her beliefs and her practices. For Paul Simpson, another troubled therapist in the US, this questioning was prompted by the realisation that there was no scientific evidence behind claims that recovered 'repressed' memories represented real events. He had been trained to do regression therapy, a form of recovered memory therapy using hypnosis, and he worked in a psychiatric hospital where some inpatients were encouraged, by this method, to remember being abused.

> I watched grown men and women turn into crying, incoherent, psychotic personalities. Clutching teddy bears, balled up in the corner of their rooms, these patients would talk with the voices of five year olds. Their stories contained imaginative horrors, ranging from being raped for years to bizarre accounts of being forced to murder and eat their own new-born children provided by powerful satanic cults... At no time were we allowed to question their validity...
>
> The patients discharged from hospital were usually prescribed volumes of psychiatric medications. Later, many had to be readmitted into the hospital because of suicide attempts, cutting themselves with razors, or simply being unable to survive in the real world. Many of these patients had a lifetime of high achievements: straight As in school, advanced college degrees and stellar success in business. These formerly high functioning individuals were now unable to keep their jobs, leave their homes, or care for their children. Divorces followed as once strong families splintered apart.
>
> Again and again it was stressed that the disintegration of these patients' lives was due to the traumas they had incurred decades ago... the "truth" had finally come to light. Their violent repudiation of a comforting façade of normalcy was the first step to recovery. I watched and waited, but oddly, their promised recovery was never forthcoming.[16]

Dr. Simpson had also been trained as a psychologist so he did what any psychologist should do: he looked for evidence. Was it possible to recover repressed memories of genuine trauma? As his disenchantment with regression therapy grew, he took himself off to a university library and looked for the research that underpinned it, imagining that 'a bit of scholarly reading' would reassure him. It did the reverse. Finding that there was no evidence that traumatic memories like these could be repressed and later recovered, he now saw the 'facts' that he had been taught in a different light. He has since dedicated himself to trying to undo some of the harm that he and others have unwittingly brought about by practising recovered memory therapy.

Some views from the clients

Most recovered memory therapists never change their minds about the value of what they are doing. The cost would be too great, not just for themselves but for the clients who depend on them and base their lives around the new beliefs that came with therapy. Therapists and clients become a mutually supportive system, strongly resistant to any doubts or questions. When most clients complain, it is not about the consequences of the therapy, but about the difficulties they had in obtaining it in the first place, and then in finding the funds to keep it going. In the UK they deplore the lack of any real understanding of dissociative disorders within the NHS. They sometimes claim that they have been 're-traumatised' by being misdiagnosed and given inappropriate treatment, and that it is only when they are able to find an independent therapist who specialises in dissociation that their problems are understood and they can start on their long journey to recovery. They are often prepared to make extreme financial sacrifices to pay for the many years of therapy that they need. They are also prepared to make fundamental changes in their beliefs and in the way they lead their lives.

When people accept that they have a Dissociative Disorder, such as DID or DDNOS, they take on a new identity. They become survivors. They are aware, for the first time, not only that they have suffered severe abuse, but also that they are possessed with many different personalities. This sets them apart from their families and also from most of the people around them. They have weird experiences which they cannot share with the rest of us. Many of them join support groups, where they can escape their isolation and share their feelings and problems with the only people who understand them, their fellow survivors. Some of these groups can be found on the internet, with websites showing us the range of serivices they offer their members.[17,18]

It becomes apparent, when we read the words of these survivors, that many of them now value their alternative personalities and do not want to lose them. The treatment goal of 'integration' has no appeal for them. This is why members of one of the support groups, First Person Plural, often do speak in the first person plural. They have a magazine, *Rainbow's End,* in which their alternative personalities, most of which seem to be children, can express themselves and share their experiences of being multiple and wanting to stay that way.

Another support group, Many Voices publishes an online 'Query of the Month' in which their members can advise each other on the problems they face. This can no longer be accessed by non-members of the group. It used to provide an illuminating view of the difficulties faced by dissociated survilvors. A repeated problem seemed to be a fear of losing their other personalities.

I was on disability for 6 years. About 8 months ago I went back to work, but it's very stressful. It seems as if my "parts" have left me to handle everything on my own. It's not like any fusion has occurred. I'm only a small fraction of a person. You might think I'd be thankful for the silence, but I'm having a hard time functioning without my parts. I don't understand why I can't communicate with them. Where did everyone go? And how can I get my parts back again so I can have help dealing with my life? Does anyone have any advice or suggestions for me? [19]

I am comfortable with being more-than-one, and do not want to integrate. I think my internal clan is normal for me. Lately though I seem to be stuck. My people still exist but seem unwilling or unable to take the front seat or be in control… I feel bad about losing my inner world. Any suggestions? [20]

Although many survivors wanted to hang on to their alternative personalities, they did find them somewhat inconvenient at times.

Doctor visits… are affected by the MPD/DID. For example, we all seem to have diabetes, but severity is different for different alters… We have very rapid switching. My internist couldn't understand this, until I told her about the MPD/DID. Now she doesn't always expect to have consistent results in blood tests. Of particular difficulty are pap smears. We have to bring a friend who distracts the 'littles' with a puppet.[21]

It's very rare that my one and only child part is fronting while driving a car, but that's what happened following a particularly triggering day at work… I found my mind dominated by my 7 year old alter, for the last hour and into the drive home. My adult self remained seated in the background of my mind, so to not only cover up my switch, but also to help operate the body's auto-pilot to drive my car and myselves home. I felt again like a novice driver while my child mind marvelled that she could drive a grown up vehicle. How do other people manage their younger parts while confronted with tasks like driving a vehicle? What sort of thing do others do to get the child part to step down at times when adult consciousness is required? [22]

Many survivors, knowing how horribly their inner children suffered in the past, feel protective towards them, and now seem prepared to indulge them, even when this is becomes inconvenient. They speak affectionately of these parts of themselves, referring to them as 'my family' or 'the littles', and try to find ways to let them express themselves. In the magazines, *Rainbow's End* and *Many Voices* there are sections that are written by these child parts and also puzzles and games that have been designed specially to entertain them. At meetings for members of support groups games and toys are often provided, so that if their inner children come out they will have something to play with.

Living with someone who is possessed by inner children must be a very strange experience. The husband of one of them set up a support organisation for people in this situation. This was originally called Partners of Dissociative Survivors, but has recently been renamed Positive Outcomes for Dissociative Survivors (PODS). It aims to provide its members with the information that they need to understand what is going on, and to enable them to meet together, to share their problems and become part of the therapeutic network that sustains the survivor. He reassures his fellow husbands and partners about what is really happening to their loved ones.

> DID is not a 'mental illness', something that has gone wrong in her brain – it is an adaptation to overwhelming trauma, a survival mechanism without which your partner would possibly be dead. Learn to respect it as a wonderful gift rather than some kind of 'madness'. Don't be ashamed of it and don't be ashamed of your partner for being dissociative. What she's going through now – the flashbacks, the panics, the triggers, the switching – is actually part of *healing*. It's the mind's way of readjusting to a new reality, a life where she isn't going to be abused any more. So all the signs that she has gone 'mad' are in fact signs that she is at last, at least in a small way, safe enough to begin to deal with stuff.[23]

Life for survivors with DID is obviously full of problems. Perhaps the most serious of these is the need to be wary at all times of 'triggers' that may set off memories of the horrific abuse that they once suffered. Since their memories always seem to involve re-experiencing the trauma, they have to be careful to protect themselves from this, and may end up leading severely restricted and lonely lives. They are repeatedly reminded that they need to be watchful for these triggers. Their various support groups encourage them to attend meetings, but usually give them a health warning first. This one came from a poster issued by the Campaign for the Recognition and Inclusion of Dissociation and Multiplicity.

> Please be warned that the day may be triggering for some survivors and you are responsible for your own safety and self-care. It may be advisable to bring a supporter with you.

Organisations promoting the dissociative disorders stress how much they value the input of the survivors. They not only have a presence at their meetings and conferences, they are often running these events themselves. They are useful there partly because they can demonstrate the reality of DID. Their childlike alters are on display when they sit through a lecture clutching a teddy bear, ask questions afterwards in the manner and voice of a six year old or simply refer to themselves in the plural. One sees in these meetings how therapists and survivors depend on each other to maintain their beliefs and also to spread them. They sustain each other with a shared sense of purpose, which must be one of the compensations for the lonely life of the DID survivor. Another one, of course, is the knowledge that the many problems she now faces are not her own fault. Of course life is difficult, but just to survive such a terrible past has been a great achievement!

Those survivors who believe that they have been ritually abused are particularly likely to see themselves as heroic. The closing speech at a conference run by one of their support groups was a rallying cry encouraging them in this view.

> Our survival is extraordinary, our experiences are not. We... have seen things we cannot bear, felt things our bodies could not endure, and been saddened beyond measure by the capacity for cruelty that some others of our kind not only have, but enjoy. And we are in the majority. Let's hold our heads high, tell our truths when we wish, and help others to heal if it helps us to heal. But let us not believe the lies

we are told about ourselves and our roles in our world. We are members of humanity more truly than those who live in lies.[24]

Sometimes survivors go on the attack and can make anyone who doubts them feel uncomfortable.

Only two sets of people know the truth about ritual abuse; the survivors and the abusers. Only one set of people will try and tell you. Only one set of people will tell you the truth. You need to listen. If we were all dead the abusers would still be here amongst you and who would be their next victims? Maybe you! Maybe your children! We are survivors. We are the living evidence of the existence of this type of abuse. Deny the abuse exists and you deny us the reality of our experiences. We would like to deny it all too. We would like to switch off the memories... The way I see it, you have only two choices; either you stand beside us and help us survive and fight back against them, help us make them stop; or you stand against us and if you do that, you are, in my eyes, one of them – the abusers.[25]

Alternative views from some of the clients

As we have seen, some clients do eventually take a different view of their therapy. In the US several hundred people have been identified as 'retractors', who now claim that what they recovered in therapy were in fact pseudo-memories; they did not represent reality at all. In a survey of 40 of these retractors, it was found that for most of them the new memories had emerged only after the therapist had suggested that they had been abused. Contact with the therapist had usually been increased following the new memories and most of this sample of clients had been advised by their therapist to cut off all contact with their families.[26] Increasing numbers of retractors are also now emerging in the UK and other countries where recovered memory therapy has been practised. Reports from these clients who did later change their minds suggest that this change always followed some movement away from the therapist and back towards the family.

For one woman this process took about twelve years. She had learnt in therapy that her father had abused her. This led her to refuse to see any of her family for eleven years. After regaining contact with them, she started questioning some of the things she had learnt in therapy, but it took her a further year and a half to change her views and believe that it was all was completely false. She then wrote this letter:

To my dear family
I apologise for taking so long to write this most important letter. After much soul searching, therapy, ego-wrestling and meditation, I have come to be certain that none of the accusations that I ever believed or made against Dad and Mom ever happened in the first place.

… I had a number of sexually abusive incidents occur as an adolescent that were very traumatic… I began attending group and individual therapy sessions at the local rape crisis center. It was enormously validating to hear other women's stories and to talk about the things I remembered. That was great for the things I remembered quite clearly, but over time, as I talked about nightmares and fears as a small child, I was constantly confronted by the other women to "face the facts" that I had initially been abused by my father… I began to doubt myself and thought that maybe they were seeing a picture emerge that, as they said, I just didn't want to face. My declarations of intense love and devotion to Dad were twisted around to appear as a co-dependent response to my "abuser"…

I can truthfully say that my therapist NEVER attempted to "plant" false memories or suggest anything to me. But once the idea of repressed memories raised its ugly head, it grew arms and legs and a tail. It was a question of constant confrontation and badgering to "remember the truth", followed by total approval and acceptance once I was able to remember again...

The thought that I was so suggestible that I could convince myself anything like that was true, sickens me... It kills me that there is no way to take back the pain, anguish and humiliation I have caused Dad and Mom and my other family members.[27]

The clients who later reject their new memories seem to have experienced similar therapeutic procedures to those used with other dissociated clients. Women in many countries have now reported similar experiences. They all consulted therapists who believed that dreams could represent reality, that any physical sensation could be a body memory and that any mental image could be a flashback. Linda, an English woman, has described to Mark Pendergrast how she was led by these methods to believe that her father had abused her. It all started with one disturbing dream which featured both her parents. During this dream she felt 'a searing pain, as if I was penetrated, almost up to my chest'. She told her therapist how confused she had been by this, and her therapist told her what it signified.

She explained that I had had a body memory, a memory of being sexually abused by my father... She explained "Your body is capable of storing the memories in a way that's so traumatic that your brain doesn't remember". I never got more than that; I just had to believe it. Then I started to have more body memories... I said "I feel like I can't breathe. I feel hot, like a hot baby in a pram". She asked how old I felt. I said I felt as if I were 18 months old, or maybe up to about four. I thought my father had actually abused me with his penis in my mouth...

I went into a severe depression, almost suicidal. I didn't want to believe it. I was paying money for absolute hell. I was desperately trying to get her to change her mind, but she wanted me to believe that she was right. It was a struggle of belief systems. And eventually she won.[28]

Linda later accepted her new perceptions to such an extent that she started along the path taken by many former clients: she decided to become a therapist herself, to move from being a survivor to being a rescuer. It was during her training for this that, for the first time, she began to question the scientific basis of body memories. She had by now confronted her family with her new beliefs, and been touched by their sorrow. It seems to have been her contact with them that led her to realise that she had some choice about what to believe, and it was a warm hug from her father that finally re-educated her and reminded her of what had been missing from her life.

> Now that I'm thinking for myself, I realise that these negative states are normal to us as human beings sometimes, and they don't necessarily indicate that we were abused. We all know what it feels like when you can't breathe because you're so stressed out. It doesn't mean it's a body memory of oral sex. I'd love to discover what it would be like to concentrate on all the *positive* aspects of your childhood and see how that was in therapy.

The therapy clients who change their minds readily admit that during therapy they did not think for themselves. They allowed themselves to follow their therapist's beliefs and to say what their therapist wanted them to say. I recently talked to Judith, another English woman, who had spent many years in close contact with a succession of therapists and social workers. They believed that she was in danger of continuing abuse and also that she had repressed some of her memories of past abuse. Judith had suffered abuse in the past. She had had a disturbed childhood and been raped when she was 13. She says she has always remembered this, and always will. What she did not remember before therapy, and what she now believes never happened, was being repeatedly raped by her father.

Judith is now 27 and talks readily about her unhappy childhood, growing up with a seriously disturbed mother and a father who was often ill, or simply not around. When I met her she told me that from childhood on she has had spells in psychiatric hospitals, has made several suicide attempts and has also harmed herself by cutting her arms. She has done things which, for some clinicians, would be definite pointers to a history of serious early abuse. She insists, however, that she has always known about any bad things that did happen to her. For many years she kept well away from her family, living in women's refuges and supervised 'safe houses'. She told me about the repeated attempts that various 'experts' had made to persuade her that her childhood had been very much worse than she had ever imagined, and also that she had DID. After a while she started telling people what they wanted to hear:

It got to the stage where you just agree with everything that they said... Then I got moved to a hostel and saw [the therapist] every single day and started accusing Dad. It was really quite bizarre because it happened so quickly and... you get to the stage when you're saying stuff and you know it's not true. It's difficult to explain, it's like... it's almost like you're automatically saying something and you can't stop, and every time you talk about it, it gets exaggerated. And I know some of it was actually impossible: one of the dates I had given, it was the day he'd had a triple bypass, so there is actually no way he could have done it...

They seem to use eating disorders and self-harm as diagnostic, so the more I self-harmed, the more they told me how bad the abuse was... At one stage I was talking about a nine-year-old daughter that I'd supposedly had when I was 13, who had been kept locked up all those years and never been allowed to eat anything. She got to the age of nine having not eaten a thing! And I watched her getting killed in one of the local parks and buried. And they arranged for the police to go and dig her up!

For the next three years Judith had daily contact either with her therapist or with other members of an organisation for ritual abuse survivors. Sometimes she did try to suggest that some of what she had said was not true, she was then accused of being in denial. During all this time she still believed her father was guilty, finding that every time she said it, it seemed to become more true. She was then encouraged to write a book.

It had a section on self-harm, a section on dissociation, how to help a survivor, a section on my experience and my alters, and it's really crazy because when I look at it now I just can't imagine why I did it. There were one or two paragraphs that are badly spelt because a five year old was typing them. [The organisation] still have a copy and every now and then I get a phone call from them asking me whether things have changed and whether they are allowed to publish it… It's actually been quite difficult making sure that they don't do it.

After a further move to yet another 'safe house', Judith finally decided, in 2004, to distance herself from three years of surveillance and to go back home. 'I was just fed up and I needed to be at home'. As with so many clients who change their minds, this distancing seems to have been crucial. It was a week after this move that she decided to satisfy her curiosity about an organisation that she had often been warned about, and told never to approach. This organisation, said to be full of abusers and intent on hurting children, turned out to be the British False Memory Society. On phoning them she discovered that they were not quite what she had been led to believe. She remained wary of them for a while, but was advised by them to read some of the literature about false memories. This began her gradual process of painfully of re-assessing her beliefs. Sadly, her father died at the time this was happening, and before Judith had a chance to say sorry to him, something she still grieves about.

When I met Judith, six years after these events, she seemed outwardly cheerful and determined to set new challenges for herself. She was studying for a degree and involved with a charity raising money for physically disabled children. She was pleased to have a flat of her own and finally to be independent of the therapeutic network. However, this has been painful for her. Although she is indignant about what happened to her, she misses the friendship and support that went with being a 'survivor'. She still feels suicidal at times. 'Sometimes I just feel I've screwed up so much that things are never going to change'. Now, however, she at last has the chance to be herself and to face her real difficulties, unencumbered by the additional imaginary horrors that were foisted upon her.

Nearly all the people who are diagnosed with DID or DDNOS and go through the recommended therapy are women. I have been told that some men go through this process as well, though in both my researches and personal contacts I have not met any. Thus, when noting the consequences of this therapy we are talking about the ways in which it radically changes the lives of women. It tells them about their past suffering and it also tells them that they have within them a host of alternative identities. They become attached to these alters or parts, and this attachment, like their attachment to their therapist, is perhaps understandable when we consider what other attachments they inevitably lose during therapy. They lose their families. During therapy they learn to see their parents (or whoever looked after them in their earliest years) in a completely new light. Sometimes they confront their parents with this new knowledge, sometimes they just break off all contact. They are often advised to distance themselves and to guard against being drawn back into abusive relationships. They may also have to reject any relatives or former friends who refuse to believe in their new memories. Their therapy has thus isolated them from their past and they desperately need their new family of therapists and fellow survivors.

For the rejected parents of these women there are no consoling new contacts. Some will have no idea why they have lost their daughter, some will know only too well, finding themselves under police investigation for specific crimes. Their anguish can be a consequence of any therapy that searches for abuse memories, but is especially likely to follow the lifechanging therapy undergone by those with a diagnosis of DID or DDNOS. The plight of these families will be described in the next chapter.

References – 5. The consequences of therapy

* Unless otherwise stated, all webpages could be accessed in August 2013.

1   Hardy D.W., Daghestani A.N. and Hutton Egan W. (1988). Multiple Personality Disorder: Failure to diagnose and the potential for malpractice liability. *Psychiatric Annals*, September, 543-548.
2   Pendergrast M. (1996). *Victims of Memory*. London: Harper Collins, p. 551.
3   Rivera M. (1991). Multiple Personality Disorder and the Social Systems: 185 cases. *Dissociation* 4 (2), 79-82.
4   Ross C.A. and Dua V. (1993). Psychiatric healthcare costs of multiple personality disorder. *American Journal of Psychotherapy*, 47, 103-112.
5   Chu J.A. et al. (2011). Guidelines for treating Dissociative Identity Disorder in adults, third revision. *Journal of Trauma and Dissociation*, 12, 115-187.
6   Brand B.L. et al (2009). A review of dissociative disorder treatment studies. *The Journal of Nervous and Mental Disease*, 197 (9), 646-654.
7   Brand B.L. (2012). What we need to know and what we need to learn about the treatment of Dissociative Disorders. *Journal of Trauma and Dissociation*. 13, 387-396.
8   Merskey H. and Piper A. (1998). Treatment of Dissociative Identity Disorder. *American Journal of Psychiatry*, 155: 1462, letter to the editor.
9   Powell R.A. and Howell A.J. (1998). Response to Ellason JW and Ross CA 1997. *American Journal of Psychiatry*, 155 (1), 303.
10 Mair K. (1999). Impact of treatment for dissociative identity disorder (multiple personality disorder) on utilisation of mental health services. Unpublished paper.
11 Fairlie J. (2010). *Unbreakable Bonds: 'They know about you Dad'*.

London: McAuley, pp.14-15.

12 False Memory Syndrome Foundation newsletter (Vol5 No5 May 1996) www.fmsfonline.org

13 Fetkewicz J., Sharma J. and Mersky H. (2000). A note on suicidal deterioration with recovered memory treatment. *Journal of Affective Disorders*, 58 (2), 155-159.

14 Brand B.L. (2012) ibid.

15 Pendergrast M. (1995) "First of all, do no harm": a recovered memory therapist recants. *Skeptic*, 3(4) 36-41.

16 Simpson P. (1996). *Second Thoughts: understanding the false memory crisis and how it could affect you.* Nashville: Thomas Nelson, pp. 12-13.

17 First Person Plural. www.firstpersonplural.org.uk/

18 Mosaic Minds. www.mosaicminds.org/

19 Many Voices. Query of the Month, June 2010 www.manyvoicespress.com/ (Access to Query of the Month no longer available).

20 Ibid Query of the Month, August 2009.

21 Ibid Many Voices, 2003.

22 Ibid Query of the Month, December 2009.

23 Spring R. (2010). The road less travelled: how to support your DID partner (part 1). *Interact*, 10 (1), 25-30.

24 Survivorship. www.survivorship.org (Follow links > articles> conference speech 2003).

25 Ritual Abuse Network Scotland. www.rans.org.uk (Accessed May 2013).

26 Lief H. and Fetkewicz J. (1995). Retraction of false memories: the evolution of pseudomemories. *Journal of Psychiatry and Law*, 411-435.

27 Parents Against Cruel Therapy. www.angryparents.net/ (Follow links > Newsletter archive >2003 > October).

28 Pendergrast (1996). ibid. Pp. 355-360.

7. BELIEF MEETS THE BACKLASH

Recovered memory therapy is seen by some as a necessary way of helping the victims of child abuse, and by others as a dangerous practice that can lead to the formation of false memories and damaging delusions. It is hard to find any common ground between these views. Some slight concessions have now been made on each side, but in many ways views have become more polarised over the years.

People on both sides of this divide probably welcome the fact that during the past 30 years we have become more aware of the prevalence of child sexual abuse and of the harm that it can cause. Credit for this must be partly due to the campaigning of the Women's Liberation Movement that gathered momentum during the 1970s, especially in the US. Women were encouraged to fight back against pervasive male dominance. Robin Morgan, in *Sisterhood is Powerful*, asserted that 'the nuclear family unit is oppressive to woman'.[1] Susan Brownmiller, in *Against Our Will: Men, Women and Rape*, launched a blistering attack on the male attitudes that underlie sexual violence towards women.[2] She suggested that these same 'patriarchal' attitudes were responsible for our failure to acknowledge the true incidence of incest. Following on from this, feminists urged all victims to speak out, to join women's groups and to write about their experiences. It was at this time that Ellen Bass, a young creative writing instructor, started collecting these women's stories. She later reproduced them to great effect in *The Courage to Heal*. A wealth of books and articles on the hidden problem of incest now began to appear.[3-5]

It seems that women incest victims were originally encouraged to speak out about abuse that they had always remembered but never told anyone about. This could only be a good thing. However, this speaking out sometimes brought about a remarkable expansion of their memories. It was this that led many therapists to extend their

137

activities to a search for 'repressed' or 'dissociated' abuse memories. In their crusade to rescue women from previously unacknowledged abuse, they eagerly used hypnosis, dream analysis, age regression and guided imagery, so that the recovery of memories now became a feature of therapy, to be worked through as part of the healing process. The new idea that some of their clients might be unknowingly suffering from dissociative disorders, characterised by hidden trauma-related memories, fitted in well with this mind-set.

It was during the 1990s that recovered memory therapists came up against the objections that they termed a 'backlash'. They argued that this was perhaps inevitable, and a sign of their success: 'every time a subordinate group begins to make progress, a backlash appears', but they protested that it was despicable to attack 'those who heroically expose the extent of sexual abuse'.[6] Although the objections to recovered memory therapy at this time came independently from many directions, the therapists claimed that this was a co-ordinated campaign and that it was spearheaded by the men who had been accused by their clients of incest. These men obviously did have a vested interest in claiming that recovered memories were false memories, but they were not alone. They were joined by many people with expert knowledge of memory and of mental health, who denied any scientific justification for the therapists' methods and beliefs. They were also joined by members of the public who judged that many of the new memories were simply unbelieveable. Thus, there are several strands to this backlash, and I will deal with each of them in turn.

The accused parents speak out

In 1991 four families in the US, with fathers who had been accused by their daughters of sexually abusing them, posted the following notice, with a contact number, as widely as they could.

Has your grown child falsely accused you as a consequence of repressed "memories"? You are not alone. Please help us document the scope of this problem.[7]

During the next few months more than 100 families responded and the False Memory Syndrome Foundation (FMSF) was born. By 1996 it had been contacted by 17,000 families, all claiming that they had been torn apart by false accusations of sexual abuse.[8] Now, more than 20 years later, the foundation still exists; families are still suffering, though fortunately the new appeals for help are arriving at a slower rate. The term 'false memory syndrome' was coined by Peter Freyd, one of the founders of FMSF, who had himself been accused of sexually abusing his daughter. The use of this term was perhaps unfortunate, as it gave the opponents of FMSF an easy target. They were quick to point out that this was not a syndrome recognised in any official classification of diseases and that it prejudged the issue by assuming that the memories in question were false. Perhaps the term 'recovered memory syndrome' would have been better. However, the rather wordy definition of this condition that was devised by the psychologist John Kihlstrom and is used by the FMSF does seem to describe quite accurately the state of mind and the way of life that can be seen in many people who have experienced recovered memory therapy. It may not be a recognised medical condition but unfortunately it does appear to exist.

When the memory is distorted or confabulated, the result can be what has been called the False Memory Syndrome, a condition in which a person's identity and interpersonal relationships are centred around a memory of traumatic experience which is objectively false but in which the person strongly *believes*. Note that the syndrome is not characterised by false memories as such. We all have memories that are inaccurate. Rather the syndrome may be diagnosed when the memory is so deeply ingrained that it orients the individual's entire personality and lifestyle, in turn disrupting all sorts of other adaptive behavior. The analogy to personality disorder is intentional. False memory syndrome is especially destructive because the person *assiduously avoids* confrontation with any evidence that might

139

challenge the memory. Thus it takes on a life of its own, encapsulated and resistant to correction. The person may become so focused on memory that he or she may be effectively distracted from coping with the real problems in his or her life.' [9] (Italics are in the original.)

In North America the FMSF was influential during the 1990s in promoting a more sceptical view of some sexual abuse allegations. They were able to point to psychological research on memory and suggestibility that supported their position, and they gained the support of many respected academics. Gradually the testimony of self-styled survivors became less likely to be enough in itself to secure convictions in the courts. Those therapists who had been searching for recovered memories now found themselves at risk of lawsuits and were sometimes more guarded in their public pronouncements, though their beliefs seemed to remain untouched by this backlash. They still worked hard to promote their ideas and also to export them worldwide. The backlash was also exported. Parents in many other countries now found it necessary to join together in a similar way, supporting each other after devastating accusations of sexual abuse. There are now False Memory Societies (they have all avoided using the term false memory syndrome) in the UK, Canada, Australia, New Zealand, the Netherlands, Scandinavia and France. All over the world hundreds of thousands of people, believing themselves to be innocent, are prepared to admit to each other, and sometimes to a wider public, that they have been accused of the despicable crime of incest.

Who are these people who have been prepared to identify themselves as alleged child abusers, or as partners of alleged child abusers? Surveys have been made of accused families in the US, the UK, Australia and New Zealand.[10-12] In all four countries those family members responding have indicated that they are mostly well educated, middle class and affluent. In the US study, 87% of fathers were in professional or white collar occupations. In the Australian study 90% of families were judged to be middle class, and only 7% to be working class, based on the father's occupation. The accusers themselves, who were almost all female and aged on average around 30, were also reported to be well educated, often to university level in each country. These families are strikingly different from those discovered in surveys of known child abuse, where poverty, low education and single parenthood are prominent features.[13,14]

It is to be expected that disadvantaged people will find it more difficult to join organisations such as false memory societies, but even so, it does seem surprising that the factors normally associated with child abuse are so strikingly absent in these families. Children are usually thought to be most at risk of abuse from stepfathers, but stepfathers comprise less than 1% of the accused abusers in the US sample and get no mention in the UK, New Zealand and Australian samples. Biological fathers were the main alleged culprits in three quarters of the US, UK and New Zealand samples, and there were accusations against mothers in about a fifth of cases. Grandparents and siblings were also sometimes implicated, but less frequently. Many of the accusations made against these men and women seem implausible because of their extreme nature. They refer to sadistic and sometimes life-threatening abuse, often occurring in infancy. Ritual abuse was alleged in 19% of the US cases, 14% of the New Zealand cases and 7% of the UK cases. In many cases, however, those accused were not given any details about their alleged offences.[15,16]

How do the promoters of recovered memory therapy meet the challenge posed by these respectable, well-educated men and women? They usually start by saying that there is no such thing as false memory syndrome. They then point out that the concept of false memory belittles and hurts the survivors of abuse and gives the perpetrators something to hide behind. They remind us that guilty as well as innocent people can claim that they have been accused as a result of false memories, and they often vilify certain individuals who are either members of, or associated with, false memory societies. However, they do usually concede that not all these men are guilty. The therapist Charles Whitfield has admitted that delusive memories could sometimes occur, but he goes on to claim that 'only 2% of parents accused on the basis of recovered memories are innocent'.[17] How he comes up with that figure is not explained. In 2009, during a conference about ritual abuse, I heard a well known expert on dissociative disorders quote this same percentage authoritatively. But she evidently saw no need to take any action over this 2% of unfortunate parents, neither did she acknowledge that there must be a corresponding number of deluded accusers who are now burdened with memories of fictitious abuse which have cut them off from any family contact or support.

Ellen Bass and Laura Davies, in the third edition of *The Courage to Heal,* published in 1994, responded to the backlash with a chapter that runs to 85 pages, entitled 'Honoring the Truth'. In it we find the usual objections to the concept of false memory syndrome and also to all who believe in it. They do then concede that there have been problems but, like Dr Whitfield, use creative accounting to suggest that these are of relatively minor importance.

> False claims of sexual abuse do exist, but compared to the astronomical numbers of survivors who were truly abused, such claims represent only a miniscule percentage of survivor accounts. Even if all 5,000 families who have contacted FMSF were indeed falsely accused that amounts to only 0.01% or one hundredth of a per cent of the estimated number of adult survivors of child sexual abuse in this country.[18]

The fact that Bass and Davis underestimated the number of families who were contacting FMSF is relatively unimportant. What does seem important is their apparent equanimity in surveying this possible amount of collateral damage. Do they have any sense of responsibility for these false accusations? Do they ever wonder whether they might themselves have set someone off on that path with the following advice in the 1988 edition of their book?

> Assume your feelings are valid. So far, no one we've talked to thought she might have been abused, and then later discovered that she hadn't been. The progression always goes the other way, from suspicion to confirmation. If you

think you were abused and your life shows the symptoms, then you were.[19]

In this edition of *The Courage to Heal*, readers were not advised to carry out any investigations to see whether there were grounds for their suspicions. In their later response to the backlash, however, Bass and Davis admit for the first time that a search for evidence can sometimes be undertaken, 'but only if you want to'. After warning that this is risky, and 'definitely not a required part of the healing process', they then give some useful suggestions:

If you look carefully at your history you may find information that helps you figure out what took place. Re-examining family photo albums, old diaries or family stories may give you clues about your past. Sometimes talking to people who were there – family members, old friends, teachers, school counsellors or neighbours – can yield valuable insights. School and medical records may also contain revealing information.[20]

This is excellent advice, but Bass and Davis insist that these investigations should not be undertaken at the stage when they are most needed. They advise readers against talking to their families while they are still uncertain about what happened. Confrontations and disclosures should be postponed 'until you are more clear'. In other words, until you have made up your mind. By this time any protestations of innocence may be seen as denial, and disconfirming evidence will either be disregarded or incorporated into an altered abuse story. We can see an example of the way this happens in a Christian counsellor's account, published elsewhere, of seven years of therapy with a client who claimed to have experienced unremitting tortures and degradation throughout her childhood. At first the therapist found it difficult to understand how such atrocities could go unnoticed in her neighbourhood, but then she and her client came up with this explanation: 'neighbours were involved in the ritual group, as were teachers at her school and the family doctor.'[21] If the evidence does not fit the story, you can always expand the story to fit the evidence.

In their response to the backlash, Bass and Davis are indignant that anyone should question the testimony of survivors or the activities of the therapists who try to help them. However, they do in places acknowledge that false memories of abuse have been damaging. Has there perhaps been a slight shift in their position? In the fourth edition of *The Courage to Heal,* published in 2008 to celebrate the 20th anniversary of its original publication, we no longer see the paragraph quoted above, with its notorious suggestion: 'if you think you were abused, and your life shows the symptoms, then you were.' There are a number of other welcome changes. In a new section, 'Finding your own truth', they admit that therapists sometimes make mistakes: 'some therapists have concluded on their own that a client had been abused, regardless of whether the person herself thought she had. This is irresponsible therapy and potentially dangerous for the client'.[22] There is another new section entitled 'Strategies for working with persistent doubt' which advises readers not to rush to any conclusions about past abuse. Doubts may result from talking to people who don't believe you, but 'consistent doubt can also be an indication that you are on the wrong track'.[23]

Despite this admission that both therapists and clients can get things wrong, we do not find any warnings about the possibilities of false memories. Bass and Davis accept that 'memory is not 100% accurate', and this means that 'survivors remember the details of their abuse with some degree of distortion'. They even give some examples of false memories of abuse, but these are seen as distortions of true abuse memories, not as fabrications, and the term 'false memory' is never used. As before, readers are encouraged to think back to their childhood and consider the possibility of sexual abuse, even if they have no memories of it. As before, they are provided throughout the book with a wealth of graphic descriptions of sexual abuse, usually incest, that may fire their imaginations.

Research psychologists question the reliability of memory

Academic psychologists who study memory have no difficulty in accepting that false autobiographical memories are a fact of life. We saw in Chapter 1 how false memories can be induced experimentally in unwitting subjects, who find them just as compelling as their true memories. One of the first psychologists to devise these experiments was Elizabeth Loftus, who had from the 1970s been an acknowledged expert on memory and had demonstrated how easily people could be misled by suggestion. By the time she started questioning claims about sexual abuse, her expertise had already made her a valuable witness in court proceedings where the accuracy of memories was in question. She has now testified in more than 250 cases, has written a vast number of books and articles and has received many awards for her work. More than anyone else, she has been influential in promoting the sceptical views that have become known as the backlash. This influence was recognised in 2010 by the American Association for the Advancement of Science, when she received their Scientific Freedom and Responsibility Award in recognition of the profound impact that her pioneering research on human memory had on the administration of justice in the United States and abroad.[24]

Perhaps it is only to be expected that Loftus's profound impact has earned her not only awards but also some venomous personal attacks and several attempts to disrupt and discredit her work. She has received hate mail and death threats and often has to have protection from security guards when giving invited addresses. For therapists and their clients she has become the enemy, a focus in the 'memory wars' in which they do battle with scientists over the nature of memory in general and the truth of recovered memories in particular. Almost 20 years ago Loftus referred to these two sides as the 'true believers' and the 'sceptics', and pointed out that they were divided by some irreconcilable convictions. One of them was belief in the concept of repression, which she dismissed as 'purely hypothetical and essentially untestable'.[25] Dissociation has now replaced repression as the process most often invoked by therapists to account for lost traumatic memories. Dissociation is another speculative concept that many people find unsatisfactory because it is a hypothetical mental state, which has to be inferred rather than directly observed.

A lot of valuable research has been generated by the memory wars. This has led to some concessions being made by both sides. As we saw in Chapter 1, the scientists discovered that some people do apparently lose their memories of childhood abuse and then recover them later.[26] They have therefore conceded that recovered memories can be true. The therapists, faced with mounting evidence of the unreliability of memory, have conceded that recovered memories can be false. In their recent Guidelines for Treating Dissociative Identity Disorder the ISST-D have included a section entitled 'Validity of Patients' Memories of Abuse'. Here they refer to statements that have been made by various professional bodies representing psychiatrists and psychologists, in which they have concluded, as above, that recovered memories can be either true or false, and that 'therapists cannot know the extent to which someone's memories are accurate in the absence of external corroboration'. Therapists are therefore advised not to make pronouncements on the truth or otherwise of their patients' memories, and to take a 'neutral stance'. This neutrality, however, seems to be rather compromised by the following advice.

> Although therapists are not responsible for determining the
> veracity of patients' memories, at times it may be therapeutic
> to communicate their professional opinion. For example, if
> the patient has developed a well-considered belief that his
> or her memories are authentic, the therapist can support this
> belief if it appears credible and consistent with the patient's
> history and clinical presentation.[27]

Since all clients with DID will be assumed by the therapist to have a history of severe abuse, it seems that any memories of this will inevitably 'appear credible and consistent'. External corroboration is no longer needed if the memory fits the therapist's theory.

Despite some concessions, no truce has been declared in the memory wars. The scientists remain sceptical of any memories that are recovered during therapy, and most therapists seem to believe that no memories of child abuse are likely to be *completely* false. As one of them said to me, 'they [her clients] do get things rather muddled up at times, but the abuse is always true.' Many of the books and papers now being used by recovered memory therapists and their supporters either make no mention of the problem of false memories, or dismiss it with a brief mention. *The Dissociative Identity Disorder Sourcebook* defined them thus:

> [False memory is] a term coined by the False Memory Syndrome Foundation to describe memories that they believe are not based on actual events. The concept is not yet proven by clinical research.[28]

Psychiatrists object to the diagnosis of DID

Recovered memory therapists have come under attack, not just from academic psychologists, but from psychiatrists. Perhaps because psychiatrists, unlike psychologists, have a medical training, their strongest objections seem to have focused on the diagnosis rather than the unreliability of memory. For many of them it was the resurgence of one particular diagnosis, Multiple Personality Disorder (MPD), that first aroused their concern. As we saw in Chapter 3, the new interest in Dissociative Disorders sprang from an original interest in MPD, and for psychiatrists this had always been a controversial condition, thought by some to be not much more than play-acting. In the 1960 edition of a widely respected psychiatric textbook the phenomenon of personality switching was described only to be briefly dismissed: 'It seems that these multiple personalities are always artificial productions, the product of the medical attention they arouse.'[29] So when psychiatrists started diagnosing an ever increasing number of cases during the 1980s, their fellow clinicians were quick to accuse them of creating this disorder themselves, and of embarking on a 'psychiatric misadventure' in which 'fictitious memories and syndromes can be created to please the therapist.'[30]

Psychiatrists also complained that the diagnostic criteria for MPD were impossibly vague. They could easily fit many patients who were really suffering from other disorders. The promoters of MPD had always claimed that, because patients with this disorder have such a wide range of symptoms, clinicians often missed the essential MPD diagnosis. Their critics stood this claim on its head and insisted that these other symptoms were the ones that required treatment, and diagnosing MPD was therefore harmful because it was a distraction that prevented clinicians treating other more serious psychological problems in the lives of patients.[31]

A further complaint was that MPD was 'culture specific': it was only diagnosed in North America, and was not found elsewhere in the world. This was certainly true in the early 1990s, but the picture now is very different. It has been discovered that MPD and DID are disorders that can be widely disseminated by international conferences and training seminars. Many of these events have now taken place with the result that Dissociative Disorders have now been discovered in countries throughout the world, including China and Japan.[32] Sometimes the concept of dissociation fails to catch on because it has to compete with an alternative local mythology. For example, in Uganda the symptoms of DID were interpreted as signs of possession by spirits.[33] In most other countries, however, contact with international experts and knowledge of the appropriate questionnaires and interview formats seems to be sufficient to enable therapists to detect many new cases of this once American disorder. It seems to be specific to the culture of the therapist rather than the client.

The therapists who treat the Dissociative Disorders point out that these are officially recognised. The American Psychiatric Association has included them since 1980 in their DSM classification of disorders. This has had the great advantage in some countries of making medical insurance companies liable for treatment costs; it has also given them a much needed stamp of legitimacy. In Europe the preferred classification system is the

International Classification of Diseases (ICD) developed by the World Health Organisation. Here we also find some recognition of Dissociative Disorders, but with a different emphasis. As in DSM, they are said to be characterised by a lack of integration between various mental functions, but here the concept is extended to include un-integrated physical functions. This means that unexplained physical dysfunctions are seen as further examples of dissociation. These are also described as Conversion Disorders, in which mental disturbance is converted into a physical symptom. The concept of dissociation is thus somewhat broadened.

Table 2 shows how the disorders have been listed in recent revisions of both classifications.

Table 2: Classification of Dissociative Disorders in DSM-IV and ICD-10	
DSM-IV 1994	**ICD-10 1992**
Dissociative amnesia	Dissociative amnesia
Dissociative fugue	Dissociative fugue
Dissociative identity disorder	Dissociative motor disorders
Depersonalisation disorder	Dissociative convulsions
Dissociative disorder NOS	Dissociative anaesthesia and sensory loss
	Dissociative stupor
	Trance and possession disorders
	Mixed dissociative (conversion) disorders
	Other dissociative (conversion) disorders
	Dissociative (conversion) disorder unspecified

The most striking difference here is that ICD lists twice as many disorders as DSM but makes no mention of the one that has always attracted the most attention and has seemed to be the raison d'être of the dissociative disorders in general. Where is dissociative identity disorder (DID)? In the full document it does creep in as a subheading, under 'Other dissociative (conversion) disorders', where it carries its former title of multiple personality disorder, but it also carries a health warning: 'This disorder is rare, and controversy exists about the extent to which it is iatrogenic or culture specific'.[34] This suggests that when ICD was last revised 20 years ago the new interpretation of DID faced considerable scepticism in countries outside North America. Dissociation seems to have had a wider meaning outside America, incorporating many strange physical states that have not generally been associated with childhood trauma.

Both classification systems have to be repeatedly revised to reflect new findings and changing attitudes. Thus DSM-IV becomes DSM-5 in 2013, and ICD-10 will become ICD-11 in 2015. Years of argument and energetic lobbying always seem to precede these revisions, with psychiatrists and others trying to influence the relevant committees to include or exclude various disorders or to describe them in particular ways. Already by 2007 representatives of the International Society for the Study of Trauma and Dissociation (ISST-D), were contacting the chair of the group revising ICD-10, asking to be involved in any discussions about the dissociative disorders. This letter could be seen on their website during 2012, but has now been removed.[35] They welcomed the fact that physical dissociative states had for some time been included in ICD, and they also stressed, without mentioning DID specifically, that the dissociative disorders in general were a public health problem that could be 'prevented and treated effectively' but had many serious outcomes without treatment. The opposing sceptics were less quick off the mark, but in 2009 a group of American psychiatrists asked the chair of the DSM-5 committee to exclude the troublesome DID diagnosis altogether from the new revision, claiming that its inclusion had damaged the reputation of psychiatry and had 'grave ill effects on many patients and their families'. Once again this letter could be viewed online up to 2012 only.[36]

These sceptical psychiatrists will be disappointed with DSM-5. DID is not only still there, but the criteria for its diagnosis have now been widened. 'The presence of two or more distinct personality states' is no longer a prime requirement, 'an experience of possession' may be substituted, and many additional symptoms of mental confusion are listed which do not have to be observed but may simply be reported. During 2012 it was possible to view online The American Psychiatric Association's account of their reasons for this and other changes. They explained that they wanted to reduce the use of Dissociative Disorder Not Otherwise Specified (DDNOS), the curiously negative diagnosis which was previously used more frequently than DID. They also hoped that the changes would increase the 'global utility' of DID, and they pointed out that physical conversion symptoms are a common feature, thus further widening the net.[37] These changes will be welcomed by the promoters of the dissociative disorders, who have been arguing for many years that we should not always expect to see the classic features of MPD in people diagnosed with DID. They have also insisted that this is a common condition occurring throughout the world. The new revision should certainly help them in their efforts to increase the known prevalence of DID, and to defy the scepticism of their fellow clinicians.

Reports of ritual abuse lead to public scepticism

It has been said that accounts of ritual abuse are the Achilles heel of recovered memory therapy. These reported traumatic experiences recovered during therapy are judged by some people to be so unbelievable that they cast doubt on the reliability of recovered memories in general. Ritual abuse can be defined as abuse carried out by a group of people in a ceremonial or circumscribed manner, with the aim of maintaining power over the victim. It involves all or some of the following: rape by many perpetrators, imprisonment, torture, cannibalism, bestiality, drinking bodily fluids, witnessing or being forced to participate in murder and/or animal sacrifice and giving birth to a baby or foetus which is then ritually sacrificed. Therapists first began to be told about these experiences during the 1980s. This development, like the renewed interest in MPD, can be traced back to the publication of a single influential book.

Michelle Remembers was published in the US in 1980. It was co-written by an MPD client and her Canadian psychiatrist, Laurence Pazder, who had previously worked in West Africa studying black magic rituals.[38] During her therapy Michelle apparently remembered being raped and tortured by both her parents and by their fellow members of a cult of Satanists. She had seen this cult ritually murder babies and adults, and on one occasion slice up a foetus and rub it on her body. She had also been caged, tormented with spiders and snakes and visited by the devil. This book became a best-seller, avidly read by thousands in Canada and the US. Pazder and Michelle later got married and together continued to publicise their remarkable story with great success. They performed nationwide on radio and television, and their story later spawned other survivor accounts and also TV shows with titles such as *Satanic Breeders: Babies for Sacrifice* and *Investigating multiple personalities: did the Devil make them do it?*".[39]

In North America at that time there were growing anxieties about the activities of bizarre cults. The horrific multiple murders committed in 1969 by Charles Manson's 'family' of groupies had been followed by sensational reports about other cults such as the Moonies and the Hare Krishnas. Then in 1978 the mass suicide of 913 followers of the Rev. Jim Jones in Jamestown, Guyana strengthened public fears about the power of cults. The fascination and horror that greeted *Michelle Remembers* thus fed into a general mood of alarm, in which the practice of black magic and gruesome satanic rituals was thought to threaten the everyday lives of ordinary people.[40]

It was against this background that some parents with young children in daycare centres began to worry that when they showed disturbed behaviour this might be a sign that they were being maltreated there. These frightened parents contacted the police and social services, and the children, who mostly denied any abuse at first, were subjected to prolonged and suggestive questioning. They became increasingly disturbed and eventually reported many bizarre assaults by the daycare staff, which included physical and sexual tortures carried out during satanic rituals. This was the beginning of a widespread panic in North America about ritual abuse in daycare centres. In 1983 the first arrests were made at the McMartin pre-school nursery in California, where seven of the staff there were accused of carrying out sexual and physical assaults on 360 children over a period of five years. This set the pattern for no fewer than 12 trials in the US alone, and some also in Canada, in which many more carers of young children were charged with abusing their charges in sadistic and sexual rituals. Some were convicted and spent years in prison, but all were later acquitted because it turned out that there was no evidence for any of these crimes beyond the testimony of the alleged young victims.[41]

How did this come about? After the publication of *Michelle Remembers*, stories of ritual abuse were proliferating and MPD was starting to be seen as a response to severe trauma and was being increasingly diagnosed. The first reports of experiencing ritual abuse came from people (nearly all of them women) who had been diagnosed with MPD. It was thus the promotion of MPD as a trauma-related disorder that enabled beliefs about ritual abuse to gain ground, and later to be transported, like MPD itself, across the world. MPD could only be caused by severe trauma, so the horrific nature of these tales of torture and killings helped to justify the diagnosis. It also explained why the victims were unaware of these experiences before they entered therapy. As one psychotherapist explained, 'the normative response to severe trauma, especially in early childhood, is dissociation and amnesia for the traumatic events'.[42] The public had been urged to 'believe the children' when allegations were made about abuse in daycare centres. They were now urged to believe the therapy clients who, having lived through these unspeakable atrocities, formed an elite among abuse survivors. Sceptics were reminded that people had previously refused to believe that incest was a real problem; so it was now necessary to face up to the reality of child abuse, however painful this might be. Belief came more easily for the therapists as they witnessed their clients' distress and terror while recalling, through their alternative personalities, the horrors of ritual abuse. Why would they put themselves through all this if it wasn't true?

The US government was sufficiently concerned by stories of ritual abuse to set up a large scale investigation into its occurrence. When this was finally completed the team of researchers reported that, after investigating over 12,000 alleged cases of ritual abuse, they could find only one that was confirmed.[43] This one case involved ritualised sexual activity, but without any of the killing, torturing and other gruesome activities that are usually said to occur. There were interesting discrepancies between the stories given by alleged child victims and those given by adults. Child victims' reports were usually restricted to scary activities, such as being put in a coffin, or frightened with spiders. It was always the adult survivors who reported the most extreme forms of abuse, including the killing of humans and animals. A third of these self-styled survivors claimed they had been forced to eat human flesh and almost as many reported the breeding of babies for sacrifice. These disclosures were typically made while undergoing therapy for MPD. At this time, two therapists, warning of the dangers of ritual abuse, quoted an estimate that '25% of clients with MPD have experienced ritualistic sexual abuse in their childhood'.[43] Another researcher suggested that during the late 1980s in North America some therapists were reporting that as many as 50% of their MPD clients had recovered memories of ritual abuse.[45]

A similar pattern of events, though on a smaller scale, was later seen in the UK, when some of the American therapists who believed their MPD clients to be ritual abuse survivors started travelling abroad. During 1989 there were several influential seminars on ritual abuse throughout the UK, informing health service and social work professionals that the horrific practices of these powerful cults were not restricted to North America but were a worldwide phenomenon. I attended one of these myself, in Dundee, and experienced its powerful effect. This was the first time I had heard of ritual abuse, and I was impressed by the American experts. Pamela Klein, a social worker and therapist, spoke movingly of her traumatised clients; and Jerry Simandl, a police detective, who seemed very level-headed and therefore convincing, spoke authoritatively on the practices of these cults. We were told to look out for certain signs and symbols which were the clues to their existence. It was easy to believe and it seemed somewhat callous not to. Only later did it occur to me that all the shocking information that we had been given came, not from facts on the ground, but solely from disturbed women who were undergoing therapy.

I lost my initial belief and gradually became more sceptical, but for many of the other clinical psychologists and social workers who attended, this event was a turning point. In Orkney and Rochdale children were suddenly taken away from their parents because social workers, having attended this and other similar seminars, became convinced that they had seen the effects of ritual abuse in the children in their care. As in North America, many legal proceedings were started, only to be dropped later for want of evidence.[46] As in America, the government became so concerned that it sponsored an investigation into the occurrence of organised ritual abuse in the UK, and, as in America, no evidence of this was found.[47]

During the same year that the American ritual abuse experts were spreading their horrifying message abroad, a US police officer with special experience of investigating ritual crimes presented Americans with a different perspective on these alleged occurrences. After pointing out how unlikely it was that such widespread brutal crimes would leave behind no forensic evidence (bodies, fluids, fibres or hairs), or that such mass conspiracy should never be betrayed by any of those involved, he gave this reassuring message:

Until more evidence is obtained and corroborated, the American people should not be frightened into believing that babies are being bred and eaten, that 50,000 missing children are being murdered in human sacrifices, or that Satanists are taking over America's day-care centres. No one can prove with absolute certainty that such activity has NOT

155

occurred. The burden of proof, however, as it would be in a criminal prosecution, is on those who claim that it has occurred.[48]

More than 20 years after that statement, we still have none of the evidence that would be needed to support the claims of those who believe in ritual abuse, despite determined searches by some people. Yet many people refuse to be reassured. In England a senior policeman, now retired, laments this lack of evidence, though in his case this had not dented his belief.

> I've never come across a case of ritual abuse that was proven. People have been named, but it's not been possible to identify them. Usually the name cannot be traced, the address does not exist, or the phone number is wrong. I've been looking for 15 years, and I've tried very hard to find proof. I've dug up fields, set up cameras, and looked down wells where bones were supposed to have been thrown, and I've found nothing that can be independently linked to the allegations.[49]

The believing therapists are undeterred by this because they are able to find sufficient evidence in the testimony of their clients. However, only a minority of recovered memory therapists do discover any ritual abuse. I have been told that this is because clients are very wary of reporting it, and usually offer the therapist only brief snippets of information that then have to be built upon by a therapist who understands what they represent. The clients need a therapist who is informed enough to be able to join the dots. In a US survey of reports of ritual abuse, it was found that less than a third of responding therapists had encountered any cases of ritual- or religion-related abuse, and mostly they had seen only one or two cases. However a tiny proportion of these therapists reported that they had each encountered more than 100 cases.[50]

There are now many organisations that can help therapists acquire this specialist skill of detecting ritual abuse. They also try to spread the word that ritual abuse really does exist. In England one of the first of these, established in 1989, was the Ritual Abuse Support and Information Network (RAINS), which aimed to support therapists who felt isolated by the widespread scepticism that met their claims about ritual abuse. In Scotland in 2001 the Tayside Ritual Abuse and Support and Help Project (TRASH) was set up. It has now changed its name to Izzy's Promise and continues to expand. It was greatly helped in 2007 by an award of £267,054 from the big lottery fund to develop their telephone helpline for people who have suffered ritual abuse.[51] At about the same time the Association of Christian Counsellors established the Trauma and Abuse Group (TAG) to provide guidelines for its members who were working with 'survivors of ritual or extreme childhood abuse'. This group has now expanded to provide information, support and training for anyone working with survivors of severe trauma.[52]

In 2009 TAG joined forces with RAINS to hold a conference on ritual abuse. One of the many invited speakers, the Canadian psychotherapist Alison Miller, started by warning her large audience, mainly made up of therapists, not to get caught up in the false memory controversy, but to take a 'neutral stance' on the accuracy of their clients' memories and to avoid any leading questions. So far, so good! However, she also told these therapists that clients might need help in overcoming their reluctance to disclose any experience of ritual abuse. To this end she gave them a list of things that their clients should know they were 'open to hear about'. This included: 'Multiple perpetrators, deliberate creation of alters [alternative personalities], torture of infants and children, years of deliberate planned abuse, sexual perversion, murders, children forced to participate'. Her proposed neutral stance seemed to be further eroded when she told them how they should respond to any disclosures.

> Most survivors are their own greatest critics when it comes to doubting their memories. They have been programmed to distrust them. They hate and fear them and want them to be untrue. They have been invalidated by others their whole

lives. To be healing, we must be deeply honest. If an account seems contrived, fear driven, impossible, etc. we can say "it does not ring true to me". And when reality is very unclear, we may say "let's see what happens as this unfolds". But when clients overcome tremendous trepidation, and finally share an account of unspeakable horrors, with vivid multisensory details, and matching somatic flashbacks, and matching affects of fear, disgust, rage, and grief, pieces of other memories match, and they both wish it wasn't true and long to be believed, and they say "Could this be real?" or "Do you think I am making this up?" we must speak the truth from our heart, and say "It all seems to fit," or "It rings true to me". To say "What matters is what is your truth" is a lie. It is dissociogenic. And it leaves them alone in the ritual or laboratory.[53]

Therapists with ritually abused clients are usually advised that they do not have to believe everything that their clients tell them. Most of seem to them draw the line at tales of alien abduction or memories from past lives. Reports of these experiences can, however, conveniently be attributed to 'programming' by the cult. Apparently this involves the deliberate implanting of false beliefs in order to discredit the victim's testimony. The concept of programming is also very useful when lack of evidence for certain activities becomes embarrassing. I have been told that many of the reported murders never really happened, but were staged, using bags of pretend blood, to convince and terrify the victim. That is why no bodies or body parts have ever been found. An alternative convenient concept is that of the 'screen memory', in which a fictitious memory, associated with childhood trauma, has a protective function in blocking the formation of the real memory.[54] Therapists are here recognising the existence of false memories, but only when they fail to fit in with their expectations. The client may be mistaken when she remembers being abused by aliens, but not when she remembers being abused by Dad.

The dissociative disorder experts are interestingly divided in assessing the credibility of accounts of ritual abuse. The International Society for the Study of Trauma and Dissociation (ISST-D) admits in its 'Guidelines for treating Dissociative Identity Disorder in Adults' that not all its members think that these accounts are literally true. They could be 'misremembered' experiences of real sadistic events, or might even be explained in some cases as 'unconscious defensive elaborations, false memory, delusion or deliberate confabulation'.[55] These explanations for what is said during therapy seem remarkably similar to those that are suggested by the recovered memory sceptics. There is common ground here, and we have seen this before. Some of the initial promoters of dissociative disorders did engage with the problem of false memories to some extent. Robert Kluft recognised that they posed serious difficulties for therapists.

> It often seems necessary to work through traumatic material that appears likely to be historically inaccurate... There is virtually no way to avoid the risk of investigating inaccurate recall, simply by declining to use one technique or another. In an era in which accounts of abuse and its consequences are media staples, the patient who enters treatment with an uncontaminated memory is more a myth than an accurate baseline. [56]

Colin Ross, another of the prime movers of the promotion of these disorders, made the following admissions in his textbook on DID:

> It is true that iatrogenic cases of DID are a serious problem; it is true that memory is reconstructive, error prone, and highly influenced by socio-psychological variables; it is true that DID patients can construct elaborate and detailed false memories; it is true that DID can be used for secondary gain; it is true that incompetent therapists are practising in the field... The sceptics need to be cured of their excesses, so that the therapists can hear what they have to say.[57]

Sadly, more than a decade after these statements, the therapists have no wish to listen to the sceptics. The common ground has not been built on, and the gulf between the two sides seems to be wider than ever. Therapists can now turn to many supporting organisations that insulate them from any criticism. Cautionary advice about the unreliability of memory has been issued by both the Royal College of Psychiatrists and the British Psychological Society.[57,58] This may have made psychiatrists and clinical psychologists working within the NHS more wary of diagnosing dissociative disorders or even of practising any recovered memory therapy. However, it has had the effect of moving the practice out to the private sector, where therapists can work independently, undisturbed and unsupervised by colleagues who might not share their beliefs. Although some of those now treating dissociative disorders did once work in the NHS, many of them would never have been qualified to do this and have come into this work from a diverse range of experiences and educational backgrounds.

Therapists who specialise in treating dissociative disorders are stuck with a theory that insists that their clients *must* have been abused as children. Their theory also instructs them to probe for new memories of childhood abuse. So although some of them have admitted that false memories are a real problem, they cannot afford to listen to the sceptics and change the way they operate. When therapists believe that their clients have suffered ritual abuse they are especially likely to be ridiculed by the sceptics, and to react with indignant affirmations of their faith. There are now many internet sites where we can see this battle being played out, as it has been for years. We know that when www.stopbadtherapy.com/ confronts www.endritualabuse.org/ neither side will ever call a truce.

References – 7. Belief meets the backlash

* Unless otherwise stated, all webpages could be accessed in August 2013.

1 Morgan R. (1970). *Sisterhood is Powerful*. New York: Vintage.
2 Brownmiller S. (1975). *Against Our Will: Men, Women and Rape*. New York: Simon and Schuster.
3 Butler S. (1978). *The Conspiracy of Silence: The Trauma of Incest*. San Francisco: New Glide Publications.
4 Armstrong L. (1978). *Kiss Daddy Goodnight: A Speak-Out on Incest*. New York: Hawthorn Books.
5 Herman J.L. and Hirschman L. (1981). *Father-Daughter Incest*. Cambridge: Harvard University Press.
6 Herman J.L. and Harvey M.R. (1993). The False Memory Debate: Social Science or Social Backlash? *Harvard Mental Health Review*, April, 4-6.
7 False Memory Syndrome Foundation. www.fmsfonline.org. Follow link > FMSF newsletter archive, Vol 1 No 1 March 1992.
8 Ibid. (Follow link > FMFS newsletter archive, Vol 5 No 3 March, 1996).
9 Pendergrast M. (1996). *Victims of Memory*. London: Harper Collins, p. 556.
10 McHugh P.R. et al. (2004). From refusal to reconciliation: family relationships after an accusation based on recovered memories. *Journal of Nervous and Mental Diseases*, 192(8), 525-531.
11 Goodyear Smith F., Laidlaw T.M. and Large R.G. (1997). Surveying families accused of child sexual abuse: a comparison of British and New Zealand results. *Applied Cognitive Psychology*, 11 (1), 31-34.
12 Elson M. (1998). Accusations of childhood sexual abuse based on recovered memories: a family survey. http://www.afma.asn.au/ELSONREP1.html

13 Grief Green J. et al. (2010). Childhood adversities and adult psychiatric disorders in the national comorbidity survey replication I. *Archives of General Psychiatry,* 67 (2), 113-123.

14 Sedlack A.S. and Broadhurst D.D. (1996). *Executive Summary of the Third National Incidence Study of Child Abuse and Neglect.* Washington DC: US Dept. of Human Services.

15 McHugh P.R.(2004) ibid.

16 Goodyear Smith F.(1997) ibid.

17 Whitfield C.L. (1995). *Memory and Abuse: Remembering and Healing the Effects of Trauma.* Deerfield Branch: Health Communications.

18 Bass E. and Davies L. (1994). www.fsa-cc.org/wordpress/wp-content/uploads/2012/07/HONORING-THE-TRUTH.pdf

19 Bass E. and Davies L. (1988). *The Courage to Heal.* (British Edition) London: Vermillion, p. 22.

20 Bass E. and Davis L. (1994), ibid.

21 Cook S. (2008). Opening Pandora's Box. In Sachs A and Galton G (Eds). *Forensic Aspects of Dissociative Identity Disorder.* London: Karnac, p. 160.

22 Bass E. and Davis L. (2008). *The courage to Heal.* New York: Harper, p. 49

23 Ibid, p.100.

24 Wikipedia. en.wikipedia.org/wiki/Elizabeth_Loftus.

25 Loftus E. and Ketcham K. (1994). *The Myth of Repressed Memory: false memories and allegations of sexual abuse.* New York: St Martin Press, p. 34.

26 Geraerts E et al (2007). The reality of recovered memories: corroborating continuous and discontinuous memories of child sexual abuse. *Psychological Science,* 18 (7), 564-567.

27 Chu J.A. et al (2011). Guidelines for Treating Dissociative identity Disorder in Adults, third revision. *Journal of Trauma and Dissociation*, 12, 115-187.

28 Haddock D.B. (2001). *The Dissociative Identity Disorder Sourcebook.* New York: McGraw Hill, p. 6.

29 Mayer-Gross W., Slater E. and Roth M. (1960). *Clinical Psychiatry.* London: Cassel and Co, p. 241.

30 Seltzer A. (1994). Multiple personality: a psychiatric

misadventure. *Canadian Journal of Psychiatry*, 39, 442-445.

31 Merskey H. (1992). The Manufacture of Personalities: the production of multiple personality disorder. *British Journal of Psychiatry*, 160, 327-340.

32 Escobar J.I. (1995). Transcultural aspects of dissociative and somatoform disorders. *Cultural Psychiatry*, 18, 555-569.

33 Van Duigi M., Cardena E. and de Jong J.T.M. (2005). Validity of DSM IV Dissociative Disorders categories in SW Uganda. *Transcultural Psychiatry*, 42, 219-224.

34 *The ICD 10 Classification of Mental and Behavioural Disorders* (1992). Geneva: WHO. Pp. 152-161.

35 Sar V., President ISST-D (2007). Letter to Steven Hyman, Chair, International advisory group for the revision of ICD-10 Mental and Behavioural Disorders. (Accessed September 2012 from ISST-D website, no longer available.)

36 Doug Bremner's website www.beforeyoutakethatpill.com/2009/4/DIDinDSM_V (Accessed September 2012, no longer available).

37 American Psychiatric Association. www.dsm5.org/Proposed Revision/pages (Accessed September 2012, no longer available).

38 Smith M. and Pazder L. (1980). *Michelle Remembers.* New York: Pocket Books.

39 Victor J.S. (1993). *Satanic Panic.* Chicago: Open Court, p. 82.

40 Victor JS (1993) ibid.

41 Wikipedia. http://en.wikipedia.org/wiki/Day-care_sex-abuse_hysteria.

42 Gould C (1995). Denying ritual abuse of children. *Journal of Psychohistory*, 22, 329-339.

43 Bottoms B.L., Shaver P.R. and Goodman G.S. (1996). An Analysis of Ritualistic and Religion Related Child Abuse Allegations. *Law and human Behaviour*, 20 (1), 1-34.

44 Snow B. and Sorensen T. (1990). Ritualistic child abuse in a neighbourhood setting. *Journal of Interpersonal Violence*, 5 (4), 474-487.

45 Mulhern S. (1994). Satanism, ritual abuse, and multiple personality disorder: a sociohistorical perspective. *International*

Journal of Clinical and Experimental Hypnosis, 42 (4), 265-288.

46 Pendergrast M. (1996). ibid, pp. 415-419.

47 La Fontaine J.S. (1994). *The extent and nature of organised ritual abuse*: *research findings.* London: HMSO.

48 Lanning K.V. (1991). Ritual abuse: a law enforcement perspective. *Child Abuse and Neglect*, 15, 171-173.

49 Healey C. (2008). Unsolved: investigating allegations of ritual abuse. In Sachs A and Galton G (Eds). *Forensic Aspects of Dissociative Identity Disorder.* London: Karnac Books, p. 28.

50 Bottoms B.L., Shaver P.R. and Goodman G.S. (1996) Ibid.

51 www.biglotteryfund.org.uk/global-content/pressreleases/ scotland/lottery-support-for-tayside-trio

52 Trauma and Abuse Group. www.tag-uk.net >about us

53 Miller A. (2009). Mind control: diagnosis and treatment. Presentation at TAG and RAINS conference, Hayes Conference Centre, Swanwick, May.

54 Steinberg M. and Schnall M. (2001). *The Stranger in the Mirror.* New York: Harper, pp. 275-293.

55 Chu J.A. et al (2011) ibid.

56 Kluft R.P. (1996). Treating the traumatic memories of patients with dissociative identity disorder. *American Journal of Psychiatry,* 153, 103-110.

57 Ross CA (1997). *Dissociative Identity Disorder: diagnosis, clinical features and treatment of multiple personality.* New York: John Wiley and Sons, p. 244.

58 Brandon S. et al (1998). Recovered memories of child sexual abuse: implications for clinical practice. *British Journal of Psychiatry*, 172, 296-307.

59 *Guidelines for psychologists working with clients in contexts in which issues relating to recovered memories may arise* (2000). Leicester: British Psychological Society.

8. ALTERNATIVE APPROACHES TO DISSOCIATION

There can be no doubt that Dissociative Identity Disorder (DID) does exist. The many people who tell us that they 'live with DID' have habits, experiences and beliefs that set them apart from most other people. What has caused their strange condition? Sceptics believe that it can develop in some susceptible people who are looking for answers to their problems. Uneasy feelings of being out of touch, forgetful or absent minded are built upon, and further imaginative introspection, especially if encouraged by a therapist, can do the rest. This has been called the 'socio-cultural' account of dissociative disorders. It is proposed as an alternative to the believers' view, that they result from childhood trauma, which has been called 'trauma-genic'. According to the socio-cultural account, dissociative disorders result from the interaction between personal characteristics of the client and her therapist's beliefs.

It is easy to forget that dissociation is also a common feature of many mental conditions not usually associated with childhood sexual abuse. A neurologist specialising in unexplained abnormal mental states urges his colleagues to be more alert to signs of dissociation, but only in order that they can offer some reassurance and symptomatic relief.

> Dissociation is a common symptom in psychiatric disorders. If you ask patients with depression, anxiety, schizophrenia, and personality disorders about dissociative symptoms, you'll find them reasonably frequently. Depersonalisation and derealisation are especially common during panic attacks, during hyperventilation and in people with post-traumatic stress symptoms.... Understanding what dissociative symptoms are – that they can come out of the blue for no good reason, and that they do not indicate madness or impending disease, can go a long way to helping

solve the patient's concern about the symptom. Treating anxiety, panic, or depression (if present) may also help.[1]

Dissociation can be seen as a marker for many kinds of distress. It thus seems strange that it can be linked, not to what is happening to people now, but to what is believed to have happened to them long ago. We may get a better understanding of the circumstances that can lead some people to develop dissociative disorders if we look at some of the conditions that have been associated with them.

Schizophrenia

More than a hundred years ago, soon after Janet had used the term 'désagrégation' to describe the mental state of his patients with unexplained physical symptoms, the Swiss psychiatrist Eugen Bleuler introduced the term 'schizophrenia' to describe the more drastic loss of normal functioning that he saw in some of his patients. The English translations of these terms – 'dissociation' and 'split mind'– might be thought to refer to the same thing, and for Bleuler this was one of the most important characteristics of the disorder that we now know as schizophrenia.

> In every case we are confronted with a more or less clear cut splitting of the psychic functions. If the disease is marked the personality loses its unity; at different times different psychic complexes seem to represent the personality. Integration of different complexes and strivings appears insufficient or even lacking... one set of complexes dominates the personality for a time, while other groups of ideas or drives are "split off" and seem either partly or completely impotent.[2]

This sounds remarkably like what happens in DID. Bleuler is clearly using the same metaphor of dissociation to describe this condition. Could he be describing the same pathological process? During the 1980s, when North American psychiatrists began to diagnose

Multiple Personality Disorder with increasing frequency, they commented on how easily it could be confused with schizophrenia. They particularly noted the presence of what had become known as schizophrenia's 'first rank symptoms' in their clients. In repeated samples of people with MPD they found that all of them had several of these symptoms, and they therefore made the audacious suggestion that they should now be thought of as diagnostic of MPD rather than schizophrenia.[3,4] The symptoms in question had been identified by the German psychiatrist Kurt Schneider in 1939. Declaring them to be the most important indicators of schizophrenia, he described them thus:

> Audible thoughts, voices heard arguing; voices heard commenting on one's actions; the experiences of influences playing on one's body... thought withdrawal and other interferences with thought; delusional perceptions and all feelings, impulses (drives) and volitional acts that are experienced by the patient as the work or influence of others.[5]

These auditory hallucinations, paranoid delusions and disordered thoughts are severely disabling, leading to a weakened grasp of reality. They are often referred to as Schneiderian symptoms, and are considered by most psychiatrists to indicate a diagnosis of schizophrenia. Many now argue that schizophrenia is best thought of, not as a specific disorder, but as a spectrum of disorders for which unfortunate life events may be important predisposing factors.[6-8] Nevertheless, the mainstream view remains that schizophrenia is a serious organic illness which may be genetic in origin. Those suffering from it are usually thought to require care and protection to save them from acting on their unrealistic and sometimes dangerous perceptions and ideas, for which they are commonly given long-term medication with powerful drugs.

If people with Schneiderian symptoms are believed to be suffering from DID rather than schizophrenia, these symptoms are less likely to be considered pathological. Their poor grasp of reality may be thought to be a consequence of their having been so severely traumatised in their early years that reality then became unbearable for them. If treated in accordance with the ISST-D guidelines, they will be encouraged to revisit that unbearable reality and gain new ideas about the source of their problems. It is hard to think of a more hazardous form of therapy for people who may already be tormented by unwanted and intrusive thoughts, delusions and hallucinations.

Schizophrenia has probably been the most frequently listed previous diagnosis for those with DID. In two large samples of cases in Canada in the 1980s, it was found that almost half had been previously diagnosed with schizophrenia.[9] Psychiatrists' preferences for different diagnoses change with time, and differ between countries, so we cannot be certain which disorder now occupies that position. But a disorder more recently recognised, and once thought to be a subtype of schizophrenia, is now increasingly mentioned.

Borderline Personality Disorder.

The curious name of this disorder is due to its original supposed link with schizophrenia. Borderline Personality Disorder is now usually seen as a separate condition, and many people prefer to use its alternative name of 'Emotionally Unstable Personality Disorder'. It has been said to affect 4-6% of the population, and to be seen in almost a fifth of psychiatric in-patients.[10] It is one of a range of personality disorders which have been formulated by psychiatrists. They identify various persistent, characteristic and maladaptive ways of behaving. Borderline Personality Disorder (BPD) has been used as a diagnostic label for people who are impulsive, unstable and insecure. They have intense and difficult social relationships and a history of disturbed and self-destructive behaviour, often with suicide attempts, self-injury or drug abuse. They also have confused ideas about themselves, with low self-esteem, rigid ways of thinking and an intense fear of abandonment.

These negative characteristics, seen here as psychiatric symptoms, have been noted in many people with dissociative disorders. Conversely, dissociative symptoms have been noted in people with BPD.[11] It seems therefore that many people could equally well be diagnosed with either disorder. In the early days of MPD, some psychiatrists were asking whether this was in fact a separate condition or just a variation of BPD.[12] People diagnosed with MPD or with BPD have been found to respond to personality questionnaires and enquiries about their personal backgrounds and histories in a remarkably similar way.[13]

Therapists often see the angry, self-destructive outbursts of clients with BPD as re-enactments of the physical, sexual and emotional abuse that they suffered as very young children. It has been claimed that nearly all these clients have a trauma history and that this must be addressed in therapy.[14] Like people with DID, they will be encouraged to see themselves as trauma survivors who were betrayed by their early caregivers. The therapeutic relationship is then seen as a way of repairing this damage and gradually teaching them to trust other people through first trusting their therapist. The belief that BPD is caused by early trauma is often strengthened by reports of this from clients in therapy, but we always have to ask, as we do with DID clients, how much they in turn have been influenced by the prior assumptions of the therapist.

It is easy to believe that people with the serious emotional and behavioural problems that can earn them the diagnosis of BPD have had troubled childhoods. Many of them may have been abused or neglected. The same may be true for those who are diagnosed with DID and are found to have similar emotional problems. However we have no evidence that being reminded of past trauma helps these people cope with life when they are adults. Their vulnerability and poor judgement must make this an especially risky undertaking.

Post Traumatic Stress Disorder

Many people who have been diagnosed with DID, schizophrenia or BPD would be much happier to be told that they have Post Traumatic Stress Disorder (PTSD). This diagnosis is now used far more frequently than it was when given its first official listing in the

1980 DSM-III at the same time as both MPD and BPD. At that time it was supposed to be diagnosed only when a known trauma had been identified. The victim had to have been exposed to a 'traumatic stressor that would evoke significant symptoms of distress in almost everyone' and 'is generally outside the range of human experience'.[15] Similarly the ICD 10 classification later specified 'an event or situation… of an exceptionally threatening or catastrophic nature'.[16] PTSD was described as an anxiety disorder, with symptoms that included repeated re-experiencing of the trauma in dreams or intrusive flashbacks, an emotional numbing, feelings of estrangement from others, hypervigilance for threat, sleep disturbance and obsessive avoidance of all reminders of the trauma. This disabling condition, which could persist for a month or more, was first identified after observing the behaviour of soldiers returning from combat in Vietnam, and also of victims of disasters such as bombings or earthquakes. It was seen as a response to unusual and intensely horrific events.

There has been a marked change in the use of this diagnosis. In a later revision of the DSM classification, the range of possible traumatic stressors was extended to include less unusual events, among them 'developmentally inappropriate sexual experiences', thus introducing child sexual abuse as a possible cause.[17] Widening the diagnostic criteria for PTSD was first suggested by Judith Herman in 1992. She claimed that prolonged abuse, especially in childhood, could lead to a severe post-traumatic syndrome, complex PTSD, and that some of its symptoms were similar to those found in dissociative disorders.[18] In complex PTSD the diagnostic criteria have been stretched in two directions. Not only is the original trauma extended from an unusual catastrophe to long-lasting mistreatment, but an increased range of symptoms have been listed, which can now apparently be delayed, perhaps for many years. Initially PTSD was diagnosed only if symptoms appeared within three months of the trauma.

Extending the concept of PTSD in this way has made it a very popular diagnosis. In the UK the National Institute for Clinical Excellence (NICE), though still advising that PTSD should only be diagnosed in people who have experienced 'exceptionally threatening and distressing events', quotes estimates that 10% of women and 5% of men may be expected to suffer from it at some time in their lives. Men are apparently more likely to be exposed to traumatic events, but women have a far lower threshold for reacting with PTSD.[19] The UK's leading mental health charity, Mind, claims that simply hearing about shocking events, such as bombings or earthquakes, may be enough to bring on this disorder.[20] By widening the criteria in this way we have come a long way from the original concept of PTSD. This diagnosis has now become so user-friendly that it can be turned to as an explanation for an ever-increasing range of symptoms.

Dissociation, in the sense of an emotional detachment from the trauma, was originally identified as one of the symptoms of PTSD. This has encouraged people to see a link between PTSD and DID, and even to claim that DID is a form of PTSD. There is an important difference however. The dissociation that is seen in people with PTSD has emphatically *not* involved any loss of memory of the trauma. The recommended treatment for PTSD does not involve any search for memories, because unavoidable traumatic memories are usually an important part of the problem. People with PTSD may be confused about the circumstances surrounding the traumatic event, but are not amnesic for the event itself. People with PTSD usually complain about finding themselves perpetually burdened with their unwelcome memories.[21]

Another crucial difference between the two disorders is that in PTSD the intrusive trauma memories, flashbacks and general hyperarousal are there from the start, whereas the DID sufferer, before she has therapy, is detached from the trauma she is assumed to have experienced, and is said to be protected by her separate identities from any conscious memory of it. It is only after she goes into therapy and is encouraged to search for memories that she acquires some of the disabling symptoms of PTSD. In a recent study of women in treatment for DID, all of them were also said to be suffering from PTSD. The researchers claimed that this was 'consistent with the conceptualisation of dissociative identity disorder as an extreme form of early-abuse-related PTSD'.[22] But perhaps what we are seeing here is therapy-related PTSD. We have seen that the recommended treatment for DID is extremely stressful and even carries a risk of suicide.[23] When clients recover memories of abuse they always seem to re-experience it, and are often heard to scream out during their treatment sessions. They then find themselves living in fear of any situations that may trigger these traumatic memories. These are indeed some of the classic PTSD symptoms, but I suggest that they are due to the therapy rather than anything that happened before. We need to formulate a completely new form of PTSD: Post *Therapy* Stress Disorder, in which clients develop intrusive memories and flashbacks and become increasingly disturbed and dissociated as their alternative personalities emerge.

Neurological impairment

In the 1980s, when Multiple Personality Disorder first started to be more frequently diagnosed, several neurologists said that they had seen this condition in patients with Temporal Lobe Epilepsy. One of them, after noting that he had seen 'a clinical picture consistent with multiple personality' in seven of his patients, and the 'illusion of supernatural possession' in a further five, suggested that 'dissociated states may constitute complex behavioural manifestations of chronic limbic epilepsy'.[24] Others, claiming the same causal link, noted that a third of their clinic patients with Temporal Lobe Epilepsy appeared to experience dissociative episodes, including multiple personality, and that these occurred independently of their seizures.[25] In subsequent years an association between multiple personality and Temporal Lobe Epilepsy became more widely accepted, and it was found that the experience of having multiple personalities could be induced in people with Temporal Lobe Epilepsy by injecting a barbiturate drug.[26]

During the current century further neurological investigations have been carried out, using increasingly sophisticated brain imaging techniques. It has been possible to examine the brain structure of people with DID and with other psychiatric disorders. Some of the structures in the limbic system, notably the hippocampus and the amygdala, have been of special interest because they are involved in emotional reactions and the laying down of memories and are thought to be affected by stress. Animal experiments have demonstrated that chronic, severe stress can impair development here, and when this happens early in life it will lead to irreversible changes, such as reduced size of the hippocampus and amygdala.[27] This finding has been seized upon by those who want to stress the importance of childhood trauma in causing adult disorders. They argue that if early exposure to stress has the same effect in humans, producing abnormalities in brain development that can be measured in adulthood, and if people with these 'trauma-related' disorders are found to show these abnormalities, then their case has been made: the neurological damage is evidence that the trauma was experienced.

Many studies have now been undertaken using magnetic resonance imaging (MRI) to scan the brains of women with disorders thought to have been caused by childhood abuse, and to compare these scans with those of women who are free from any psychiatric disorder. In one of the first of these, it was a found that a sample of women diagnosed with PTSD due to childhood abuse did indeed have a significantly reduced size of hippocampus when compared to a group of healthy women.[28] Two later studies have shown similar reductions in the size of both the hippocampus and the amygdala in women whose BPD was thought to be related to child abuse.[29,30] A further study showed these same deficits in women with DID who had all reported child abuse,[31] and a later study found them in women with abuse-related PTSD though not in women with DID.[32]

Do these findings support the view that severe early child abuse is a cause of these later disorders? Once again we are faced with the problem of confounding variables. Child abuse is not the only factor that can lead to a reduced size of hippocampus or amygdala. Similar neurological deficits occur with age, in other psychiatric conditions including schizophrenia, with chronic alcohol abuse and in people exposed to a variety of stressful situations.[33-35]

PTSD was first diagnosed in American soldiers returning from Vietnam. Because so many of them were affected, we have been able to learn a lot from them about adult reactions to trauma. Several studies have now shown that Vietnam veterans suffering from PTSD show reductions in hippocampal size.[36,37] These deficits sometimes seemed to be related as much to the severity of the PTSD symptoms as to the amount of stressful combat that the men had experienced. Some soldiers were even found to have developed PTSD without having had any exposure to combat. Because these men differed so much in their susceptibility to PTSD, it was thought that reduced hippocampal volume might be a sign of pre-existing vulnerability to this disorder, rather than a consequence of suffering from it. To see if this was so, a team of researchers studied a series of identical twins.[38] They were all Vietnam veterans, but only one of each pair had been exposed to combat. Of those who were exposed to combat, only some had succumbed to PTSD. The MRI scans of these men revealed a variety of neurological abnormalities, including reduced hippocampal volume. However, in each case their co-twin, who had never been exposed to combat and did not suffer from PTSD, was found to show the same deficits. Some residual symptoms of PTSD, such as an increased startle response, were seen only in the twin who had been in combat and developed PTSD. This suggested that these symptoms had resulted from their traumatic experiences. The neurological signs however appeared to reflect a pre-existing inherited predisposition. Those veterans who had been exposed to combat but had not developed PTSD were free of any neurological abnormalities, and so were their co-twins.

We see an interesting parallel to this in one of the studies which compared women with DID with women who had no psychiatric disorder. The women with DID, who were said also to suffer from PTSD and who all reported that they had suffered childhood abuse, showed the expected reductions in size of the hippocampus and amygdala. However, almost half of the control group of healthy women reported that they too had suffered childhood abuse, and they showed no reductions in size of hippocampus or amygdala. In this group there was no difference between those who had reported abuse and those who had not.[39] It does therefore seem possible that women who succumb to BPD, DID or PTSD sometimes have inborn neurological deficits which increase their vulnerability to these disorders and may also account for some of the many other problems which they have. In the studies in which these women were compared with control samples of healthy women it was never possible to match these two groups so that they were truly comparable. Women in the control samples were always selected to be free of any current psychiatric disorder and not taking any drugs. Those with trauma-related disorders usually had other psychiatric disorders in addition, were taking a variety of drugs and often had different social and educational backgrounds.[40,41] Well women were being compared with sick women who were currently undergoing treatment. In one study they were recruited from a Trauma Disorders Program, which suggests that they may have been under considerable stress at the time of testing.[42]

At this stage it is impossible to know which comes first: the neurological impairment or the experience of trauma. All that we do know is that some women who have been exposed to stress show measurable neurological abnormality. This could be an inborn characteristic, it could be the result of stress experienced during childhood or it could be the result of stress experienced later, including during therapy. As already mentioned, recovered memory therapy is extremely stressful. It involves exposure to imagined traumatic events which can be very vivid and powerful. If the observed neurological impairment is acquired rather than inborn, could my newly coined 'Post Therapy Stress Disorder' have helped to bring this about?

Strange experiences

We have seen that DID can be confused with other disorders such as schizophrenia, Borderline Personality Disorder and Post Traumatic Stress Disorder, and that the neurological deficits that have been detected in people with DID have also been detected in people with each of these disorders.[43-45] People with DID can thus share many characteristics with those who suffer from these disorders. They do, however, appear to have one characteristic that makes them rather special: their imaginative creativity and susceptibility to hypnosis. Dissociation has been described as 'a brilliantly creative survival device' and it appears to be facilitated by hypnosis.[46] The ISST-D recommends, in its treatment guidelines, that the client's hypnotic susceptibility should be exploited. They remind therapists that, whether or not they deliberately induce hypnosis, their clients will usually be in a hypnotic state when speaking through their alternative personalities.[47] While they are in this state, they often report some very bizarre experiences. One of these is the well-known hypnotic phenomenon of age regression; a state in which people behave as though they have become young children again. They are able to mimic the voices and actions of young children in an uncannily convincing way. The alternative identities in DID are often very young and seem to represent the host personality herself as a child. Many therapists believe that when their client is in this childlike state she really has become a real rather than an imagined child.

The phenomenon of age regression has fascinated people for a long time. Those who experience it have a compellingly real experience of recapturing the state of mind that they once had as a child. Observers may also be convinced that this age regression has brought with it a genuine reinstatement of the past. However, a review of more than 70 studies, that tested this belief by examining the physiological and mental processes of age regressed adults, concluded that this does not in fact happen. Many of the observed changes seemed to have been willed by the hypnotic subject rather than occurring spontaneously, and reports of dramatically increased accuracy of recall for childhood events under hypnosis did not stand up to later scrutiny. Although the behaviour of hypnotically age regressed subjects often appeared uncannily childlike, well-motivated actors were found to do just as well, and both failed to match the typical behaviour of real children. This review reported that equally compelling instances of age progression had been observed, in which people appeared to become themselves as they would be when they were 20 or more years older. Time travel has not been so eagerly invoked to explain this phenomenon.[48]

Some highly hypnotisable subjects can regress, not just to childhood, but beyond it to previous lives, and this can certainly happen in DID. Colourful past life experiences have been reported, as have memories of being in the womb, being born and being an infant, often with support from a believing therapist. These reported experiences are, however, at times so bizarre that even the therapists become sceptical, though, as noted earlier, they can sometimes explain them away as examples of 'programming' by members of a powerful cult. Some therapists are able to view unlikely or paranormal experiences as imaginative metaphors for more credible abuse. Though a further group of therapists apparently believe that there really is a strangely different world out there to which dissociated clients have access.

It has been suggested that a heightened ability to dissociate can bring about a special sensitivity to paranormal phenomena, and that this may explain some of the strange experiences reported by people with DID.[49] During the 1990s many people in the US were reporting that their lives had changed radically after they had encountered or been abducted by aliens.[50] Two psychologists, Kenneth Ring and Christopher Rosing, were curious about the characteristics of these people and of others with similarly strange experiences. In an intriguing investigation that they labelled The Omega Project, they used questionnaires to compare the psychological profiles of people who had these paranormal experiences (experiencers) with those who did not (controls).[51] The two experiences they were interested in were alien abduction and near death experiences (NDEs). People who claimed that they had undergone alien abduction or strange near death phenomena were compared with people with an interest in but no experience of these things. This experiment is of interest here because Ring and Rosing believed that dissociation would play a part in bringing about both of these experiences. They reasoned that if this was so, childhood abuse and trauma, which they believed to be 'one of the most common antecedents to dissociation' might be implicated. They thought this would be specially likely in the case of alien abduction because of the sexual symbolism involved.

When they analysed questionnaire responses from their 353 subjects, Ring and Rosing discovered that the experiencers in both the abduction and the NDE groups often responded similarly. They gained higher scores on a dissociation questionnaire and were significantly more likely to report various types of childhood abuse. They were also more likely to report that they had suffered life-threatening illnesses as children. This strengthened the researchers' belief that the experience of childhood trauma could lead to a habit of dissociating, which could in turn enable people to become sensitive to paranormal phenomena.

> Dissociation would be predicted to allow relatively easy access to alternate, non-ordinary realities. When therefore in later life, such persons undergo the trauma of either a near death incident or one involving a UFO, they are more likely than others, because of their prior familiarity with non-ordinary realities, to be able to flip into that state of consciousness which, like a special lens, affords a glimpse of these remarkable occurrences.
>
> What we are suggesting, then, is that such persons are what we might call *psychological sensitives* with low stress thresholds, and that it is their traumatic childhood that has helped to make them so... these individuals... are the unwitting beneficiaries of a kind of compensatory gift in return for the wounds they have incurred while growing up... They may experience directly what the rest of us with unexceptional childhoods may only wonder at.[52] (Original italics.)

Colin Ross, a prominent campaigner for the recognition of dissociative disorders has also noticed that dissociation is often accompanied by reports of very strange experiences. He has a similar explanation for this.

I hypothesise that severe, chronic childhood trauma interrupts the closing of the window to ESP [extra sensory perception]... In our culture paranormal experience is suppressed or ignored, as it is in mainstream psychiatry... The window is closed during "normal" development in the absence of trauma...

The dissociative mind seems to be very open to unusual experiences.[53]

Are we then expected to believe in these experiences? An alternative explanation is that the dissociative mind is very open to fantasy. We saw above that the ability to dissociate has been hailed as 'brilliantly creative', and we know from several studies that people who have high scores on measures of dissociation also score highly on measures of a tendency to fantasise.[54,55] This tendency is perhaps shared by some of the promoters of the dissociative disorders.

For those therapists who cannot bring themselves to share their clients' beliefs in paranormal experiences, a convenient alternative explanation has been provided. The tendency to believe in paranormal experiences can itself be seen as one of the symptoms of dissociation. Marlene Steinberg tells us that this has been proved through the use of her SCID-D interview schedule:

Before the advent of the SCID-D clinicians were faced with a dubious choice regarding patients who spoke of past lives or abductions by aliens: either proclaim these people crazy or accept their accounts as descriptions of real events. Today, the SCID-D assessment process shows that these people are attesting to symptoms of dissociation and could benefit from therapies designed to treat dissociative disorders. The phenomena they describe are... yet another example of the power of the human mind to protect itself by creating imaginative metaphorical symbols for memories of unthinkable childhood trauma.[56]

Steinberg evidently believes that because people who dissociate use fanciful metaphors when talking about their experiences, we can permit ourselves to be sceptical about many of the things that they tell us. What we cannot do, of course, is to extend this scepticism to any reports of early childhood sexual abuse.

Accepting uncertainty and moving on

The trauma-related explanation for DID was never based on evidence. Instead it gained ground following the publication of one book, *Sybil*, which has now been discredited. Attempts to find evidence of a causal link between high levels of dissociation, whether revealed by DES scores or seen in people with DID or DDNOS, and childhood trauma have not been successful. Dissociation does, however, appear to be associated with a variety of psychiatric disorders and with other problems in adulthood. It is possible that some of these may result from childhood trauma, but we can never be sure about this. Given this uncertainty, we should be aware that investigating this unknown territory may do far more harm than good, and prevent clients getting the help they need to tackle their current problems. We have seen some of the damaging consequences of trauma-based treatments for dissociative disorders; we need to look for alternatives.

Most diagnoses of DID are made by therapists convinced of its traumatic origins, who then pass on this conviction to their clients. But we should not assume that this diagnosis is always imposed on an unwilling client by an overzealous therapist, because people are now increasingly able to diagnose DID in themselves, having learnt about it from books and websites. Anyone asking Google 'do I have DID?' will be offered a wealth of information, including the suggestion that a wide variety of common symptoms may be masking this condition. They will probably also learn that it is caused by childhood trauma, and that they will have to revisit this trauma during treatment. However, we can see from many internet blogs and postings that people do sometimes accept the diagnosis but struggle with the alleged cause and proposed treatment. Alternatives could be available for them.

Three psychologists recently reported their joint treatment of a client who had diagnosed her own DID many years previously.[57] They were confident that she did now experience this condition, that she was fragmented into various 'parts'. They then confirmed her diagnosis with the standard assessments, DES and SCID-D. Their client was 49 years old, had had a difficult childhood and also had symptoms of Post Traumatic Stress Disorder following some distressing incidents in adulthood. What made their treatment different was that none of them viewed her condition as a response to early childhood trauma. They saw it as a way of avoiding distress and distracting herself from current problems.

> Our treatment concept centred on the idea that the core symptoms of DID... can often be understood as the manifestations of a dysfunctional avoidance-based coping strategy associated with a failure to acknowledge and/or take responsibility for puzzling and self-defeating behaviours, troubling cognitions and negative feelings... abetted by the use of imaginative and attention regulating strategies to create a credible feeling of distance or separation from aversive personal or interpersonal events.

By encouraging their client to tolerate unpleasant emotions and restructure her self-defeating thoughts, these therapists eventually enabled her to face her continuing problems without using distancing strategies or imagining herself to have any separate identities. The treatment took several years and did not resolve all her difficulties, but it did bring about great improvement and gave her the means of facing the world once more as an integrated individual. More importantly, it did not subject her to any new memories of trauma. These therapists thought they were able to help their client deal with what was happening now because they made no assumptions about what had happened in the past. They viewed dissociation as a maladaptive way of coping with present problems, rather than a defence that had once been necessary to survive childhood trauma.

This is an example of cognitive-behavioural therapy (CBT), in which the client is given practical help in changing the thoughts and behaviours that are keeping the problem going. Unlike the recommended trauma-based treatment for dissociative disrders, CBT has been shown to have measurable benefits, and has been used for many psychiatric disorders, including schizophrenia.[58] It has also been used to treat dissociative symptoms in PTSD.[59]

An original form of CBT has been devised specially for Borderline Peersonality Disorder (BPD). This has been called dialectical behaviour therapy (DBT) and, like other forms of CBT it addresses only the current behaviour of the clients, who are taught to regulate their emotions, to accept themselves but also to work towards change.[60] It was devised during the 1980s by Marsha Linehan, an American psychologist, and combines a rigorous analysis of current maladaptive behaviour with some meditative techniques to increase self awareness. A recent review concluded that DBT was the only form of therapy that had shown any measurable success in treating BPD.[61] The author of this review suggested that the narrow focus of this therapy was one of the reasons for its success. By restricting attention to current problems and avoiding any reference to past trauma, therapists protected their challenging and needy clients from many unhelpful and dangerous experiences.

> Methods in which patients re-experience traumatic events from childhood may be particularly counterproductive and have never been tested empirically... BPD patients do not habituate to stressful thoughts but become increasingly activated and disturbed. This may help explain the regression and increasing symptom levels seen in therapies that focus on traumatic events.

Marsha Linehan has recently revealed that her internationally acclaimed work in developing and testing this therapy for BPD sprang from a determination to rescue others from the condition that she herself had suffered from in her youth.[61] In an interview with the *New York Times*, she told of her unhappy childhood, with repeated suicide attempts, psychosomatic illnesses and self-harming episodes, which led to lengthy hospitalisation when she was 17. Her extensive studies in psychology and her catholic faith then gradually enabled her to accept herself as she was and to learn ways in which she could change. Her story is noteworthy because she takes full responsibility for her childhood unhappiness. She says that she suffered from feelings of inadequacy compared to others in her family. She did not see herself as a victim or as a survivor, but as her own worst enemy. She learnt to defeat this enemy by confronting it. Her therapy reflects the same disciplined, realistic approach.

The neurologist quoted at the start of this chapter regarded dissociation as a common feature of psychiatric disorders. It is worth remembering that it is also a common feature of many people's lives. We all dissociate to some extent, though some of us do it more than others. This can be a deliberate indulgence, giving a welcome break from everyday reality; but it can also be an affliction, causing confusion and anxiety. When people indicate, perhaps by giving themselve high scores on the DES, that they are dissociating to an unusual extent, we need to ask some important questions. Why are they are doing this now? Is there something happening in their lives that might explain it? Is this really a problem for them, or is it a way of alerting us to other difficulties? It is paradoxical that the people who are most eager to diagnose dissociation seem to have the least interest in investigating the present circumstances that may lead people to adopt this state of mind. Their trauma-genic theory has closed their minds and prevents them from seeing the full picture and learning from their clients. It also prevents them from offering the types of therapy that might be far more effective and less hazardous.

References – 8. Alternative approaches to dissociation

1   Stone J. (2006). Dissociation: what is it and why is it important? *Practical Neurology*, 6 (5), 308.
2   Bleuler E. (1950). *Dementia Praecox or the group of schizophrenias.* (U. Zinkin, trans.) New York: MacMillan, pp.8-9.
3   Kluft R.P. (1987). First-rank symptoms as a diagnostic clue to Multiple Personality Disorder. *American Journal of Psychiatry,* 114, 293-298.
4   Ross C.A. (1989). *Multiple Personality Disorder: Diagnosis, Clinical Features and Treatment.* Oxford: John Wiley and Sons.
5   Schneider K. (1939). *Psychiser befund und Psychiaerissche Diagnose.* English translation (1959), *Clinical Psychopathology* (fifth edition). New York: Grune and Stratton, pp. 133-34.
6   Boyle M. (2002). *Schizophrenia: A scientific delusion.* London: Routledge.
7   Bentall R.P. (2004). *Madness Explained: psychosis and human nature.* London: Penguin Books.
8   Read J. et al (2005). Childhood trauma, psychosis and Schizophrenia: a literature review with theoretical and clinical implications. *Acta Psychiatrica Scandinavia*, 112, 330-350.
9   Ross C.A. and Norton G.R. (1988). Multiple personality disorder patients with a prior diagnosis of schizophrenia. *Dissociation,* 1 (2), 39-42.
10 Linehan M.M. (1993). *Cognitive Behavioural Therapy of Borderline Personality Therapy.* New York: Guilford Press.
11 Boon S. and Draijer N. (1993). The differentiation of patients with MPD or DDNOS from patients with a cluster B personality disorder. *Dissociation,* VI (2), 126-135.
12 Horvitz R.P. and Braun B.G. (1984). Are Multiple Personalities Borderline? *Psychiatric Clinics of North America*, 7, 69-87.
13 Kemp K., Gilberson A.D. and Toren M. (1988). The differential diagnosis of Multiple Personality Disorder from Borderline Personality Disorder. *Dissociation*, 1 (4), 41-46.

14 Herman J.L., Perry C.J. and Van der Kolk B.A. (1989). Childhood Trauma in Borderline Personality Disorder. *American Journal of Psychiatry*, 146, 490-495.

15 *Diagnostic and Statistical Manual of Mental Disorder, DSM-III* (1980). Third edition. Washington, DC: American Medical Association.

16 *The ICD-10 Classification of Mental and Behavioural Disorders* (1992). Geneva: World Health Organisation, p. 147.

17 *Diagnostic and Statistical Manual of Mental disorders DSM-IV* (1994). Fourth edition. Washington DC: American Psychiatric Association.

18 Herman J. (1992). Complex PTSD: a syndrome in survivors of prolonged and repeated trauma. *Journal of Traumatic Stress.* 5 (3), 377-391.

19 National Institute for Clinical Excellence (2005). The management of PTSD in adults and children in primary and secondary care. *National Clinical Practice Guideline 26.*

20 Mind. www.mind.org.uk Follow links to information and advice > mental health A to Z > Post Traumatic Stress Disorder. (Accessed August 2013).

21 McNally (2005). *Remembering Trauma.* Cambridge, Mass: Harvard University Press, p. 152.

22 Vermetten E., Schmahl C., Lindner S. et al (2006). Hippocampal and Amygdalar Volumes in Dissociative Identity Disorder. *American Journal of Psychiatry*, 163 (4), 630-636.

23 Fetkewicz J., Sharma V. and Merskey H. (2000). A note on suicidal deterioration with recovered memory treatment. *Journal of Affective Disorders*, 58, 155-159.

24 Mesulam M. (1981). Dissociative states with abnormal temporal lobe EEG: multiple personality and the illusion of possession. *Archives of Neurology*, 38 (3), 176-181.

25 Schenk L. and Bear D. (1981). Multiple personality and related dissociative phenomena in patients with temporal lobe epilepsy. *American Journal of Psychiatry*, 138 (10), 1311-1316.

26 Ahern G.L., Herring A.M. and Tackenberg J. (1995). An association of multiple personality and temporolimbic epilepsy:

intracarotid amylobarbital test observations. *Archives of Neurology,* 50 (10), 1020-1025.

27 Brunson K.L. et al (2003). Stress and the developing hippocampus: a double edged sword? *Molecular Neurobiology,* 27, 121-136.

28 Bremner J.D. et al (1997). Magnetic resonance imaging-based measurement of hippocampal volume in post traumatic stress disorder related to childhood physical and sexual abuse: a preliminary report. *Biological Psychiatry,* 41, 23-32.

29 Dreissen M. et al (2000). Magnetic resonance imaging volumes of the hippocampus and the amygdala in women with borderline personality disorder and early traumatisation. *Archives of General Psychiatry,* 57 (12), 1115-1122.

30 Schmahl C.G. et al (2003). Magnetic Resonance Imaging of hippocampus and amygdala volume in women with childhood abuse and Borderline Personality Disorder. *Psychiatric Research: Neuroimaging,* 122, 193-198.

31 Vermetten E. et al. (2006). Hippcampal and amygdala volumes in dissociative identity disorder. *American Journal of Psychiatry,* 163, 630-636.

32 Weniger G. et al (2008). Amygdala and hippocampal volumes and cognition in adult survivors of childhood abuse with dissociative disorders. *Acta Psychiatrica Scandinavica,* 118 (4), 281-290.

33 Narr K.L. et al (2004). Regional specification of hippocampal volume reductions in first-episode schizophrenia. *Neurological Imaging,* 21 (4), 1563-1575.

34 Agartz I. et al (1999). Hippocampal volume in patients with alcohol dependency. *Archives of General Psychiatry,* 54 (4), 356-363.

35 Lindaur R.J. et al (2004). Smaller hippocampal volume in Dutch police officers with posttraumatic stress disorder. *Biological Psychiatry,* 56, 356-363.

36 Gurvits T. et al (1996). Magnetic Resonance imaging Study of Hippocampal Volume in Chronic, Combat-related Post Traumatic Stress Disorder. *Biological Psychiatry,* 40 (11), 1091-1099.

37 Gilbertson M.W. et al (2002). Smaller hippocampal volume predicts pathologic vulnerability to psychological trauma. *Nature Neuroscience*, 5, 1242-1247.

38 Pitman R.K. et al (2006). Clarifying the origin of Biological Abnormalities in PTSD Through the Study of Identical Twins Discordant for Combat Exposure. *Annals of the New York Academy of Sciences*, 1071, 242-254.

39 Vermetten E. et al (2006) ibid.

40 Driessen M. et al (2000) ibid.

41 Schmahl C.G. et al (2003) ibid.

42 Vermetten E. et al (2006) ibid.

43 Narr K.L. et al (2004) ibid.

44 Dreissen M. et al (2000) ibid.

45 Gurvits T. et al (1996) ibid.

46 Sinason V. (2011). Quoted by Amanda Mitchison, Guardian Weekend, October 20.

47 Chu J.A. et al (2011). Guidelines for Treatment of Dissociative Identity Disorder in Adults. *Journal of Trauma and Dissociation*, 6(4), 69-149.

48 Nash M. (1987). What, if anything is regressed about hypnotic age regression? A review of the empirical literature. *Psychological Bulletin,* 102 (1), 42-52.

49 Ross C.A. (1997). *Dissociative Identity Disorder: diagnosis, clinical features and treatment of multiple personalities.* New York: Wiley and Sons.

50 Mack J.E. (1994). *Abduction: Human Encounters with Aliens.* New York: Wheeler Publications.

51 Ring K. and Rosing C.J. (1990). The Omega Project: a psychological survey of persons reporting abductions and other UFO encounters. *Journal of UFO Studies,* 2, 59-98.

52 Ibid p. 75.

53 Ross C.A. (1997) ibid, p. 223-224.

54 Merckelbach H. et al (2000). Dissociative experiences, response bias, and fantasy proneness in college students. *Personality and Individual Differences*, 28, 49-58.

55 Giesbrecht T. et al (2008). Cognitive Processes in Dissociation:

an analysis of core theoretical assumptions. *Psychological Bulletin*, 134 (5), 617-647.

56 Steinberg M. and Schnall M. (2001). *The Stranger in the Mirror.* New York: Harper, p 293.

57 Lynn S.J., Condon L. and Colletti G. (2013). Treatment of Dissociative Identity Disorder: an evidence based approach. In O Donohue and SO Lilienfeld (Eds.) *Case Studies in Clinical Science: Bridging the gap from science to practice.* New York: Oxford.

58 Pilling S. et al (2002). Psychological treatments in schizophrenia: meta-analysis of family intervention and cognitive behavioural therapy. *Psychological Medicine,* 32 (05), 763-782.

59 Kennerley H. (1996). Cognitive therapy of dissociative symptoms associated with trauma. *British Journal of Psychology*, 35 (3), 325-340.

60 Linehan M.M. (1993) ibid.

61 Paris J. (2010). Effectiveness of different therapy approaches in the treatment of Borderline Personality Disorder. *Current Psychiatry Reports*, 12 (1), 56-60.

62 Benedict Carey (2011). Expert on mental illness reveals her own fight. *New York Times*, June 23.

63 Chu J.A. et al (2011) ibid.

9. THE CAMPAIGN

In March 2011 the Campaign for the Recognition and Inclusion of Dissociation and Multiplicity was launched with a meeting in London attended by more than 200 survivors, therapists and sympathisers. There has, of course, been a continuing worldwide campaign along these lines ever since the 1980s, when some North American psychiatrists first declared that multiple personality was a trauma-related disorder that should be more widely diagnosed and treated. There are now organisations all over the world whose purpose is to counter the scepticism of professional colleagues and to win acceptance from a wider public for the recognition of dissociative disorders as trauma-related. What they mean by dissociative disorders always seems to be just DID or DDNOS and what they mean by trauma is severe sexual and physical abuse starting in infancy or early childhood. To spread their message they organise a variety of conferences and training events for psychiatrists, other healthcare professionals and also for any volunteers who want to help distressed people. The aim is to educate as many people as possible in methods of detecting and treating these hidden disorders and gain support for the growing numbers of survivors who will, as a consequence, be discovered. In recent years pressure to promote the diagnosis of dissociative disorders seems to have come as much from those who have them as from those who treat them. The two groups are to some extent intermingled, as many survivors go on to form self-help groups or to become therapists themselves. They are then respected as 'experts by experience' and can be very influential.

Dissociative Disorders and the National Health Service

Delegates at the 2011 campaign meeting wanted Dissociative Identity Disorder to be officially recognised within the NHS as a disorder requiring treatment. The National Institute of Clinical

Excellence, NICE, which provides professionals working in the NHS with guidelines for treating a wide range of mental and behavioural conditions, makes no mention of DID or of any dissociative disorders. There is also no DID diagnosis computer code available for GPs. The delegates wanted dissociative disorders to be included in all lists of treatable disorders, but they were in a difficult position here. Many of those who said they were 'living with DID' objected to having their condition labelled as a disorder. They agreed with the speaker who insisted, 'I haven't got a disorder. I find that offensive. I have lots of different parts.' People with DID see it as a life-saving reaction to the overwhelming trauma that they suffered as children. Thus in some way it was an achievement; it had protected them then and remained a necessary way of coping with their adult lives. Despite this, they still needed support and recognition of the difficulties that they faced, and suggested that the acronym DID might be better understood if the final 'D' could stand for 'defence' or 'diagnosis' rather than disorder. They were unable to agree about this but were all very content to have their condition defined as an aspect of Post Traumatic Stress Disorder.

We see here a combined effort by therapists and survivors to promote a new understanding of some mental problems. This has interesting parallels with the anti-psychiatry movement that emerged in several countries during the 1960s and 1970s. This movement, like the current campaign, was initially led by psychiatrists but later joined by a wider range of activists. The leading lights of the earlier movement (Cooper, Laing, Szasz, Foucault and Breggin) had many different agendas, but they appeared united in their view that psychiatry, by using a medical model to identify specific disorders, ignored the complexity of human distress and society's responsibility in causing it. They accused orthodox psychiatrists of mis-classifying as illnesses many normal reactions to difficult situations. This was said to be a misuse of power which stigmatised people and prevented them from finding alternative ways out of their difficulties. Psychiatrists were criticised for treating symptoms, usually with drugs, and not looking at what might have caused these symptoms. Although child abuse was rarely mentioned at this time, adult problems were sometimes traced back to difficulties that had been imposed on the growing child. Pressure to meet the family's conflicting demands was thought by some to be enough to lead certain people to psychosis.[1]

Orthodox psychiatry in the UK appears to have largely weathered this challenge. Many disorders are now thought to have some genetic component, and symptoms remain the focus of most psychiatric interventions within the NHS. Patients are encouraged to overcome their current problems, and to fit in with society rather than to change it. To carry out this symptomatic treatment, psychiatrists have been provided with an ever-growing range of drugs. Various talking therapies, such as cognitive behavioural therapy, are sometimes used as an alternative, or in addition. But, as the campaigners for dissociation have noted, the aim is usually to keep the patient firmly in the here and now, and to encourage a pragmatic approach to present problems. For most people living with DID this completely misses the point. They claim that it is not only unhelpful but 're-traumatising', and are extremely critical of the way the NHS deals with dissociative disorders. Since this overburdened service is under pressure to provide treatment that is both economical and 'evidence-based' it is not surprising that the type of treatment recommended by the ISST-D is not available. Despite the hopes of some of the campaigners, it is only when we look beyond the confines of the NHS that we are likely to find the therapists who are willing and able to meet the extreme needs of those who live with DID. It is also here that we find the many organisations that are encouraging more and more people to join these therapists and so become part of an expanding service.

Expanding the treatment for dissociative disorders

There has recently been a noticeable growth in services for people who have suffered sexual abuse. In the UK most of this seems to have developed outside the NHS, with the establishment of many charities, often staffed by volunteers. In 2002 The Survivors Trust was launched as an umbrella organisation to support five specialist agencies for the survivors of rape and sexual abuse. By 2011 they were supporting more than 130 of these agencies. A trawl through The Survivors Trust's website reveals that most of these agencies deal only with women, and that their focus is more often on child sexual abuse than on rape or sexual abuse in adulthood.[2] This applies even to the many rape crisis centres throughout the UK, who announce that, despite their name, they are not just for women in crisis, and that 65% of the women who consult them are now survivors of child sexual abuse.[3] Twelve of the agencies supported by The Survivors Trust indicate on their websites that they are willing to help women who have previously suffered ritual abuse, either by treating them directly or by referring them on to ritual abuse experts.

Many organisations running courses to promote the dissociative disorders make a special effort to attract rape crisis centre staff, whom they regard as 'gatekeepers' because of the people they meet in the course of their work. They want to teach them to recognise the subtle signs of dissociation, so that potential therapy clients can be detected. This seems to be happening worldwide. The International Society for the Study of Trauma and Dissociation (ISST-D) is quite explicit about its expansionist aims, and declares that 'We must teach other professionals how trauma is relevant to what they do every day'.[4] In the UK a wide variety of workshops, study days and training courses have now been organised in pursuit of this goal. The Trauma and Abuse Support Centre (TASC) runs training days every month. During 2010, a day devoted to 'Dissociation, Trauma and Time Travelling… or Living and Working with Dissociative Identity Disorder' was said to be

> Suitable for counsellors, therapists, partners, pastoral workers, Rape Crisis Centre staff, and anyone else interested in or involved in the field of sexual abuse, trauma and dissociation.[5]

The European Society for Trauma and Dissociation UK Network has also been running frequent courses. In 2010 they advertised their three day foundation course in 'Understanding and Working with Dissociation' and gave an exhaustive list of the people that they were hoping to attract:

This workshop series has been designed for anyone in the statutory, voluntary or private sector whose work may bring them into contact with individuals whose lives may be affected by childhood trauma and/or a dissociative disorder. It will benefit anyone working in health or adult or children's mental health (including commissioners; managers; clinicians of all disciplines; supervisors; support workers and NHS counselling/psychotherapy co-ordinators). Those working in education (e.g. schoolteachers, university and college lecturers, tutors and supervisors on PG/ Masters counselling and psychotherapy courses); social care (e.g. adult and children's social workers, anyone working in child protection, fostering and adoption services) and pastoral care will also find the programme useful. It may be suitable for those who have lived experience of complex dissociative conditions and their non-abusing family and friends.[6]

Potential participants, many of whom had no clinical background, were assured that, after completing this course, they would not only 'understand the developmental origins of dissociation', but would be able to start diagnosing it. They would be able to 'draw on a range of treatment strategies' and 'be equipped for multi-disciplinary work'. The organisers also hoped that they would be able to inform colleagues and others about dissociation and will take further, more advanced courses run by ESTD UK.

DID survivors themselves often play an important role in training events. They refer to themselves as 'experts by experience' and are eager to share their expertise with as many people as possible. The survivor led support group First Person Plural (FPP) is proud of its record of training.

Over the last ten years we have delivered training to multi-disciplinary mental health teams, rape crisis centres, solicitors, a prison-based trauma team and housing associations, to name just a few. These wide audiences reflect a need for a working knowledge of dissociation to become mainstream training for most people whose jobs bring them into contact with vulnerable people.[7]

FPP still has hopes of gaining more NHS support for people with DID. In 2011 they launched a DVD called *A Logical Way of Being*, in which they described their experiences of living with DID. Its purpose was to provide 'an introduction to dissociative identity disorder and other complex disorders'.[8] Their aim was to distribute this to each of the several hundred community health teams within the UK. So far, however, their most impressive achievement has been persuading the National Association of Mental Health, known as Mind to publish the booklet *Understanding dissociative disorders*. This appears to reflect the Association's impartial and professional point of view, but it was in fact written by one of FPP's members, and disseminates only the believers' views on the subject.[9]

Another active support group, Positive Outcomes for Dissociative Survivors (PODS), is run by a husband and wife team: Rob Spring and his wife, Carolyn, who was diagnosed with DID in 2005. PODS runs a helpline, has a regular newsletter and holds 'awareness and information workshops' during most months at various UK locations. These are aimed at attracting the usual wide range of people, including, once again, rape crisis staff.[10]

Rape crisis centres are usually thought to be there for women who are already aware that they have been sexually abused. Do these women really need to be made aware of any further, unsuspected horrors? Most rape crisis staff are unpaid volunteers without any special educational qualifications. The only training they are required to undertake can usually be completed in just a few weeks. After this they will find themselves conducting telephone or face-to-face counselling. If they are also to be involved in diagnosing or treating dissociative disorders they will have taken on an unexpectedly heavy burden. The fact that at least three rape crisis centres now make specific mention of ritual abuse on their websites, is perhaps some indication that in places this has indeed happened.[11-13]

Dissociation and ritual abuse also feature in the slightly longer training courses that are run by the Association of Christian Counsellors (ACC), which was formed in 1992 to 'facilitate provision by Christians of quality counselling and pastoral care'. Because so many of their graduates were found to be treating dissociated survivors, this association set up a working group to provide specific training guidelines for counsellors 'working with survivors of ritual or extreme abuse or those working with DID'. In 2000 this working group became the Trauma and Abuse Group (TAG). TAG is now yet another organisation busy running study days, training courses and conferences, all said to be suitable for a wide range of people, including rape crisis staff.[14]

For those wanting a quick route to working with trauma survivors another Christian organisation offers 'some of the most innovative and exciting training courses currently available in the UK'. This is Deep Release, founded in 1994 by Chris and Pauline Andrew. Their courses take just one weekend, but trainees have the option of continuing with further weekends, during which more advanced techniques may be taught. The 'deep release interventions' certainly sound original, since they include instruction in 'pre- and perinatal psychotherapy (in-womb and very early trauma)', 'duvet work and how to use the conception to birth journey', 'the baptismal model', 'therapeutic touch and holding' and 'inner child work'. Dr Chris Andrew, who was once a consultant psychiatrist working in the NHS, claims to 'place a strong emphasis on research, particularly in the areas of neuroscience, bodywork and trauma'. It is hard to imagine what research can underpin his therapeutic methods, but very easy to imagine the powerful effect they must have on some clients. The co-director of Deep Release explains, in a journal published by TAG, why she recommends the use of therapeutic touch.

To experience safe, non-sexual touch for the first time in their lives can be both terrifying (at first) and extraordinarily healing (eventually)… Reliving the trauma in safe arms, realising that *this time* they are not alone, *this time* someone is there who sees and cares, can begin a deeply restorative process. *This time* someone is bringing comforting words and sometimes even shedding tears. *This time* there is a sense of profound hope that it will not all end here – or worse, be never ending.[15]

Finally, for those unable to get to any of the above study days or courses, there is always home study. The UK College of Holistic Training offers, among its many distance learning courses, an open entry three month course that can lead to a Certificate in Dissociative Disorders Awareness.[16]

Because the promoters of dissociative disorders usually have a strong belief in body memories, they have been able to spread their message to people whose work on physical problems puts them in contact with their clients' bodies. This can enable aromatherapists, reflexologists and osteopaths to make new interpretations of their clients' experiences of physical discomfort or incapacity. These can now be seen as examples of the body remembering something that the mind has forgotten. An osteopath has written that he finds the idea that organs and other tissues can hold specific memories of life events quite believable, and that 'it is often the subject of clinical discussion between osteopaths'. He has thus been able to treat a number of people with DID, sometimes finding, in the state of their muscles or other soft tissues, corroboration for their otherwise unbelievable stories, and sometimes discovering there the evidence of some past trauma of which they had been quite unaware.[17]

A clear effect of the current campaign has been to enable an ever-widening range of people to treat dissociative disorders. Their backgrounds, both personal and educational, vary greatly. Although there are people with full professional experience of mental health problems who have chosen to work in this area, they have been joined by many others with no clinical experience who seem to be woefully ignorant of the wide variety of disabling mental conditions that can afflict people. If they interpret any strange behaviour that they observe in their clients as the understandable consequence of childhood trauma they may be seriously led astray, putting both themselves and their clients at grave risk. I have yet to see any warnings about this. It is also worrying that so often these therapists seem to be volunteers who are willing to undertake this arduous work free of charge for clients they regard as specially in need of help. Their dedication is impressive but also very worrying.

The willingness of volunteers is, of course, very opportune. Funding the intensive, long-term treatment of people with DID has always been a problem.

Making it easier to diagnose the Dissociative Disorders

The message given by the many training courses available is that there are countless people out there silently suffering with an undiagnosed dissociative disorder. These potential clients are not easy to identify, and they often appear to have rather different problems. However, help is at hand, with the diagnostic tools that were described in Chapter 4. These take the form of either self-report questionnaires or structured interviews, and are surprisingly easy to administer and score. In all of these the symptoms of dissociation are described, so that the client knows what the clinician is looking for. The client can then say whether or not he or she has experienced these symptoms. By adding up the number of times the client endorses them, a score can then be arrived at, which is compared against norms, i.e. the scores from a large sample of people. This use of norms and numbers gives an appearance of objectivity, but, as we saw earlier, these scores reflect only the personal decisions of the client, her interpretation of the questions and the impression she wants to make. In a structured interview, such as the SCID-D, the clients' responses can be explored further, and the campaigners claim that this is now the 'gold standard' for diagnosis of dissociative disorders. Its originator, Marlene Steinberg, is confident of its accuracy.

People suffering from dissociative disorders can now be identified with the same degree of accuracy as people suffering from other psychiatric or medical disorders. Just like an electrocardiogram can diagnose heart rhythm world-wide, individuals who are suffering from a dissociative disorder can now be accurately identified with the SCID-D.[18]

What Steinberg ignores here is that a medical test, such as an electrocardiogram, measures something objective, that does not respond to the expectations or wishes of either clinician or client. The SCID-D measures something that is very subjective: the client's response to repeated enquiries about private, unobserved experiences. Moreover it is a dialogue that can take up to five hours, between a clinician who is on the lookout for positive answers and a client who may be hoping to engage the interest and help of that clinician. As I noted in Chapter 4, it was developed in the hope that it might be able to detect dissociative symptoms that were missed by the DES.[19] It is probably very effective in doing this since any positive response will be followed by an invitation to elaborate ('What was that experience like?' 'How often does that occur?'). Thus, once clients have endorsed a dissociative symptom they have the opportunity to start talking about their experiences, in their own words, rather than just answering questions. This must be rewarding for many people who are seeking help.

The Pottergate Centre for Trauma and Dissociation, in Norwich, uses SCID-D as part of its helpful diagnostic service.[20] They invite anyone wanting to know whether they have a dissociative disorder to contact this centre, which will then send them copies of two self-report questionnaires, the DES and a version of the Somatoform Dissociation Questionnaire (SDQ-20), and score them free of charge. These questionnaires, described in Chapter 4, were each designed to measure different dissociative symptoms. The DES enquires about psychological experiences and the SDQ-20 about physical experiences. If scores of either of the returned questionnaires suggest the presence of a dissociative disorder, the enquirer will be invited to attend the centre so that, for a fee, a full assessment can be made using SCID-D. I know of one woman who was invited for this assessment after getting a borderline score on just one of these two very different questionnaires. What would have been the outcome if she had accepted this invitation? The Pottergate Centre told me that roughly 90% of those who accept its offer of an assessment are found to have a dissociative disorder, and most are referred on for treatment. About 60% of these will have DID, 30% DDNOS and 10% have either depersonalisation disorder or dissociative fugue. They report that they have seen a steady growth in the number of assessments they make over the past seven years.[21] Their use of SCID-D thus seems guaranteed to identify many more trauma survivors and to increase significantly the apparent prevalence of the dissociative disorders within the UK.

The SCID-D, which was originally developed in the hope that it would identify potential clients who might be missed by questionnaires, has now been in use for more than 20 years. Its originator, Marlene Steinberg, describes it as a 'breakthrough diagnostic test which allows therapists worldwide to diagnose dissociative disorders based on rigorous scientific testing'.[22] I can think of no rigorous scientific testing that has ever demonstrated that the subjective feelings tapped by this test represent a defence used against trauma occurring in early life. It is easy to imagine many other reasons for experiencing, or claiming to experience, these feelings. But although the test includes some questions about drug use and head injury, it avoids any exploration of the many other ways in which a high score might be interpreted.

Some time ago a message was posted on the internet asking if an online SCID-D was available. This was from someone who thought she might have some of the symptoms but was too busy to see a therapist. She would be pleased to know that this test, though originally intended to be used only by specially trained mental health professionals, is now available for use by anyone who can afford to buy it. Both the interview schedule and the interviewer's guide can be bought from Amazon, or, more cheaply, from the Pottergate Centre shop.[23] No special expertise is needed to follow the directions given, to talk someone through the interview or to score their responses. It has never been easier to diagnose the dissociative disorders!

Telling the public about dissociative disorders

The promoters of dissociation believe that at least 1% of the population have DID, and that as many as 10% may have DDNOS.[24] If the general public is to accept that so many people among them are harbouring alternative personalities within themselves, they must first be made more familiar with this strange phenomenon. One way that this can be done is by public appearances of the people who live with DID.

At the 2011 London campaign meeting, one of the speakers was Kim Noble. She had been diagnosed with schizophrenia in the past, but had later become a star demonstrator of DID. She gave delegates a PowerPoint presentation of the many paintings that had been produced, in a variety of different styles, by some of her 20 different personalities. We learn from her website that these paintings have now been widely exhibited and her shows sympathetically reviewed in the national press (*The Telegraph* and *The Guardian*), each time with an explanation of DID as a trauma-related disorder.[25] Kim has also performed on the US television programme, *The Oprah Show*. There she appeared with her 12 year old daughter, Aimee, and demonstrated several of her personalities. The interviewer gave each of these a separate introduction, and her daughter helped by explaining who they were and reacting appropriately to each of them. She laughed when Ken, a young gay man, insisted he did not look like a woman and was not a transvestite, and she cried when Dawn, a personality who was living in the past, declared that Aimee was not her daughter, because her daughter had been taken away at birth.[26]

It seems that in the US this type of dramatic personality switching has come to be accepted as entertaining television. Until recently millions of viewers every week enjoyed watching *The United States of Tara*. This was described as a comedy-drama based on an idea by Steven Spielberg. Perhaps he had been inspired by the box-office success of the film of *Sybil*. The series featured an off-beat family coping with the DID of Tara, the mother. Or, as a reviewer described it: 'adult victims of abuse awkwardly adapting to seeming normalcy.' Tara's contrasting personalities, both male and female, provided her family with some hilarious situations. The message seemed to be that, if you were open-minded enough, living with DID could be perplexing but also quite amusing at times. The show ran for three seasons, but was finally axed in 2010, when the viewing ratings were beginning to fall.[27]

DID is not yet regular family entertainment on UK television, but it does get some recognition. Many people may have learnt about it in 2011, when Channel 4's *4thought* series of short daily programmes was devoted to the question 'Is mental illness ever a gift?' In each programme someone who had been affected by mental illness was invited to give their answer to this question. These answers ranged from seeing it as a curse, a wake-up call, a way of learning about life, of finding God or of being more creative. Only one person said that it had been an unequivocal gift. This was Melanie Goodwin, one of the founders of First Person Plural. Talking straight to camera, she gave a sober account of living with DID, which had a very different flavour from that of Kim Noble's *Oprah Show* performance.

> I've never seen myself as suffering from an illness. I see it as a gift that's been given me to help me survive a life that I wouldn't have survived otherwise...
>
> For the past 18 years I've been coming to terms with surviving an abusive childhood through developing Dissociative Identity Disorder. I began to realise that I had many different parts inside. These were children who had been abused, who were still back in time, so they had a sense of their own identity... I'm very aware that these parts are very much part of me...
>
> I could go to the sea with my four external children and other parts of me could enjoy paddling and playing in the sand quite safely with my children without them being aware that it wasn't actually always me in the body fully...

> To be able to become DID as a child and do what I did, to be able to separate the brain and fragment it into so many parts was an absolute gift.[28]

This positive image of DID, here conveyed by an apparently calm and rational woman, may be very effective in spreading the word that this disorder is not freakish and weird, but an understandable response to childhood trauma.

People may also be influenced by books which give detailed firsthand accounts of surviving a traumatic childhood by developing DID. These graphic tales of triumph over adversity, misery memoirs with an interesting new slant, now seem to be published with increasing frequency. An organisation for the survivors of ritual abuse advertises that it has a ghostwriter available to help any members who wish to tell their stories to a wider public.[29] During 2009 alone at least six of these books were published, and three of them were reviewed at length in UK newspapers.

Today I'm Alice: Nine personalities one tortured mind by Alice Jamieson was favourably reviewed in both the *Daily Express* and *The Sunday Times*. It later featured as one of *The Sunday Times* 'Top Ten Best-sellers'. *Precious: a true story* by Precious Williams was also featured by both *The Sunday Times* and *The Daily Express*. The author told Fleur Britten of *The Sunday Times*, how glad she was that she had been enabled to survive her childhood by developing DID. She had been in treatment for one and a half years and was eager to continue, despite realising that treatment could take up to ten years and was 'extremely painful and expensive'.[30]

In the third book, *Fractured: living nine lives to escape my own abuse,* Ruth Dee told a similar story. She was grateful both for the dissociation and for the many years of therapy that had followed her diagnosis. In her sympathetic review in *The Telegraph* Cassandra Jardine showed us that she had completely accepted her subject's story of developing DID as a result of a horrific childhood that was remembered only by her alternative personalities. She told readers: 'In the last 20 years scepticism has given way to a widespread (but still not universal) acceptance of the existence – even the benefits –

of this response to early events too traumatic to process.'[31]

Journalists have thus been playing a part in promoting this acceptance. Colourful ghostwritten autobiographies by people living with DID continue to be published, and apparently provide very good copy. Kim Noble has now followed up her television performance and painting exhibitions with her own book and has so gained yet another sympathetic *Guardian* interview, this time with Amanda Mitchison, who seems quite unfazed by the fact that Kim is now sporting not 20 but over 100 personalities. She tells us of Kim's long fight to have her condition recognised and uncritically reviews her book *All Of Me*. Her article includes testimony from Dr Valerie Sinason, a well known expert on ritual abuse, who tells us that DID is 'a brilliantly creative survival device'.[32]

The new orthodoxy

The US-based International Society for the Study of Trauma and Dissociation (ISST-D), which has for many years been making authoritative statements about the dissociative disorders and issuing guidelines for their treatment, had more than 1,200 members in 2008, and claimed at that time that these numbers were growing. Nearly 1,000 therapists had graduated from their psychotherapy programme, and more courses and conferences were planned. Its affiliated subgroup, the European Society for Trauma and Dissociation (ESTD), which was founded in 2006, now has members in 17 countries and also appears to be growing. These organisations advertise themselves as intended mainly for professionally qualified therapists, researchers or teachers who work 'in the field of (chronic) trauma, dissociation and disorders related to chronic traumatisation'.[33]

This organisation has undergone some interesting name changes since it started life as the International Society for the Study of Multiple Personality and Dissociation in 1984. After MPD became DID in 1993, the reference to multiple personality was dropped and it became the ISSD. It later introduced the important word 'trauma' to become the ISST-D of today. With our present day awareness of the emotional havoc wrought by wars, torture and natural disasters, trauma has now become a mainstream concern, so this presentational shift has made the organisation appear more orthodox. They advertise a course that provides 'An introduction to the diagnosis and treatment of chronic complex post-traumatic disorders'. No mention of dissociation or of child abuse here. However, the ISST-D has not changed. It is still only interested in one type of trauma: severe early childhood sexual and physical abuse. Its use of the words 'chronic' and 'complex' should tell us it is not interested in the original type of Post Traumatic Stress Disorder (PTSD), in which people are reacting to a known, unforgettable trauma. The interest of ISST-D is still firmly centred on the multiple personalities seen in DID, though other disorders are now drawn into the net if they are thought to have dissociative features.

Many dissociation campaigners now seem to use deliberately vague terms. They talk about a range of 'trauma-related' disorders. The term 'complex dissociation' is increasingly used, which sometimes seems to be a euphemism for DID or DDNOS, and sometimes seems to refer to any form of dissociation that they have declared to be trauma-related. As mentioned before, a far wider range of symptoms now seem to qualify. This may be partly due to the work of Ellert Nijenhuis, the Dutch psychologist who developed the Somatoform Dissociation Questionnaire.[34] His focus on physical symptoms has been welcomed by ISST-D, who have granted him four separate awards for his 'scientific excellence' and his ability to promote his ideas. His most significant achievement, however, was the knighthood that was conferred on him in 2004 by Queen Beatrix of the Netherlands for an 'outstanding contribution to the study and treatment of chronically traumatised individuals'. For 'chronically traumatised individuals' one could substitute 'clients with dissociative disorders' but maybe that would not have gone down so well with Queen Beatrix! In 2005, Nijenhuis founded the Psychotraumatology Institute Europe,[35] and we now find that some of the dissociation campaigners are referring to themselves as traumatologists. Are they deliberately trying to confuse us? There is an Institute of Psychotrauma in London, but this is a very different organisation. Here the staff really do qualify for this title by dealing with the full a range of traumas, and by treating PTSD rather than dissociative disorders.

Therapists now have the confidence to refer to the dissociation-trauma link as an established fact, a given. This makes them less concerned about the continuing reports of false memories. If some memories of abuse are shown to be inaccurate, that does not mean that no abuse took place, since according to this new orthodoxy, dissociation itself can now be seen as evidence of abuse. When the reported details of abuse become embarrassingly improbable they can even be explained away as 'screen memories', in which the true details of the abuse have been distorted.[36] Sometimes therapists and clients no longer need recognisable memories at all, but find evidence of abuse in the physical sensations they see as body memories and in the fleeting images they see as flashbacks. These have been referred to as 'alternative memories'. Women who have these memories are sometimes found to regard them as sufficient evidence that some sort of trauma must have occurred, so that, without any further details, they are prepared to reframe their lives and see themselves as trauma survivors.[37]

This expansion of symptoms and sensations into evidence of child abuse can be seen as an amazing achievement on the part of the dissociation campaigners. They have been campaigning for a long time now, first in North America, then in the UK and across the world. They were checked to some extent during the 1990s by the backlash that was described in Chapter 7. During these years several therapists in North America were successfully sued for the harm they had done to their clients and their families. In the UK the threat of lawsuits has had less impact in restraining the activities of therapists, though a large out of court settlement was recently awarded to one wronged client.[38] Despite these setbacks, many of the original promoters of dissociative disorders are still in business, and newer supporting organisations seem to be springing up all the time and gaining new members.

It is not possible to assess how many new clients are reached by the growing number of independent therapists. However, one barometer of growth in the population of people now living with

DID may be a rise in demand for services for those who believe they have been ritually abused. The Scottish charity Izzy's Promise was set up in 2002 to cater for them. By 2009 it was supporting 70 ritual abuse survivors, and since then it has reported that many more surviviors have been seen every year, most of them with DID. In 2010 they had to take on an extra 14 volunteers to help the 10 who were already hard at work with this very needy group of people. As already mentioned, they were greatly helped by their award in 2007 of a £267,054 grant from the National Lottery to support their work for the survivors of ritual and organised abuse.[39] In England a further charity for these survivors was set up in 2006. The Paracelsus Trust aims to raise funds for the treatment and protection of 'patients at risk of continuing ritual abuse'. It also appears to have been successful; between 2007 and 2011 it was able to increased its annual income tenfold.[40]

Although the existence of organised ritual abuse was refuted many years ago in Government-sponsored reports,[41,42] these now seem to have been forgotten, and the believers are increasingly determined to re-educate the general public. Like the ISST-D they have changed some of the terms they use. The abuse that they report now sounds more secular but no less horrific. There is less mention of the satanic or supernatural aspects of ritual abuse, and more emphasis on 'mind control', in which torture and programming techniques are used to promote lifelong servitude to the cult. Sometimes links are made to political brainwashing techniques, child trafficking or pornography, and the abuse is often referred to as 'extreme' rather than 'ritual'.

The Extreme Abuse Survey, launched in 2007, formed part of this educational project. It was designed to demonstrate once and for all the reality of ritual abuse. Using the internet, some psychologists joined forces with a ritual abuse survivor to devise a 248-item questionnaire, which they posted online in English and in German. It drew positive responses from 1471 participants from more than 30 countries. Participants were asked if they had experienced a wide range of activities that have been associated with ritual abuse. These included participating in animal mutilations or killings, witnessing murder, bestiality, being raped by many people, being caged and suffering sensory and/or sleep deprivation. More than half the respondents endorsed at least one of these experiences, and often many more. The Extreme Abuse Survey thus demonstrated a widespread belief in the reality of ritual abuse and mind control. Its compilers hope that survivors will now be encouraged by knowing that their sufferings have been shared by so many others, so that they will have more confidence to speak out and challenge the sceptics.

> The survey is your opportunity to prove that Ritual Abuse, Mind Control and/or Government Experimentation are not "Urban Legends", fantasy or implanted memories. We can show a skeptical public that our numbers are beyond their wildest imaginations and that regardless of their belief or non-belief we need recognition and respect for having survived the most atrocious events known to humankind, hidden behind a mask of secrecy and disbelief... Your voice will not be silenced or altered by anyone who has tried to discredit your experiences.[43]

It is well known that religious movements thrive under persecution. We see the same thing happening here. Scepticism appears to have energised the believers and to have encouraged a new militancy. With an increasing public recognition of the prevalence of child abuse and the devastating consequences that can follow from it, those of us who question some accounts of it are accused of callously turning our back on its victims, and denying a grim reality. Rather than denying the damage that really is caused by child abuse, we are pointing to the further damage that can be caused by reckless assumptions about its place in the lives of the many people who seek our help.

References – 9. The campaign

* Unless otherwise stated, all webpages could be accessed in August 2013.

1   Laing R.D. and Esterson A. (1964). *Sanity, Madness and the Family.* London: Penguin Books.
2   The Survivors Trust. www.thesurvivorstrust.org/
3   Rape Crisis. www.rapecrisis.org.uk/ (Follow link > child sexual abuse).
4   ISST-D. www.isst-d.org/development/case-statement.htm (Accessed May 2013)
5   Trauma and Abuse Support Centre. www.tasc-online.org.uk/ (conference details no longer available).
6   European Society for Trauma and Dissociation UK Network. www.estd.org/countries/united-kingdom/ (Conference details no longer available).
7   FPP statement to the Campaign for Recognition and Inclusion of Dissociation and Multiplicity, London Conference, 2011.
8   FPP. www.firstpersonplural.org.uk/training
9   Livingstone K. (2004). *Understanding dissociative disorders.* London: Mind.
10   PODS. www.pods-online.org.uk
11   www.caraessex.org.uk/ (Follow links> Information >ritual abuse).
12   www.bristolrapecrisis.org.uk
13   www.wrc-info.org
14   TAG. www.tag-uk.net
15   Andrew P. (2010). What I have learned through working with DID. *Interact*, 10 (1), 35-37.
16   UK College of Holistic Training. www.ukcollege-holistic.co.uk/dissoc-aware.html
17   Silverstone J. (2008). Corroboration in the body tissues. In Sachs A. and Galson G. (Eds). *Forensic Aspects of Dissociative Identity Disorder*. London: Karnac.

18 Steinberg M. www.strangerinthemirror.com/dissociative.html

19 Steinberg M, Rounsaville S and Cichetti DV (1990). The Structured Clinical interview for DSM-III Dissociative Disorders: preliminary report on a new diagnostic instrument. *American Journal of Psychiatry*, 147, (I), 76-82.

20 The Pottergate Centre. www.dissociation.co.uk/

21 Reme Aquarone, personal communication, July 2011.

22 Steinberg M. www.strangerinthemirror.com

23 The Pottergate Centre. www.dissociation.co.uk/ (Follow link> the Pottergate shop).

24 Boon S, Steele K and van der Hart O (2011). *Coping with Trauma-Related Dissociation*. London: WW Norton and Co.

25 Kim Noble. www.kimnoble.com/ (Follow link>articles and reviews).

26 Oprah Show. www.oprah.com/oprahshow/kim-noble-multiple personality-artist (Aired October 6, 2010).

27 Tara. wikipedia.org/wiki/united-states-of-tara

28 Melanie Goodwin. www.channel4.com/programmes/4thoughttv /episode-12 (Accessed October 2011)

29 Izzy's Promise. www.izzyspromise.org.uk/ (Accessed March 2012).

30 Fleur Britten. www.thesundaytimes.co.uk/sto/style/living/ emotions/article355663.ece (Accessed July 2011).

31 Ruth Dee. www.telegraph.co.uk/health/4540255/getting-to-know-my-true-self.html

32 Amanda Mitchison. *Guardian Weekend*, 20 October, 2011.

33 European Society for Trauma and Dissociation. www.estd.org

34 E.R.S. Nijenhuis website. www.enijenhuis.nl/

35 psychotraumatology-institute-europe.com

36 Steinberg M and Schall M (2001). *The Stranger in the Mirror: Dissociation – the hidden epidemic*. New York: Harper, pp. 275-293.

37 Woodiwiss J (2010). 'Alternative memories' and the construction of a sexual abuse narrative. In Haaken J and Reavey P (Eds). *Memory Matters*. London: Routledge.

38 Fairlie J (2010). *Unbreakable Bonds: they know about you dad*. London: Austin and McAulay.

39 www.biglotteryfund.org.uk/global-content/press-releases/scotland/
    lottery-support-for-tayside-trio
40 Paracelsus Trust. http://opencharities.org/charities/1114980
41 La Fontaine J.S. (1994). *The extent and nature of organised and ritual
    abuse.* London: HMSO.
42 Bottoms B.L., Shaver P.R. and Goodman G.S. (1996). An
    analysis of ritualistic and religion related child abuse allegations.
    Law and Human Behaviour, 20 (1), 1-34.
43 Rutz C., Becker T., Overkamp B. and Karriker W. (2008).
    Exploring Commonalities Reported by Adult Survivors of
    Extreme Abuse: Preliminary Empirical Findings. In Noblitt R.
    and Perskin Noblitt P. (Eds). *Ritual Abuse in the Twenty-First
    Century.* Bandon: Karnac, p. 56.

10. THE DAMAGE

Does searching for childhood trauma have to damage adult lives? Possibly not, when the investigation is carried out in good faith, and when failure to find any trauma is readily accepted. However, we know how difficult this acceptance can be. We all suffer from a bias that leads us to see what we are looking for, and ignore any troublesome facts that get in the way. To counter this tendency, and keep in touch with the reality, we have to stand back and be prepared to change our minds. This is never easy.

Psychotherapy should be seen as a co-operative enterprise, in which both parties inform each other. But therapists with fixed ideas about the cause of a client's present problems are unlikely to hear any contradictory voices, and leave their client with no chance of putting them right about anything. In physical medicine a laboratory test may either confirm or refute the doctor's initial hunch. Unfortunately this cannot happen in psychotherapy, where the hunch so often becomes a self-fulfilling prophesy. We saw something of this one-way process in the therapists' notes reproduced in Chapter 6. Because these therapists expected to encounter disbelief they were not deflected by it, and remained determined to learn nothing from their clients' doubts.

Theories can be dangerous. The theory that certain adult disorders are caused by severe childhood trauma has encouraged a use of recovered memory therapy that is both unscientific and damaging. Its use is not restricted to the dissociative disorders, though it is here that it is likely to have the most devastating effects. As I pointed out in Chapter 2, no specific post-abuse syndrome has ever been identified, yet it has been suggested that eating disorders,[1] self-harming,[2] pseudo-epileptic seizures,[3] and several other conditions can be seen as indicators that abuse has occurred. Therapists with these assumptions can then use recovered memory therapy to confirm them. Their clients, like those with DID or

211

DDNOS, will be encouraged to fantasise about what might have happened to them when they were very young. Fantasy and theory will then meet and blend together, reinforcing each other, and leading therapist and client into a disturbing new world that can damage them both.

Therapists often speak of the 'vicarious traumatisation' that they suffer, when clients describe and even seem to re-live the horrors that they now believe in. No one could remain emotionally detached from the nightmarish images of sexual perversion, cruelty and paranoia that must pervade their therapy sessions. There is an obvious danger that both parties can become unbalanced, first by the search for something horrible and then by finding it. I have heard more than one therapist confess that they were now starting to have doubts about their own childhood. They live in a world in which anything is possible. Dreams, fantasies and even physical sensations can all be an indication that there was something very nasty indeed in the woodshed.

Therapists treating dissociative disorders can find themselves committed to many years of listening to unspeakable horrors. Sue Cook, a Christian counsellor, tells us in a chapter appropriately entitled 'Opening Pandora's box' how this affected her.

> I experienced a degree of contamination and violation just listening to these things. Laura told me that she would leave my house after a session and often by the time she had reached the end of my road she would be shaking or be sick. What I did not tell her was that my response was not much different! Many times after she left I would sit on my sofa and cry…

> Often I would think I could never hear anything more shocking and sickening than what Laura disclosed in our current session, and then the following week she would describe something even worse. So my level of tolerance was continually being stretched. Accounts of torture were followed by being buried alive, followed by cannibalism and

child sacrifice, and so it went on… I was not listening to just hours of details of abuse… but hundreds of hours of hard-core criminal acts, which takes its toll.[4]

By the time this was written Sue Cook and Laura had been enduring seven years of this, with additional treatment being provided over the last three years at the Clinic for Dissociative Studies in London. Did all this do either of them any good? During this time Laura had reported, through her other personalities, that she and many others were still in the power of her abusers and at risk from them. This left her alarmed therapist wanting to go to the police but acknowledging that no one other than a therapist would believe a word of this story. Like many other DID therapists she was trapped and agonised by her own belief and powerless to change anything.

Many times I wonder if I and others have done the right thing in lifting the lid off this box of horrors. The level of suffering and pain continues to be so great, as Laura and other DID clients recover co-consciousness and are no longer largely protected from their history, but are having to face it and own it as theirs and integrate it… Seven years on, I still find it hard at times to keep going in this work. Even as I close my office door, these amazing survivors stay in my thoughts and disturb my sleep with the compelling, and at times seemingly impossible task of bringing the torture to an end and enabling them to reach a place of safety at last.[5]

The world of ritual abuse is like an alien religion. It is very hard for the uninitiated to understand how intelligent people are able to maintain their belief in it. It appears to consume the lives of its believers, giving some of them a new sense of purpose but robbing them of their critical faculties. It is especially sad when therapists seem to fly in the face of any scientific education they may have received. Wanda Karriker, a retired psychologist who spent much of her career working with ritual abuse survivors, tells us that this work led her to suspect that she too might be a ritual abuse survivor, because the recollections of one of her clients matched some childhood memories of her own. She then decided to test these suspicions, but chose a method that was almost guaranteed to confirm them.

> Realising any validation of my own history would probably have to come from within me, I entered therapy with an expert in clinical hypnosis for the express purpose of figuring out the truth about my childhood... Although I had hoped I would find well developed alters who could tell me about any dissociated segments of my childhood, it never happened. Perhaps I had multiple personalities as a child who integrated when I was 13 and the abuse ended. Along my journey, I accumulated tons of circumstantial evidence that my memories of a totally wonderful childhood had been an illusion. Unfortunately I have never been able to reconstruct a single event in narrative form. But fortunately I have never suffered the experience of having to live again the torture inherent in the rape of a child's body, mind, and soul. Hence the sometimes controversy in my mind. If the productions of my unconscious via flashes, dreams, automatic writing, body memories, and general feelings of 'knowing' are true, why was I left relatively unscathed mentally, physically, and emotionally?[6]

Exactly! How was it possible for Dr Wanda Karriker, like so many ritual abuse survivors, to complete her education and believe in a happy childhood right up to the time she entered therapy? Her testimony gives a chilling indication of the way the habitual search for trauma can corrupt an educated mind. She has now resolved the 'sometimes controversy' in her mind and joined the ranks of the survivor therapists who battle against the denial of the sceptics.

The clients who break free from recovered memory therapy often tell us that their therapists robbed them for a while of their ability to think for themselves. Their therapists also seem to lose this ability at times, as both parties become traumatised by the horrors they are discovering. When these include crimes that are still being perpetrated their anxious involvement is intensified. It was because of therapists' fears that their clients continued to be at risk of suffering ritual abuse that the Paracelsus Trust was recently established, to provide funds that would enable these clients to have 'urgent respite', assistance for housing and night-time protection. They have been increasingly successful in raising these funds.[7] The original chair of this trust was Pat Frankish, a distinguished clinical psychologist and former president of the British Psychological Society. It seems surprising that anyone with this background should be able to believe that the heinous but undetected crimes of ritual abuse are still being committed in nearby locations and often on particular known dates. Why don't the believers have the courage of their convictions and go out there to try to stop them, or at least gather some evidence of their existence?

Belief in widespread and continuing ritual abuse is an extreme example of a more general flight from reason that can result from recovered memory therapy. Therapists feel under pressure to accept what their clients are telling them, and insist that it is not their job to act as police. They are advised to take a neutral stance on the truth of what they hear, leaving it up to the client to decide what to believe, though they do seem prepared to give them some helpful hints when things fit in with their theory. I find this abdication of reason and responsibility quite shocking. When a client's imaginings are of a real person committing a serious crime isn't it essential that both client and therapist work together, from the start, to discover whether such a thing could have happened? Therapists may not always care whether recovered memories represent a literal or a metaphorical truth, but the clients certainly do care. When they repeatedly ask 'Do you believe me?' and 'Do you think I am making this up?' they are pleading for something other than a neutral stance.

Therapists can be impressed by the internal consistency of their clients' reports, but seem to have no interest in investigating their far more important external consistency. Yet so often the relevant information can be found, in medical and school records, from family members and from people who were there at the time.

Instead of encouraging their clients to investigate, therapists usually advise them to distance themselves from their families and any alleged abuser until they are more sure. By this time any meeting will be a confrontation rather than an enquiry. Of course guilty people will often, though not always, deny what they have done, and the whole truth may never be known. Even when this is the case, some useful information may be gathered, and therapist and client may get nearer to discovering how well the memories fit, not just the theory, but the circumstances. Some of the saddest of the stories told by accused parents are of their repeated attempts to contact their daughter's, or son's, therapist, convinced that if only this person knew more about the family's history and circumstances, he or she would accept that the events in question could never have happened; they must have been imagined rather than remembered.

In the first chapter I described some painstaking studies confirming that it is possible for people to suffer abuse in childhood and then forget about it, and also that *some* memories of childhood abuse recovered in adulthood may indeed be true. Does this justify searching for more memories during therapy? Does new knowledge about past ill treatment, even when it is true, ever help people deal with their present problems? We now have unequivocal evidence that many of these memories recovered during therapy are far from true. Furthermore, recovered memory therapy, despite being intensive and long-lasting, has not been shown to have any measurable benefits.

At the start of this book two fathers told us something of the costs of this therapy. They and their families have suffered anguish and confusion as a result of it, and they know that there is no easy way out. In the UK alone countless families have had similar experiences.[8] If the current campaign to promote the diagnosis and treatment of dissociative disorders succeeds, many more families will suffer the inevitable consequences. The practice of recovered memory therapy carries with it terrible risks, not just for the families of its clients, but for everyone else who is involved. A client who is persuaded to renounce her kith and kin loses the love and support that once sustained her. She also loses her freedom to think

216

independently, a loss she shares with her therapist. Once she has taken the radical step of repudiating her family, neither she nor her therapist can afford to question their conviction that her problems were caused by childhood sexual abuse. Any doubts have to be dismissed as 'denial'. Shackled together, client and therapist are imprisoned by their shared beliefs. Therapy has become tragedy, no less for the well-meaning therapist than for the unknowing client.

References – 10. The damage

1   Rader W.C. (1992). Incest and eating disorders. *Professional Counsellor*, 6 (4), p. 16.
2   Cavanaugh R.M. (2002) Self mutilation as a manifestation of child sexual abuse in adolescent girls. *Pediatric Adolescent Gynecology*, 15, 97-100.
3   Reilly J. et al (1999). The association of physical abuse with somatisation: characteristics of patients presenting with irritable bowel syndrome and non-epileptic attack disorder. *Psychological Medicine*, 29, 339-406.
4   Cook S. (2008). Opening Pandora's box. In Sachs A. and Galton G. (Eds). *Forensic Aspects of Dissociative Identity Disorder*, pp. 160-161.
5   Ibid, p. 166.
6   Karriker W. (2011). The ritual abuse controversy: personal observations. *Interact*, 11 (1), 28-32.
7   Paracelsus Trust. http://opencharities.org/charities/1114980 (Accessed August 2013).
8   BFMS (2007). *Fractured Families: the untold anguish of the falsely accused.* Bradford on Avon: BFMS.

APPENDIX

Dissociative Experiences Scale-II (DES-II)
Eve Bernstein Carlson, Ph.D. & Frank W. Putnam, M.D.

Directions: This questionnaire consists of twenty-eight questions about experiences that you may have in your daily life. We are interested in how often you have these experiences. It is important, however, that your answers show how often these experiences happen to you when you are not under the influence of alcohol or drugs. To answer the questions, please determine to what degree the experience described in the question applies to you, and circle the number to show what percentage of the time you have the experience.

For example: 0% 10 20 30 40 50 60 70 80 90 100%
                (Never)   (Always)

1. Some people have the experience of driving or riding in a car or bus or subway and suddenly realizing that they don't remember what has happened during all or part of the trip. Circle a number to show what percentage of the time this happens to you.
    0% 10 20 30 40 50 60 70 80 90 100%

2. Some people find that sometimes they are listening to someone talk and they suddenly realize that they did not hear part or all of what was said. Circle the number to show what percentage of the time this happens to you.
    0% 10 20 30 40 50 60 70 80 90 100%

3. Some people have the experience of finding themselves in a place and have no idea how they got there. Circle a number to show what percentage of the time this happens to you.
    0% 10 20 30 40 50 60 70 80 90 100%

4. Some people have the experience of finding themselves dressed in clothes that they don't remember putting on. Circle the number to show what percentage of the time this happens to you.
0% 10 20 30 40 50 60 70 80 90 100%

5. Some people have the experience of finding new things among their belongings that they do not remember buying. Circle the number to show what percentage of the time this happens to you.
0% 10 20 30 40 50 60 70 80 90 100%

6. Some people sometimes find that they are approached by people that they do not know, who call them by another name or insist that they have met them before. Circle the number to show what percentage of the time this happens to you
0% 10 20 30 40 50 60 70 80 90 100%

7. Some people sometimes have the experience of feeling as though they are standing next to themselves or watching themselves do something and they actually see themselves as if they were looking at another person. Circle the number to show what percentage of the time this happens to you.
0% 10 20 30 40 50 60 70 80 90 100%

8. Some people are told that they sometimes do not recognize friends of family members. Circle the number to show what percentage of the time this happens to you.
0% 10 20 30 40 50 60 70 80 90 100%

9. Some people find that they have no memory for some important events in their lives (for example, a wedding or graduation). Circle the number to show what percentage of the time this happens to you.
0% 10 20 30 40 50 60 70 80 90 100%

10. Some people have the experience of being accused of lying when they do not think that they have lied. Circle the number to show what percentage of the time this happens to you.
0% 10 20 30 40 50 60 70 80 90 100%

11. Some people have the experience of looking in a mirror and not recognizing themselves. Circle the number to show what percentage of the time this happens to you.
0% 10 20 30 40 50 60 70 80 90 100%

12. Some people have the experience of feeling that other people, objects, and the world around them are not real. Circle the number to show what percentage of the time this happens to you.
0% 10 20 30 40 50 60 70 80 90 100%

13. Some people have the experience of feeling that their body does not seem to belong to them. Circle the number to show what percentage of the time this happens to you.
0% 10 20 30 40 50 60 70 80 90 100%

14. Some people have the experience of sometimes remembering a past event so vividly that they feel as if they were reliving that event. Circle the number to show what percentage of the time this happens to you.
0% 10 20 30 40 50 60 70 80 90 100%

15. Some people have the experience of not being sure whether things that they remember happening really did happen or whether they just dreamed them. Circle the number to show what percentage of the time this happens to you.
0% 10 20 30 40 50 60 70 80 90 100%

16. Some people have the experience of being in a familiar place but finding it strange and unfamiliar. Circle the number to show what percentage of the time this happens to you.
0% 10 20 30 40 50 60 70 80 90 100%

17. Some people find that when they are watching television or a movie they become so absorbed in the story that they are unaware of other events happening around them. Circle the number to show what percentage of the time this happens to you.
0% 10 20 30 40 50 60 70 80 90 100%

18. Some people find that they become so involved in a fantasy or daydream that it feels as though it were really happening to them. Circle the number to show what percentage of the time this happens to you.
0% 10 20 30 40 50 60 70 80 90 100%

19. Some people find that they sometimes are able to ignore pain. Circle the number to show what percentage of the time this happens to you.
0% 10 20 30 40 50 60 70 80 90 100%

20. Some people find that they sometimes sit staring off into space, thinking of nothing, and are not aware of the passage of time. Circle the number to show what percentage of the time this happens to you.
0% 10 20 30 40 50 60 70 80 90 100%

21. Some people sometimes find that when they are alone they talk out loud to themselves. Circle the number to show what percentage of the time this happens to you.
0% 10 20 30 40 50 60 70 80 90 100%

22. Some people find that in one situation they may act so differently compared with another situation that they feel almost as if they were two different people. Circle the number to show what percentage of the time this happens to you.
0% 10 20 30 40 50 60 70 80 90 100%

23. Some people sometimes find that in certain situations they are able to do things with amazing ease and spontaneity that would usually be difficult for them (for example, sports, work, social situations, etc.). Circle the number to show what percentage of the time this happens to you.

0%   10   20   30   40   50   60   70   80   90   100%

24. Some people sometimes find that they cannot remember whether they have done something or have just thought about doing that thing (for example, not knowing whether they have just mailed a letter or have just thought about mailing it). Circle the number to show what percentage of the time this happens to you.

0%   10   20   30   40   50   60   70   80   90   100%

24. Some people find evidence that they have done things that they do not remember doing. Circle the number to show what percentage of the time this happens to you.

0%   10   20   30   40   50   60   70   80   90   100%

25. Some people sometimes find writings, drawings, or notes among their belongings that they must have done but cannot remember doing. Circle the number to show what percentage of the time this happens to you.

0%   10   20   30   40   50   60   70   80   90   100%

26. Some people sometimes find that they hear voices inside their head that tell them to do things or comment on things that they are doing. Circle the number to show what percentage of the time this happens to you.

0%   10   20   30   40   50   60   70   80   90   100%

27. Some people sometimes feel as if they are looking at the world through a fog, so that people and objects appear far away or unclear. Circle the number to show what percentage of the time this happens to you.

0%   10   20   30   40   50   60   70   80   90   100%

Dissociative Experiences Scale II (DES II)
Description and Interpretation

Description: The Dissociative Experiences Scale II (DES II) is a copyright-free, screening instrument. According to its authors, Carlson and Putnam, "it is a brief, self-report measure of the frequency of dissociative experiences. The scale was developed to provide a reliable, valid, and convenient way to quantify dissociative experiences. A response scale that allows subject to quantify their experiences for each item was used so that scores could reflect a wider range of dissociative symptomatology than possible using a dichotomous (yes/no) format." (see Dissociation 6 (1): 16-23)

Interpretation: The Dissociative Experiences Scale II (DES II): When scoring, drop the zero on the percentage e.g. 30%=3; 80%=8 then add up single digits for client score.

Items from the DES for Each of the Three Main Factors of Dissociation:

Amnesia Factor: This factor measures memory loss, i.e., not knowing how you got somewhere, being dressed in clothes you don't remember putting on, finding new things among belongings you don't remember buying, not recognizing friends or family members, finding evidence of having done things you don't remember doing, finding writings, drawings or notes you must have done but don't remember doing. **Items — 3, 4, 5, 8, 25, 26**.

Depersonalization/Derealization Factor: Depersonalization is characterized by the recurrent experience of feeling detached from one's self and mental processes or a sense of unreality of the self. Items relating to this factor include feeling that you are standing next to yourself or watching yourself do something and seeing yourself as if you were looking at another person, feeling your body does not belong to you, and looking in a mirror and not recognizing yourself. Derealization is the sense of a loss of reality of the immediate environment. These items include feeling that other people, objects, and the world around them is not real, hearing voices inside your head that tell you to do things or comment on things you are doing, and feeling like you are looking at the world through a fog, so that people and objects appear far away or unclear.

Items — **7, 11, 12, 13, 27, 28**.

Absorption Factor: This factor includes being so preoccupied or absorbed by something that you are distracted from what is going on around you. The absorption primarily has to do with one's traumatic experiences. Items of this factor include realizing that you did not hear part or all of what was said by another, remembering a past event so vividly that you feel as if you are reliving the event, not being sure whether things that they remember happening really did happen or whether they just dreamed them, when you are watching television or a movie you become so absorbed in the story you are unaware of other events happening around you, becoming so involved in a fantasy or daydream that it feels as though it were really happening to you, and sometimes sitting, staring off into space, thinking of nothing, and being unaware of the passage of time.

Items — **2, 14, 15, 17, 18, 20**.

INDEX

Absorption *see* Fantasy proneness
Acquiescence bias 77
Age regression 138, 176
Alien abduction *vii*, 158, 177-8
Amygdala *see* Hippocampus
Anti-Psychiatry Movement 190
Attachment theory 63
Autobiographies of DID survivors 202-3

Bass, E and Davis, L 40-1, 137, 142-4
Bleuler, E 166
Body memories 79, 101, 108, 129-130, 196, 205
Borch-Jacobson, M 54-5
Borderline Personality Disorder 46, 72, 168-9, 175
Bowlby, J 63

British False Memory Society (BFMS) 132
British Psychological Society (BPS) 9-10, 160, 215
Brownmiller, S 137

Cheit, R 15
Childhood amnesia 9-10
Christian Counsellors *xviii*, 143, 212
          Association 157, 195
Clancy, S 28-9
Cognitive behavioural therapy (CBT) *v*, 20, 181-2, 191
Compensation claims 113, 117-9
Confirmation bias 87, 211
Conversion disorder 79, 149-50
Cook, S 212-3
Corroboration of recovered memories 15-19, 60
Courage to Heal (The) see Bass, E and Davis, L
Cults *see* Ritual abuse

Dalenberg, F 18-19
Day-care centre abuse allegations 152-3
Denial 54, 96-7, 99-100, 107-9
Diagnostic and Statistical Manual of Mental Disorders (DSM)
          DSM III 47, 56
          DSM IV 47, 69, 149-50
          DSM-5 150-1
Dialectical Behaviour Therapy (DBT) 182
Discontinuous memories 15-17

227

Dissociation
     Pathological 74-6
Dissociative disorders *also* Dissociative Identity Disorder DID
     Definition 46-8
     Dissociative Disorder not Otherwise Specified (DDNOS) 68-9, 86, 151
     Dissociative Disorders Interview Schedule (DDIS) 80-1
     Prevalence 84-6
Dissociative Experiences Scale (DES) 61, 73-8
     Surveys using DES 61-3
Deep Release 195
Delusions *see* Hallucinations
Depersonalisation (*also* Derealisation) 75, 78, 81, 165
Dreams 101, 106, 129, 170, 212 *see also* Nightmares

Eating disorders 25, 117
Experts by experience 189, 193
Extreme Abuse Survey 206-7
European Society for Trauma and Dissociation (ESTD) 192-3, 203

False memory
     Experiments 6-9, 17
     Societies 132, 138-41
     Syndrome 139-40
     Syndrome Foundation (FMSF) *see* Societies
False positive diagnosis 70, 75, 80-2, 87
Fantasy proneness 75-6, 179
Finkelhor, D 27
First Person Plural (FPP) 123, 193, 201-2
First rank symptoms of schizophrenia 167, 72
Flashbacks 13-4, 101-2, 125, 129, 158, 170-2
Follow-up studies *see* Outcome studies
Forgotten childhood abuse 10-2
4thought (Channel 4 television) 201-2
Free association 3, 51
Freud *v-vii,* 3-5, 12, 51
Fusion (of alternative identities) 97, 123

Greaves, G 56-7
Goodwin, M 201-2
Guided imagery *vii,* 19, 100, 138

Hall, L and Lloyd, S 24
Hallucinations 72, 167-8
Herman, J 170
Hippocampus 173-5
Hypnosis 48-50, 51, 54, 96, 175-7, 214

Hysteria 49-50, 55

Iatrogenesis 47, 58, 147-8, 150, 159
Implicit (traumatic) memories 13-4
Incest 4, 25, 137-8, 140, 144, 153
Inner children 107, 124-5
Integration (of alternative identities) *see* Fusion
International Classification of Diseases (ICD)
      ICD-10 69, 149
      ICD-11 150
International Society for Trauma and Dissociation (ISST-D) 94, 150, 192, 203-5
      Treatment guidelines 94-8, 146
Izzy's Promise 157, 206

Janet, P 12, 48-51

Karriker, W 213-4
Kihlstrom, J 139
Klein, P 155
Kluft, R 72, 78, 159,

Linehan, M 182-3
Loftus, E 118-9, 145
Logical Way of being (A) 194

Magnetic Resonance Imaging (MRI) 173-4
Many Voices 123-5
McNally, R 14
Memory wars 145-7
Michelle Remembers 152
Miller, A 157-8
Mind (National Association for Mental Health) 25, 194
Morgan, R 137
Multiple Personality Disorder (MPD)
      Early cases 48-51, 57-8

Nathan, D 55-6
National Health Service (NHS) 59, 101, 117, 122, 160, 189-90, 191, 193, 194
National Institute for Clinical Excellence (NICE) 170, 189-90
Near death experiences *see* Paranormal experiences
Neurological impairment 172-5
Newsome, R 100-1, 119-20
Nightmares 13, 101, 103, 119, 128
Nijenhuis, E 78-9, 204
Noble, K 200, 203

Osteopathy 196

Outcome studies 20, 114-6

Paracelsus Trust 206, 215
Paranormal experiences *also* Past life experiences *xii*, 177-9
Pazder, L *see Michelle Remembers*
Pendergrast, M 100, 129
Positive Outcomes for Dissociative Survivors (PODS) 194
Post Therapy Stress Disorder 172, 175
Post Traumatic Stress Disorder (PTSD) 14, 169-75
        In Vietnam veterans 174
Pottergate Centre for Trauma and Dissociation 198-9
Prince, M 48
Prospective studies 26-7, 35-6, 63
Psychoanalysis *v*, 3, 12, 51-2
Psychosis and childhood abuse *see* Schizophrenia

Randomised controlled trials 112-3
Rape Crisis Centres 192, 194-5
Repression *v-vii*, 3, 12-3, 15, 145
Retractors
        Clients 117-9, 127-33
        Therapists 100-1, 119-20
Rind, B, Tromovitch, P and Bausermean, R 37-9
Ring, K and Rosing, C 177-8
Ritual abuse
        Continuing danger 213, 215
        Definition 151-2
        Official investigations 154, 155
        Programming 108-9, 158
        Seminars, conferences, support organisations 154-8, 206-7
Ross, C 80, 85, 114, 159, 178
Royal College of Psychiatrists 160

Schizophrenia
        Association with child sexual abuse 34-6
        Symptoms similar to DID 56, 72, 166-8
Schreiber, F *see Sybil*
Screen memories 158, 205
Seduction theory 3-5
Self-harm 25, 118, 131
Simandl J 155
Simpson, P 120-2
Sinason, V 203
Socio-cultural (explanation of dissociative disorders) 165
Somatoform Dissociation Questionnaire (SDQ) 78-9, 198, 204

Spiegel, H 54-5
Steinberg, M *see next entry*
Structured Clinical interview for Dissociative Disorders (SCID-D) 81-4, 85, 179-80, 197-8
Suicide *xiv, xvii,* 116, 118-9, 168, 172
Survivors' self-help literature 25, 40 *see also* Bass E and Davis L
Survivors Trust 191-2
Sutcliffe, J and Jones, J 57-8
Switching (between identities) 124-5, 147, 200
Sybil 51-6

Temporal lobe epilepsy 172
Trauma and Abuse Support Centre (TASC) 192
Trauma and Abuse Group (TAG) 157, 195
Triggers (for re-experiencing trauma) 125-6

Understanding dissociative disorders see Mind
United states of Tara (The) 200-1

Van der Kolk, B 13-4, 95
Vicarious traumatisation 212-3
Vietnam veterans 174

Women's Liberation Movement 137
Whitfield, C 142
Wilbur, C *see Sybil*
Williams, L 80-81